Umberto Eco

FAITH IN FAKES
Travels in Hyperreality

TRANSLATED FROM THE ITALIAN BY
William Weaver

VINTAGE

Published by Vintage 1998

14 16 18 20 19 17 15 13

Copyright © 1983, 1976, 1973 by
Gruppo Editoriale Fabbri-Bompiani, Sonzogno, Etas S.p.A.
English translation copyright © 1986 by
Harcourt Brace Jovanovich, Inc

First published in Great Britain by
Martin Secker & Warburg Limited 1986

Vintage
Random House, 20 Vauxhall Bridge Road,
London SW1V 2SA

www.vintage-books.co.uk

Addresses for companies within The Random House Group
Limited can be found at: www.randomhouse.co.uk/offices.htm

The Random House Group Limited Reg. No. 954009

A CIP catalogue record for this book
is available from the British Library

ISBN 9780749396282

The Random House Group Limited makes every effort to ensure
that the papers used in its books are made from trees that have
been legally sourced from well-managed and credibly certified
forests. Our paper procurement policy can be found at:
www.randomhouse.co.uk/paper.htm

Printed in the UK by CPI Bookmarque, Croydon, CR0 4TD

CONTENTS

Contents

Preface

An American interviewer once asked me how I managed to reconcile my work as a scholar and university professor, author of books published by university presses, with my other work as what would be called in the United States a "columnist" — not to mention the fact that, once in my life, I even wrote a novel (a negligible incident and, in any case, an activity allowed by the constitution of every democratic nation). It is true that along with my academic job, I also write regularly for newspapers and magazines, where, in terms less technical than in my books on semiotics, I discuss various aspects of daily life, ranging from sport to politics and culture.

My answer was that this habit is common to all European intellectuals, in Germany, France, Spain, and, naturally, Italy: all countries where a scholar or scientist often feels required to speak out in the papers, to comment, if only from the point of view of his own interests and special field, on events that concern all citizens. And I added, somewhat maliciously, that if there was any problem with this it was not my problem as a European intellectual; it was more a problem of American intellectuals, who live in a country where the division of labor between university professors and militant intellectuals is much more strict than in our countries.

It is true that many American university professors write for cultural reviews or for the book page of the daily papers. But many Italian scholars and literary critics also write columns where they take a stand on political questions, and they do this not only as a natural part of their work, but also as a duty. There is, then, a difference in "patterns of culture." Cultural anthropologists accept cultures in which people eat dogs, monkeys, frogs, and snakes, and even cultures where adults chew gum, so it should be all right for countries to exist where university professors contribute to the newspapers.

The essays chosen for this book are articles that, over the years, I wrote for daily papers and weekly magazines (or, on occasion, monthly reviews, but not strictly academic journals). Some of them may discuss, perhaps over a period of time, the same problems. Others are mutually contradictory (but, again, always over a period of time). I believe that an intellectual should use newspapers the way private diaries and personal letters were once used. At white heat, in the rush of an emotion, stimulated by an event, you write your reflections, hoping that someone will read them and then forget them. I don't believe there is any gap between what I write in my "academic" books and what I write in the papers. I cannot say precisely whether, for the papers, I try to translate into language accessible to all and apply to the events under consideration the ideas I later develop in my academic books, or whether it is the opposite that happens. Probably many of the theories expounded in my academic books grew gradually, on the basis of the observations I wrote down as I followed current events.

At the academic level I concern myself with the problems of language, communication, organization of the systems of signs that we use to describe the world and to tell it to one another. The fact that what I do is called "semiotics" should not frighten anyone. I would still do it if it were called something else.

When my novel came out in the United States, the newspapers referred to semiotics as an "arcane discipline." I would not want to do anything here to dispel the arcanum and reveal what semiotics is to those who perhaps have no need to know. I will say only that if, in these travel notes, these thoughts about politics, these invectives against sport, these meditations on television, I have said things that may interest somebody, it is also because I look at the world through the eyes of a semiologist.

In these pages I try to interpret and to help others interpret some "signs." These signs are not only words, or images; they can also be forms of social behavior, political acts, artificial landscapes. As Charles S. Peirce once said, "A sign is something by knowing which we know something more."

But this is not a book of semiotics. God forbid. There already exist too many people who present as semiotics things that are not semiotics, all over the world; I do not want to make matters worse.

There is another reason why I write these things. I believe it is my political duty. Here again I owe the American reader an explanation. In the United States politics is a profession, whereas in Europe it is a right and a duty. Perhaps we make too much of it, and use it badly; but each of us feels the moral obligation to be involved in it in some way. My way of being involved in politics consists of telling others how I see daily life, political events, the language of the mass media, sometimes the way I look at a movie. I believe it is my job as a scholar and a citizen to show how we are surrounded by "messages," products of political power, of economic power, of the entertainment industry and the revolution industry, and to say that we must know how to analyze and criticize them.

Perhaps I have written these things, and go on writing similar things, for other reasons. I am anxious, insecure, and always afraid of being wrong. What is worse, I am always afraid that the person who says I am wrong is better than I am. I need to check quickly the ideas that come into my head. It takes years to write an "academic" book, and then you have to wait for the reviews, and then correct your own thinking in the later editions. It is work that demands time, peace of mind, patience. I am capable of doing it, I believe, but in the meanwhile I have to allay my anxiety. Insecure persons often cannot delay for years, and it is hard for them to develop their ideas in silence, waiting for the "truth" to be suddenly revealed to them. That is why I like to teach, to expound still-imperfect ideas and hear the students' reaction. That is why I like to write for the newspapers, to reread myself the next day, and to read the reactions of others. A difficult game, because it does not always consist of being reassured when you meet with agreement and having doubts when you are faced with dissent. Sometimes you have to follow the opposite course: Distrust agreement and find in dissent the confirmation of your own intuitions. There is no rule; there is only the risk of contradiction. But sometimes you have to speak because you feel the moral obligation to say something, not because you have the "scientific" certainty that you are saying it in an unassailable way.

1

TRAVELS
IN
HYPER
REALITY

Travels in
Hyperreality

The Fortresses of Solitude

Two very beautiful naked girls are crouched facing each other.
They touch each other sensually, they kiss each other's breasts
lightly, with the tip of the tongue. They are enclosed in a kind of
cylinder of transparent plastic. Even someone who is not a professional voyeur is tempted to circle the cylinder in order to see the
girls from behind, in profile, from the other side. The next temptation is to approach the cylinder, which stands on a little column
and is only a few inches in diameter, in order to look down from
above: But the girls are no longer there. This was one of the many
works displayed in New York by the School of Holography.

Holography, the latest technical miracle of laser rays, was invented back in the '50's by Dennis Gabor; it achieves a full-color
photographic representation that is more than three-dimensional.
You look into a magic box and a miniature train or horse appears;
as you shift your gaze you can see those parts of the object that
you were prevented from glimpsing by the laws of perspective. If
the box is circular you can see the object from all sides. If the

object was filmed, thanks to various devices, in motion, then it moves before your eyes, or else you move, and as you change position, you can see the girl wink or the fisherman drain the can of beer in his hand. It isn't cinema, but rather a kind of virtual object in three dimensions that exists even where you don't see it, and if you move you can see it there, too.

Holography isn't a toy: NASA has studied it and employed it in space exploration. It is used in medicine to achieve realistic depictions of anatomical changes; it has applications in aerial cartography, and in many industries for the study of physical processes. But it is now being taken up by artists who formerly might have been photorealists, and it satisfies the most ambitious ambitions of photorealism. In San Francisco, at the door of the Museum of Witchcraft, the biggest hologram ever made is on display: of the Devil, with a very beautiful witch.

Holography could prosper only in America, a country obsessed with realism, where, if a reconstruction is to be credible, it must be absolutely iconic, a perfect likeness, a "real" copy of the reality being represented.

Cultivated Europeans and Europeanized Americans think of the United States as the home of the glass-and-steel skyscraper and of abstract expressionism. But the United States is also the home of Superman, the superhuman comic-strip hero who has been in existence since 1938. Every now and then Superman feels a need to be alone with his memories, and he flies off to an inaccessible mountain range where, in the heart of the rock, protected by a huge steel door, is the Fortress of Solitude.

Here Superman keeps his robots, completely faithful copies of himself, miracles of electronic technology, which from time to time he sends out into the world to fulfill a pardonable desire for ubiquity. And the robots are incredible, because their resemblance to reality is absolute; they are not mechanical men, all cogs and beeps, but perfect "copies" of human beings, with skin, voice, movements, and the ability to make decisions. For Superman the fortress is a museum of memories: Everything that has happened in his adventurous life is recorded here in perfect copies or preserved in a miniaturized form of the original. Thus he keeps the city of Kandor, a survival from the destruction of the planet Krypton, under a glass bell of the sort familiar from your great-aunt's Victorian parlor. Here, on a reduced scale, are Kandor's buildings, highways, men, and women. Superman's scrupulousness in preserving all the mementoes of his past recalls those private museums, or *Wunderkammern*, so frequent in German baroque civilization, which originated in the treasure chambers of medieval lords and perhaps, before that, with Roman and Hellenistic collections. In those old collections a unicorn's horn would be found next to the copy of a Greek statue, and, later, among mechanical crèches and wondrous automata, cocks of precious metal that sang, clocks with a procession of little figures that paraded at noon. But at first Superman's fussiness seemed incredible because, we thought, in our day a *Wunderkammer* would no longer fascinate anybody. Postinformal art hadn't yet adopted practices such as Arman's crammed assemblage of watchcases arranged in a glass case, or Spoerri's fragments of everyday life (a dinner table after an untidy meal, an unmade bed), or the postconceptual exercises of an artist like Annette Messanger, who accumulates memories of her childhood in neurotically archivistic notebooks which she exhibits as works of art.

The most incredible thing was that, to record some past events, Superman reproduced them in the form of life-size wax statues, rather macabre, very Musée Grévin. Naturally the statues of the photorealists had not yet come on the scene, but even when they did it was normal to think of their creators as bizarre avant-garde artists, who had developed as a reaction to the civilization of the abstract or to the Pop aberration. To the reader of "Superman" it seemed that his museographical quirks had no real connection with American taste and mentality.

And yet in America there are many Fortresses of Solitude,

with their wax statues, their automata, their collections of inconsequential wonders. You have only to go beyond the Museum of Modern Art and the art galleries, and you enter another universe, the preserve of the average family, the tourist, the politician.

The most amazing Fortress of Solitude was erected in Austin, Texas, by President Lyndon Johnson, during his own lifetime, as monument, pyramid, personal mausoleum. I'm not referring to the immense imperial-modern–style construction or to the forty-thousand red containers that hold all the documents of his political life, or to the half million documentary photographs, the portraits, the voice of Mrs. Johnson narrating her late husband's life for visitors. No, I am referring to the mass of souvenirs of the Man's scholastic career, the honeymoon snapshots, the nonstop series of films that tell visitors of the presidential couple's foreign trips, and the wax statues that wear the wedding dresses of the daughters Luci and Lynda, the full-scale reproduction of the Oval Office, the red shoes of the ballerina Maria Tallchief, the pianist Van Cliburn's autograph on a piece of music, the plumed hat worn by Carol Channing in *Hello, Dolly!* (all mementoes justified by the fact that the artists in question performed at the White House), and the gifts proffered by envoys of various countries, an Indian feather headdress, testimonial panels in the form of ten-gallon hats, doilies embroidered with the American flag, a sword given by the king of Thailand, and the moon rock brought back by the astronauts. The Lyndon B. Johnson Library is a true Fortress of Solitude: a *Wunderkammer*, an ingenious example of narrative art, wax museum, cave of robots. And it suggests that there is a constant in the average American imagination and taste, for which the past must be preserved and celebrated in full-scale authentic copy; a philosophy of immortality as duplication. It dominates the relation with the self, with the past, not infrequently with the present, always with History and, even, with the European tradition.

Constructing a full-scale model of the Oval Office (using the same materials, the same colors, but with everything obviously more polished, shinier, protected against deterioration) means that for historical information to be absorbed, it has to assume the aspect of a reincarnation. To speak of things that one wants to connote as real, these things must seem real. The "completely real" becomes identified with the "completely fake." Absolute unreality is offered as real presence. The aim of the reconstructed Oval Office is to supply a "sign" that will then be forgotten as such: The sign aims to be the thing, to abolish the distinction of the reference, the mechanism of replacement. Not the image of the thing, but its plaster cast. Its double, in other words.

Is this the taste of America? Certainly it is not the taste of Frank Lloyd Wright, of the Seagram Building, the skyscrapers of Mies van der Rohe. Nor is it the taste of the New York School, or of Jackson Pollock. It isn't even that of the photorealists, who produce a reality so real that it proclaims its artificiality from the rooftops. We must understand, however, from what depth of popular sensibility and craftsmanship today's photorealists draw their inspiration and why they feel called upon to force this tendency to the point of exacerbation. There is, then, an America of furious hyperreality, which is not that of Pop art, of Mickey Mouse, or of Hollywood movies. There is another, more secret America (or rather, just as public, but snubbed by the European visitor and also by the American intellectual); and it creates somehow a network of references and influences that finally spread also to the products of high culture and the entertainment industry. It has to be discovered.

And so we set out on a journey, holding on to the Ariadne-thread, an open-sesame that will allow us to identify the object of this pilgrimage no matter what form it may assume. We can identify it through two typical slogans that pervade American advertising. The first, widely used by Coca-Cola but also frequent as a hyperbolic formula in everyday speech, is "the real thing"; the second, found in print and heard on TV, is "more"—in the sense of "extra." The announcer doesn't say, for example, "The program will continue" but rather that there is "More to come." In America you don't say, "Give me another coffee"; you ask for "More coffee"; you don't say that cigarette A is longer than cigarette B, but that there's "more" of it, more than you're used to having, more than you might want, leaving a surplus to throw away—that's prosperity.

This is the reason for this journey into hyperreality, in search of instances where the American imagination demands the real thing and, to attain it, must fabricate the absolute fake; where the boundaries between game and illusion are blurred, the art museum is contaminated by the freak show, and falsehood is enjoyed in a situation of "fullness," of *horror vacui*.

The first stop is the Museum of the City of New York, which relates the birth and growth of Peter Stuyvesant's metropolis, from the purchase of Manhattan by the Dutch from the Indians for the famous twenty-four dollars, down to our own time. The museum has been arranged with care, historical precision, a sense of temporal distances (which the East Coast can permit, while the West Coast, as we shall see, is unable as yet to achieve it), and with considerable didactic flair. Now there can be no doubt that one of the most effective and least boring of didactic mechanisms is the diorama, the reduced-scale reproduction, the model, the crèche. And the museum is full of little crèches in glass cases, where the visiting children—and they are numerous—say, "Look, there's Wall Street," as an Italian child would say, "Look, there's Bethlehem and the ox and the ass." But, primarily, the diorama aims to establish itself as a substitute for reality, as something even more real. When it is flanked by a document (a parchment or an engraving), the little model is undoubtedly more real even than the engraving. Where there is no engraving, there is beside the diorama a color photograph of the diorama that looks like a painting of the period, except that (naturally) the diorama is more effective, more vivid than the painting. In some cases, the period painting exists. At a certain point a card tells us that a seventeenth-century portrait of Peter Stuyvesant exists, and here a European museum with didactic aims would display a good color reproduction; but the New York museum shows us a three-dimensional statue, which reproduces Peter Stuyvesant as portrayed in the painting, except that in the painting, of course, Peter is seen only full-face or in half-profile, whereas here he is complete, buttocks included.

But the museum goes further (and it isn't the only one in the world that does this; the best ethnological museums observe the same criterion): It reconstructs interiors full-scale, like the Johnson Oval Office. Except that in other museums (for example, the splendid anthropological museum in Mexico City) the sometimes impressive reconstruction of an Aztec square (with merchants, warriors, and priests) is presented as such; the archeological finds are displayed separately and when the ancient object is represented by a perfect replica the visitor is clearly warned that he is seeing a reproduction. Now the Museum of the City of New York does not lack archeological precision, and it distinguishes genuine pieces from reconstructed pieces; but the distinction is indicated on explanatory panels beside the cases, while in the reconstruction, on the other hand, the original object and the wax figurine mingle in a continuum that the visitor is not invited to decipher. This occurs partly because, making a pedagogical decision we can hardly criticize, the designers want the visitor to feel an atmosphere and to plunge into the past without becoming a philologist or archeologist, and also because the reconstructed datum was already tainted by this original sin of "the leveling of pasts," the fusion of copy and original. In this respect, the great exhibit that reproduces completely the 1906 drawing room of Mr. and Mrs. Harkness Flagler is exemplary. It is immediately worth noting that a private home seventy years old is already archeology; and this tells us a lot about the ravenous consumption of the present and about the constant "past-izing" process carried out by American civilization in its alternate process of futuristic planning and nostalgic remorse. And it is significant that in the big record shops the section called "Nostalgia," along with racks devoted to the '40's and the '50's, has others for the '60's and '70's.

But what was the original Flagler home like? As the didactic panel explains, the living room was inspired by the Sala dello Zodiaco in the Ducal Palace of Mantua. The ceiling was copied from a Venetian ecclesiastical building's dome now preserved in the Accademia in Venice. The wall panels are in Pompeiian-pre-Raphaelite style, and the fresco over the fireplace recalls Puvis de Chavannes. Now that real fake, the 1906 home, is maniacally faked in the museum showcase, but in such a way that it is difficult to say which objects were originally part of the room and which are fakes made to serve as connective tissue in the room (and even if we knew the difference, that knowledge would change nothing, because the reproductions of the reproduction are perfect and only a thief in the pay of an antique dealer would worry about the difficulty of telling them apart). The furniture is unquestionably that of the real living room—and there was real furniture in it, of real antiquity, one presumes—but there is no telling what the ceiling is; and while the dummies of the lady of the house, her maid, and a little girl speaking with a visiting friend are obviously false, the clothes the dummies wear are obviously real, that is, dating from 1906.

What is there to complain about? The mortuary chill that seems to enfold the scene? The illusion of absolute reality that it conveys to the more naïve visitor? The "crèche-ification" of the bourgeois universe? The two-level reading the museum prompts with antiquarian information for those who choose to decipher the panels and the flattening of real against fake and the old on the modern for the more nonchalant?

The kitsch reverence that overwhelms the visitor, thrilled by his encounter with a magic past? Or the fact that, coming from the slums or from public housing projects and from schools that lack our historical dimension, he grasps, at least to a certain extent, the idea of the past? Because I have seen groups of black schoolchildren circulating here, excited and entertained, taking much more interest than a group of European white children being trundled through the Louvre . . .

At the exit, along with postcards and illustrated history books, they sell reproductions of historical documents, from the bill of sale of Manhattan to the Declaration of Independence. These are described as "looking and feeling old," because in addition to the tactile illusion, the facsimile is also scented with old spice. Almost real. Unfortunately the Manhattan purchase contract, penned in pseudo-antique characters, is in English, whereas the original was in Dutch. And so it isn't a facsimile, but—excuse the neologism—a fac-different. As in some story by Heinlein or Asimov, you have the impression of entering and leaving time in a spatial-temporal haze where the centuries are confused. The same thing will happen to us in one of the wax museums of the California coast where we will see, in a café in the seaside style of England's Brighton, Mozart and Caruso at the same table, with Hemingway standing behind them, while Shakespeare, at the next table, is conversing with Beethoven, coffee cup in hand.

And for that matter, at Old Bethpage Village, on Long Island, they try to reconstruct an early nineteenth-century farm as it was; but "as it was" means with living animals just like those of the past, while it so happens that sheep, since those days, have undergone—thanks to clever breeding—an interesting evolution. In the past they had black noses with no wool on them; now their noses are white and covered with wool, so obviously the animals are worth more. And the eco-archeologists we're talking about are working to rebreed the line to achieve an "evolutionary retrogression." But the National Breeders' Association is protesting, loudly and firmly, against this insult to zoological and technical progress. A cause is in the making: the advocates of "ever forward" against those of "backward march." And there is no telling now which are

11

the more futurological, and who are the real falsifiers of nature. But as far as battles for "the real thing" are concerned, our journey certainly doesn't end here. *More to come!*

Satan's Crèches

Fisherman's Wharf, in San Francisco, is an Eldorado of restaurants, shops selling tourist trinkets and beautiful seashells, Italian stands where you can have a crab cooked to order, or eat a lobster or a dozen oysters, all with sourdough French bread. On the sidewalks, blacks and hippies improvise concerts, against the background of a forest of sailboats on one of the world's loveliest bays, which surrounds the island of Alcatraz. At Fisherman's Wharf you find, one after another, four waxwork museums. Paris has only one, as do London, Amsterdam, and Milan, and they are negligible features in the urban landscape, on side streets. Here they are on the main tourist route. And, for that matter, the best one in Los Angeles is on Hollywood Boulevard, a stone's throw from the famous Chinese Theatre. The whole of the United States is spangled with wax museums, advertised in every hotel—in other words, attractions of considerable importance. The Los Angeles area includes the Movieland Wax Museum and the Palace of Living Arts; in New Orleans you find the Musée Conti; in Florida there is the Miami Wax Museum, Potter's Wax Museum of St. Augustine, the Stars Hall of Fame in Orlando, the Tussaud Wax Museum in St. Petersburg. Others are located in Gatlinburg, Tennessee, Atlantic City, New Jersey, Estes Park, Colorado, Chicago, and so on.

The contents of a European wax museum are well-known: "live" speaking images, from Julius Caesar to Pope John XXIII, in various settings. As a rule, the environment is squalid, always subdued, diffident. Their American counterparts are loud and aggressive, they assail you with big billboards on the freeway miles in advance, they announce themselves from the distance with glowing signs, shafts of light in the dark sky. The moment you enter you are alerted that you are about to have one of the most thrilling experiences of your life; they comment on the various scenes with long captions in sensational tones; they combine historical reconstruction with religious celebration, glorification of movie celebrities, and themes of famous fairytales and adventure stories; they dwell on the horrible, the bloody; their concern with authenticity reaches the point of reconstructive neurosis. At Buena Park, California, in the Movieland Wax Museum, Jean Harlow is lying on a divan; on the table there are copies of magazines of the period. On the walls of the room inhabited by Charlie Chaplin there are turn-of-the-century posters. The scenes unfold in a full continuum, in total darkness, so there are no gaps between the niches occupied by the waxworks, but rather a kind of connective décor that enhances the sensation. As a rule there are mirrors, so on your right you see Dracula raising the lid of a tomb, and on the left your own face reflected next to Dracula's, while at times there is the glimmering figure of Jack the Ripper or of Jesus, duplicated by an astute play of corners, curves, and perspective, until it is hard to decide which side is reality and which illusion. Sometimes you approach an especially seductive scene, a shadowy character is outlined against the background of an old cemetery, then you discover that this character is you, and the cemetery is the reflection of the next scene, which tells the pitiful and horrifying story of the grave robbers of Paris in the late nineteenth century.

Then you enter a snowy steppe where Zhivago is getting out of a sleigh, followed by Lara, but to reach it you have to pass the cabin where the lovers will go and live, and from the broken roof a mountain of snow has collected on the floor. You experience a certain emotion, you feel very Zhivago, you wonder if this involvement is due to the lifelike faces, to the natural poses, or to "Lara's Theme," which is being played with insinuating sweetness; and then you realize that the temperature really is lower, kept below zero centigrade, because everything must be like reality. Here "reality" is a movie, but another characteristic of the wax museum is that the notion of historical reality is absolutely democratized: Marie Antoinette's boudoir is recreated with fastidious attention to detail, but Alice's encounter with the Mad Hatter is done just as carefully.

When you see Tom Sawyer immediately after Mozart or you enter the cave of *The Planet of the Apes* after having witnessed the Sermon on the Mount with Jesus and the Apostles, the logical distinction between Real World and Possible Worlds has been definitively undermined. Even if a good museum (with sixty or seventy scenes and two or three hundred characters) subdivides its space, separating the movie world from religion and history, at the end of the visit the senses are still overloaded in an uncritical way; Lincoln and Dr. Faustus have appeared reconstructed in the same style, similar to Chinese socialist realism, and Hop o' My Thumb and Fidel Castro now belong forever to the same ontological area.

This anatomical precision, this maniacal chill, this exactness of even the most horrifying detail (so that a disemboweled body displays the viscera neatly laid out as if for a medical-school lecture) suggest certain models: the neoclassical waxworks of the Museo della Specola in Florence, where Canovan aspirations join with Sadean shudders; and the St. Bartholomews, flayed muscle by muscle, that adorn certain anatomy lecture-halls. And also the hyperrealistic ardors of the Neapolitan crèche. But in addition to these memories in the minor art of Mediterranean countries, there are others, more illustrious: the polychrome wood sculpture of German churches and city halls, the tomb figures of the Flemish-Burgundian Middle Ages. Not a random reference, because this exacerbated American realism may reflect the Middle European taste of various waves of immigration. Nor can one help recalling Munich's Deutsches Museum, which, in relating with absolute scientific precision the history of technology, not only uses dioramas on the order of those at the Museum of the City of New York, but even a reconstruction of a nineteenth-century mine, going dozens of meters underground, with the miners lying in passages and horses being lowered into the pits with windlasses and straps. The American wax museum is simply less hidebound; it shows Brigitte Bardot with a skimpy kerchief around her loins, it rejoices in the life of Christ with Mahler and Tchaikovsky, it reconstructs the chariot race from *Ben Hur* in a curved space to suggest panoramic VistaVision, for everything must equal reality even if, as in these cases, reality was fantasy.

The idea that the philosophy of hyperrealism guides the reconstructions is again prompted by the importance attached to the "most realistic statue in the world" displayed in the Ripley's "Believe It or Not!" Musèums. For forty years in American newspapers Ripley drew a panel in which he told of the wonders he had discovered in the course of his journeys around the world. The shrunken, embalmed heads of the Borneo wild men, a violin made entirely of matches, a calf with two heads, and a fake mermaid first brought to America around 1840: Ripley overlooked nothing in the universe of the amazing, the teratological, the incredible. At a certain point Ripley created a chain of museums, which house the objects he wrote about; and there you can see, in special display cases, the mermaid (billed as "The World's Greatest Fake!"), a guitar made from an eighteenth-century French bidet, the Iron Maiden of Nuremberg, a statue of a fakir who lived swathed in chains or of a Chinese with double pupils, and—wonder of wonders—the most realistic statue in the world, "the living statue. Hananuma Masakichi, greatest sculptor of Japan, posed for himself and carved his own image in wood. The hair, teeth, toenails, and fingernails are Masakichi's own."

Some of the curiosities in the Ripley's Museums are unique; others, displayed in several museums at once, are said to be authentic duplicates. Still others are copies. The Iron Maiden of Nuremberg, for example, can be found in six or eight different locations, even though there is only one original; the rest are copies. What counts, however, is not the authenticity of a piece, but the amazing information it conveys. A *Wunderkammer* par excellence, the Ripley's Museum has in common with the medieval and baroque collections of marvels the uncritical accumulation of every curious find; the difference lies in the more casual attitude toward the problem of authenticity. The authenticity the Ripley's Museums advertise is not historical, but visual. Everything looks real, and therefore it is real; in any case the fact that it seems real is real, and the thing is real even if, like Alice in Wonderland, it never existed.

For that matter, when the Museum of Magic and Witchcraft presents the reconstructed laboratory of a medieval witch, with dusty cabinets containing countless drawers and with cupboards from which toads and poisonous herbs emerge, and jars containing odd roots, and amulets, alembics, vials with sinister liquids, dolls pierced with needles, skeletal hands, flowers with mysterious names, eagles' beaks, infants' bones: As you confront this visual achievement that would make Louise Nevelson envious, and in the background you hear the piercing screams of young witches dragged to the stake and from the end of the dark corridor you see the flames of the auto-da-fé flicker, your chief impression is theatrical; for the cultivated visitor, the skillfulness of the reconstruction; for the ingenuous visitor, the violence of the information—there is something for everybody, so why complain? The fact is that the historical information is sensationalistic, truth is mixed with legend, Eusapia Palladino appears (in wax) after Roger Bacon and Dr. Faustus, and the end result is absolutely oneiric.

But the masterpiece of the reconstructive mania (and of giving more, and better) is found when this industry of absolute iconism has to deal with the problem of art.

Between San Francisco and Los Angeles I was able to visit seven wax versions of Leonardo's *Last Supper*. Some are crude and unwittingly caricatural; others are more accurate though no less unhappy in their violent colors, their chilling demolition of what had been Leonardo's vibrance. Each is displayed next to a version of the original. And you would naturally—but naïvely—suppose that this reference image, given the development of color photo reproduction, would be a copy of the original. Wrong: because, if compared to the original, the three-dimensional creation might come off second-best. So, in one museum after the other, the waxwork scene is compared to a reduced reproduction carved in wood, a nineteenth-century engraving, a modern tapestry, or a bronze, as the commenting voice insistently urges us to note the resemblance of the waxwork, and against such insufficient models, the waxwork, of course, wins. The falsehood has a certain justification, since the criterion of likeness, amply described and analyzed, never applies to the formal execution, but rather to the subject: "Observe how Judas is in the same position, and how Saint Matthew . . ." etc., etc.

As a rule the Last Supper is displayed in the final room, with symphonic background music and a *son et lumière* atmosphere. Not infrequently you are admitted to a room where the waxwork Supper is behind a curtain that slowly parts, as the taped voice, in deep and emotional tones, simultaneously informs you that you are having the most extraordinary spiritual experience of your life, and that you must tell your friends and acquaintances about it. Then comes some information about the redeeming mission of Christ and the exceptional character of the great event portrayed, summarized in evangelical phrases. Finally, information about Leonardo, all permeated with the intense emotion inspired by the mystery of art. At Santa Cruz the Last Supper is actually on its own, the sole attraction, in a kind of chapel erected by a committee of citizens, with the twofold aim of spiritual uplift and celebration of the glories of art. Here there are six reproductions with which to compare the waxworks (an engraving, a copperplate, a color copy, a reconstruction "in a single block of wood," a tapestry, and a printed reproduction of a reproduction on glass). There is sacred music, an emotional voice, a prim little old lady with eyeglasses to collect the visitor's offering, sales of printed reproductions of the reproduction in wax of the reproduction in wood, metal, glass. Then you step out into the sunshine of the Pacific beach, nature dazzles you, Coca-Cola invites you, the freeway awaits you with its five lanes, on the car radio Olivia Newton-John is singing *Please, Mister, Please*; but you have been touched by the thrill of artistic greatness, you have had the most stirring spiritual emotion of your life and seen the most artistic work of art in the world. It is far away, in Milan, which is a place, like Florence, all Renaissance; you may never get there, but the voice has warned you that the original fresco is by now ruined, almost invisible, unable to give you the emotion you have received from the three-dimensional wax, which is more real, and there is more of it.

But when it comes to spiritual emotions nothing can equal what you will feel at the Palace of Living Arts in Buena Park, Los Angeles. It is next to the Movieland Wax Museum and is in the form of a Chinese pagoda. In front of the Movieland Museum there is a Rolls-Royce all of gold; in front of the Palace of Living Arts there is Michelangelo's David, in marble. Himself. Or almost. An authentic copy, in this case. And for that matter he won't come as a surprise, because in the course of our trip we have been lucky enough to see at least ten Davids, plus several Pietàs and a complete set of Medici Tombs. The Palace of Living Arts is different, because it doesn't confine itself—except for some statues—to presenting reasonably faithful copies. The Palace reproduces in wax, in three dimensions, life-size and, obviously, in full color, the great masterpieces of painting of all time. Over there you see Leonardo, painting the portrait of a lady seated facing him: She is Mona Lisa, complete with chair, feet, and back. Leonardo has an easel beside him, and on the easel there is a two-dimensional copy of La Gioconda: What else did you expect? Here is the Aristotle of Rembrandt, contemplating the bust of Homer; and here is El Greco's Cardinal de Guevara, the Cardinal Richelieu of Philippe de Campaigne, the Salome of Guido Reni, the Grande Odalisque of Ingres, and the sweet Pinkie of Thomas Lawrence (she not only has a third dimension, but a silk dress that stirs slightly in the breeze from a concealed electric fan, for the figure, as everybody knows, stands against a landscape where storm clouds loom).

Beside each statue there is the "original" painting; but here, too, it is not a photographic reproduction, but a very cheap oil copy, like a sidewalk artist's; and once again the copy seems more convincing than the model as the visitor is convinced that the Palace itself replaces and improves on the National Gallery or the Prado.

The Palace's philosophy is not, "We are giving you the reproduction so that you will want the original," but rather, "We are giving you the reproduction so you will no longer feel any need for the original." But for the reproduction to be desired, the original has to be idolized, and hence the kitsch function of the inscriptions and the taped voices, which remind you of the greatness of the art of the past. In the final room you are shown a Michelangelo Pietà, a good copy this time, in marble, made (as you are duly informed) by a Florentine artisan, and, what's more, as the voice tells you, the pavement on which the statue stands is made from stones that came from the Holy Sepulcher in Jerusalem (and hence there is more here than in St. Peter's, and it is more real).

Since you have spent your five dollars and have a right not to be tricked, a photocopy next to the statue reproduces the document with which the management of the Church of the Holy Sepulcher confirms that it has allowed the Palace to remove twenty stones (from where is not clear). In the emotion of the moment, with shafts of light cleaving the darkness to illuminate the details as they are described, the visitor doesn't have time to realize that the floor is composed of far more than twenty stones and that, moreover, the said stones are also supposed to make up a facsimile of the adjacent wall of Jerusalem, and therefore the authentic archeological stones have been amply added to. But what matters is the certainty of the commercial value of the whole: the Pietà, as you see it, cost a huge sum because they had to go specially to Italy to procure an authentic copy. For that matter, next to Gains-borough's *Blue Boy* there is the notice that the original is now in the Huntington Art Gallery of San Marino, California, which paid seven hundred and fifty thousand dollars for it. So it's art. But it is also life, because the didactic panel adds, quite pointlessly: "The Blue Boy's age remains a mystery."

The acme of the Palace, however, is reached in two places. In one you see Van Gogh. This is not the reproduction of a spe-cific picture: Poor Vincent is sitting, with his electroshock look, on one of the chairs he painted elsewhere, against the background of a rumpled bed as he actually painted it, and with some little Van Goghs on the walls. But the striking thing is the face of the great lunatic: in wax, naturally, but meant to render faithfully the rapid, tormented brushstrokes of the artist, and thus the face seems devoured by some disgusting eczema, the beard is palpably moth-eaten, and the skin is flaking, with scurvy, herpes zoster, mycosis.

The second sensational moment is provided by three statues reproduced in wax, and therefore more real because they are in color whereas the originals were in marble and hence all white and lifeless. They are a Dying Slave and a David of Michelangelo. The Dying Slave is a great hulk with an undershirt rolled up over his chest and a loincloth borrowed from a semi-nudist colony; the David is a rough type with black curls, slingshot, and a green leaf against his pink belly. The printed text informs us that the wax-work portrays the model as he must have been when Michelangelo copied him. Not far off is the Venus de Milo, leaning on an Ionic column against the background of a wall with figures painted in red. I say "leaning," and in fact this polychrome unfortunate has arms. The legend explains: "Venus de Milo brought to life as she was in the days when she posed for the unknown Greek sculptor, in approximately 200 B.C."

The Palace is inspired by Don Quixote (who is also present, even if he isn't a painting), who "represents the idealistic and re-alistic nature of man and, as such, is the chosen symbol of the

Palace." I imagine that with "idealistic" they are referring to the eternal value of art, and with "realistic" to the fact that here an ancestral desire can be satisfied: to peer beyond the picture's frame, to see the feet of the portrait bust. The Palace of Living Arts achieves with masterpieces of the past what the most highly developed reproduction technique through laser beams—holography—does with original subjects.

The only thing that amazes us is that in the perfect reproduction of the Arnolfini double portrait by van Eyck, everything is three-dimensional except the one thing that the painting depicted with surprising illusory skill and that the Palace's artisans could have included without the slightest effort—namely, the convex mirror in the background that reflects the back of the painted scene, as if it were viewed through a wide-angle lens. Here, in the realm of three-dimensional wax, the mirror is painted. The only credible reasons are symbolic. Confronting an instance where Art played consciously with Illusion and admitted the vanity of images through the image of an image, the industry of the Absolute Fake didn't dare venture to copy, because it would have come too close to the revelation of its own falsehood.*

Enchanted Castles

Winding down the curves of the Pacific coast between San Francisco, Tortilla Flat, and Los Padres National Park, along shores that recall Capri and Amalfi, as the Pacific Highway descends toward Santa Barbara, you see the castle of William Randolph Hearst rise, on the gentle Mediterranean hill of San Simeon. The traveler's heart leaps, because this is the Xanadu of *Citizen Kane*, where Orson Welles brought to life his protagonist, explicitly modeled on the great newspaper magnate, ancestor of the unfortunate Symbionese Patricia.

Having reached the peak of wealth and power, Hearst built

---

*The Palace of Living Arts closed in 1982.—ED.

here his own Fortress of Solitude, which a biographer has described as a combination of palace and museum such as had not been seen since the days of the Medicis. Like someone in a René Clair movie (but here reality far outstrips fiction), Hearst bought, in bits or whole, palaces, abbeys, and convents in Europe, had them dismantled brick by numbered brick, packaged and shipped across the ocean, to be reconstructed on the enchanted hill, in the midst of free-ranging wild animals. Since he wanted not a museum but a Renaissance house, he complemented the original pieces with bold imitations, not bothering to distinguish the genuine from the copy. An incontinent collectionism, the bad taste of the nouveau riche, and a thirst for prestige led him to bring the past down to the level of today's life; but he conceived of today as worth living only if guaranteed to be "just like the past."

Amid Roman sarcophagi, and genuine exotic plants, and remade baroque stairways, you pass Neptune's Pool, a fantasy Greco-Roman temple peopled with classical statues including (as the guidebook points out with fearless candor) the famous Venus rising from the water, sculpted in 1930 by the Italian sculptor Cassou, and you reach the Great House, a Spanish-Mexican–style cathedral with two towers (equipped with a thirty-six-bell carillon), whose portal frames an iron gate brought from a sixteenth-century Spanish convent, surmounted by a Gothic tympanum with the Virgin and Child. The floor of the vestibule encloses a mosaic found in Pompeii, there are Gobelins on the walls, the door into the Meeting Hall is by Sansovino, the great hall is fake Renaissance presented as Italo-French. A series of choir stalls comes from an Italian convent (Hearst's agents sought the scattered pieces through various European dealers), the tapestries are seventeenth-century Flemish, the objects — real or fake — date from various periods, four medallions are by Thorvaldsen. The Refectory has an Italian ceiling "four hundred years old," on the walls are banners "of an old Sienese family." The bedroom contains the authentic bed of Richelieu, the billiard room has a Gothic tapestry, the projection room (where every night Hearst forced his guests to watch the films he produced, while he sat in the front row with a handy telephone linking him with the whole world) is all fake Egyptian with some Empire touches; the Library has another Italian ceiling, the study imitates a Gothic crypt, and the fireplaces of the various rooms are (real) Gothic, whereas the indoor pool invents a hybrid of the Alhambra, the Paris Métro, and a Caliph's urinal, but with greater majesty.

The striking aspect of the whole is not the quantity of antique pieces plundered from half of Europe, or the nonchalance with which the artificial tissue seamlessly connects fake and genuine, but rather the sense of fullness, the obsessive determination not to leave a single space that doesn't suggest something, and hence the masterpiece of bricolage, haunted by *horror vacui*, that is here achieved. The insane abundance makes the place unlivable, just as it is hard to eat those dishes that many classy American restaurants, all darkness and wood paneling, dotted with soft red lights and invaded by nonstop music, offer the customer as evidence of his own situation of "affluence": steaks four inches thick with lobster (and baked potato, and sour cream and melted butter, and grilled tomato and horseradish sauce) so that the customer will have "more and more," and can wish nothing further.

An incomparable collection of genuine pieces, too, the Castle of Citizen Kane achieves a psychedelic effect and a kitsch result not because the Past is not distinguished from the Present (because after all this was how the great lords of the past amassed rare objects, and the same continuum of styles can be found in many Romanesque churches where the nave is now baroque and perhaps the campanile is eighteenth century), but because what offends is the voracity of the selection, and what distresses is the fear of being caught up by this jungle of venerable beauties, which unquestionably has its own wild flavor, its own pathetic sadness, barbarian grandeur, and sensual perversity, redolent of contamination, blasphemy, the Black Mass. It is like making love in a confessional with a prostitute dressed in a prelate's liturgical robes reciting Baudelaire while ten electronic organs reproduce the *Well-Tempered Clavier* played by Scriabin.

But Hearst's castle is not an *unicum*, not a *rara avis*: It fits into the California tourist landscape with perfect coherence, among the waxwork Last Suppers and Disneyland. And so we leave the castle and travel a few dozen miles, toward San Luis Obispo. Here, on the slopes of Mount San Luis, bought entirely by Mr. Madonna in order to build a series of motels of disarming pop vulgarity, stands the Madonna Inn.

The poor words with which natural human speech is provided cannot suffice to describe the Madonna Inn. To convey its external appearance, divided into a series of constructions, which you reach by way of a filling station carved from Dolomitic rock, or through the restaurant, the bar, and the cafeteria, we can only venture some analogies. Let's say that Albert Speer, while leafing through a book on Gaudi, swallowed an overgenerous dose of LSD and began to build a nuptial catacomb for Liza Minnelli. But that doesn't give you an idea. Let's say Arcimboldi builds the Sagrada Familia for Dolly Parton. Or: Carmen Miranda designs a Tiffany locale for the Jolly Hotel chain. Or D'Annunzio's Vittoriale imagined by Bob Cratchit, Calvino's *Invisible Cities* described by Judith Krantz and executed by Leonor Fini for the plush-doll industry, Chopin's Sonata in B flat minor sung by Perry Como in an arrangement by Liberace and accompanied by the Marine Band. No, that still isn't right. Let's try telling about the rest rooms. They are an immense underground cavern, something like Altamira and Luray, with Byzantine columns supporting plaster baroque cherubs. The basins are big imitation-mother-of-pearl shells, the urinal is a fireplace carved from the rock, but when the jet of urine (sorry, but I have to explain) touches the bottom, water comes down from the wall of the hood, in a flushing cascade something like the Caves of the Planet Mongo. And on the ground floor, in keeping with the air of Tyrolean chalet and Renaissance castle, a cascade of chandeliers in the form of baskets of flowers, billows of mistletoe surmounted by opalescent bubbles, violet-suffused light among which Victorian dolls swing, while the walls are punctuated by art-nouveau windows with the colors of Chartres and hung with Regency tapestries whose pictures resemble the garish color supplements of the Twenties. The circular sofas are red and gold, the tables gold and glass, and all this amid inventions that turn the whole into a multicolor Jell-O, a box of candied fruit, a Sicilian ice, a land for Hansel and Gretel. Then there are the bedrooms, about two hundred of them, each with a different theme: for a reasonable price (which includes an enormous bed—King or Queen size—if you are on your honeymoon) you can have the Prehistoric Room, all cavern and stalactites, the Safari Room (zebra walls and bed shaped like a Bantu idol), the Kona Rock Room (Hawaiian), the California Poppy, the Old-Fashioned Honeymoon, the Irish Hills, the William Tell, the Tall and Short, for mates of different lengths, with the bed in an irregular polygon form, the Imperial Family, the Old Mill.

The Madonna Inn is the poor man's Hearst Castle; it has no artistic or philological pretensions, it appeals to the savage taste for the amazing, the overstuffed, and the absolutely sumptuous at low price. It says to its visitors: "You too can have the incredible, just like a millionaire."

This craving for opulence, which goads the millionaire as it does the middle-class tourist, seems to us a trademark of American behavior, but it is much less widespread on the Atlantic coast, and not because there are fewer millionaires. We could say that the Atlantic millionaire finds no difficulty in expressing himself through the means of essential modernity, by building in glass and reinforced concrete, or by restoring an old house in New England. But the house is already there. In other words, the Atlantic coast yearns less for Hearstian architectural expression because it has its own architecture, the historical architecture of the eighteenth century and the modern, business-district architecture. Baroque rhet-

oric, eclectic frenzy, and compulsive imitation prevail where wealth
has no history. And thus in the great expanses that were colonized
late, where the posturban civilization represented by Los Angeles
is being born, in a metropolis made up of seventy-six different
cities where alleyways are ten-lane freeways and man considers his
right foot a limb designed for pressing the accelerator, and the left
an atrophied appendix, because cars no longer have a clutch—eyes
are something to focus, at steady driving speed, on visual-mechan-
ical wonders, signs, constructions that must impress the mind in
the space of a few seconds. In fact, we find the same thing in
California's twin-state, Florida, which also seems an artificial region, an uninterrupted continuum of urban centers, great ramps
of freeways that span vast bays, artificial cities devoted to entertainment (Disneyland and Disney World are in California and
Florida, respectively, but the latter—a hundred and fifty times bigger than the former—is even more pharaonic and futuristic).

In Florida, south of St. Petersburg, crossing a series of bridges
suspended over inlets of the sea and proceeding along water-level
highways that link two cities across a bay as marvelous as it is
useless for human beings without car, boat, and private marina,
you come to Sarasota. Here the Ringling dynasty (of circus mag-
nates) has left substantial memories of itself. A circus museum, a
painting and sculpture museum complete with Renaissance villa,
the Asolo Theater, and finally the "Ca' d'Zan." The words, as the
guidebook explains, mean "House of John in Venetian dialect,"
and in fact the Ca' is a palazzo, or rather a section of Grand Canal
façade which opens on a garden of overwhelming botanical beauty,
where, for example, a banyan tree, its multiple exposed roots spill-
ing to the ground, creates a wild gazebo inhabited by a bronze
statue; and at the rear, there is an only slightly Venetian terrace
where, following a path punctuated by a Cellini, or a Giovanni da
Bologna, fake, but with the proper patina and mold in all the right
places, you gaze out on one of the bayous of Florida, once the
paradise of early explorers or the blessed land of Little Jody, where
he wept and followed Flag, the immortal yearling.

Ca' d'Zan is a Venetian palazzo that could be used for an architecture course's final exam: Describe a Venetian palazzo, symbol of the pomp and historical destiny of the Doges, meeting place of Latin civilization and Moorish barbarism. Obviously, the student aiming at an "A" emphasizes the bright colors, the Oriental influences, and produces a result that would be more pleasing to Othello than to Marco Polo. About the interior there can't be a moment's doubt: It's the Hotel Danieli. The architect Dwight James Baum deserves (in the sense that Eichmann does) to go down in history. Also because, not content with the Danieli, he overdid. He engaged an unknown Hungarian decorator to paint a coffered ceiling in a barroom-naïf style, he lavished terra-cottas, docked gondolas, Murano-style glass of pink, amethyst, and blue; but to be double-sure he decked it all with Flemish and English tapestries, French trumeaux, art-nouveau sculpture, Empire chairs, Louis XV beds, Carrara marbles (with labels guaranteeing origin), as usual carved by artisans brought specially from Venice; and into the bargain he made extra certain that the bar would have leaded glass panels, brought — note the archeological refinement — from the Cicardi Winter Palace of St. Louis. And this, to tell the truth, seems to me the maximum of sincere effort. Here again the authentic pieces, which would make Sotheby's ecstatic, are numerous, but what prevails is the connective tissue, totally reconstructed with arrogant imagination, though explanatory labels are quick to tell you that the good is good, arriving even at certain catalogue naïvetés like the legend stuck on a Dutch porcelain clock in the form of a medieval castle, which says, "Dutch, 1900 ca. ?" The portraits of the proprietors, husband and wife, now happily deceased and assumed into history, dominate the whole. For the prime aim of these wild Xanadus (as of every Xanadu) is not so much to live there, but to make posterity think how exceptional the people who did live there must have been. And, frankly, exceptional gifts would be required — steady nerves and a great love of the past or the future — to stay in these rooms, to make love, to have a pee, eat a hamburger, read the newspaper, button your fly. These eclectic

27

reconstructions are governed by a great remorse for the wealth that was acquired by methods less noble than the architecture that crowns them, a great will to expiatory sacrifice, a desire for posterity's absolution.

But it is hard to apply punishing irony to these pathetic ventures, because other powerful people have thought to assert their place in history through the Nuremberg Stadium or the Foro Mussolini, and there is something disarming about this search for glory via an unrequited love for the European past. We are tempted to feel sorry for the poor history-less millionaire who, to recreate Europe in desolate savannahs, destroys the genuine savannah and turns it into an unreal lagoon. But surely this hand-to-hand battle with history, pathetic as it may be, cannot be justified, because history will not be imitated. It has to be made, and the architecturally superior America shows this is possible.

The Wall Street area in New York is composed of skyscrapers, neo-Gothic cathedrals, neoclassical Parthenons, and primary cubelike structures. Its builders were no less daring than the Hearsts and the Ringlings, and you can also find here a Palazzo Strozzi, property of the Federal Reserve Bank of New York, complete with rustication and all. Built in 1924 of "Indiana limestone and Ohio sandstone," it ceases its Renaissance imitation at the third floor, rightly, and continues with eight more stories of its own invention, then displays Guelph battlements, then continues as skyscraper. But there is nothing to object to here, because lower Manhattan is a masterpiece of living architecture, crooked like the lower line of Cowboy Kate's teeth; skyscrapers and Gothic cathedrals compose what has been called a jam session in stone, certainly the greatest in the history of mankind. Here, moreover, the Gothic and the neoclassical do not seem the effect of cold reasoning; they illustrate the revivalist awareness of the period when they were built, and so they aren't fakes, at least no more than the Madeleine is, in Paris, and they are not incredible, any more than the Victor Emmanuel monument is, in Rome. Everything is integrated in a now homogeneous urban landscape, because real cities redeem, in their context, even what is architectonically ugly. And perhaps in New York the Ca' d'Zan of Sarasota would be acceptable, just as in Venice, on the Grand Canal, so many sibling-palazzos of the Ca' d'Zan are acceptable.

In fact, a good urban context and the history it represents teach, with a sense of humor, even kitsch how to live, and thus exorcise it. On the way between San Simeon and Sarasota I stopped in New Orleans. I was coming from the recreated New Orleans of Disneyland, and I wanted to check my reactions against the real city, which represents a still intact past, because the Vieux Carré is one of the few places that American civilization hasn't remade, flattened, replaced. The structure of the old Creole city has remained as it was, with its low houses, its cast-iron balconies and arcades, reasonably rusted and worn, its tilting buildings that mutually support one another, like buildings you see in Paris or Amsterdam, repainted perhaps, but not too much. Storyville is gone; there is no Basin Street left, no red-light district, but there are countless strip joints with doors open onto the street, in the racket of bands, of circulating tourists, strolling idlers. The Vieux Carré isn't the least like the entertainment district of an American city; it is more like a cousin of Montmartre. In this corner of pretropical Europe there are still restaurants inhabited by *Gone with the Wind* characters, where waiters in tails discuss with you the alterations in sauce béarnaise due to the impact of local spices. Other places, strangely similar to a Milanese *brasera*, know the mysteries of *bollito* with green sauce (shamelessly presented as Creole cuisine).

On the Mississippi you can take a six-hour trip on a paddle-steamer, obviously fake, constructed according to the latest mechanical criteria, but still it transports you along wild shores inhabited by alligators as far as Barataria, where Jean Lafitte and his pirates hid before joining up with Andrew Jackson to fight the British. So in New Orleans, history still exists and is tangible, and

29

under the porch of the Presbythère there stands, a forgotten archeological item, one of the first submarines in the world, with which Confederate sailors attacked Yankee vessels during the Civil War. Like New York, New Orleans knows its own fakes and historicizes them: In various patrician houses in Louisiana, for example, there exist copies of Ingres's portrait of Napoleon enthroned, because many French artists came here in the nineteenth century saying they were pupils of the great painter, and they distributed copies, more or less reduced, and more or less successful, but this was in a time when oil copies were the only way of knowing the original, and local historiography celebrates these copies as the documentation of their own "coloniality." The fake is recognized as "historical," and is thus garbed in authenticity.

Now in New Orleans, too, there is a wax museum, devoted to the history of Louisiana. The figures are well made, the costumes and furnishings are honestly precise. But the atmosphere is different; the circus feeling, the magic aura are absent. The explanatory panels have an undertone of skepticism and humor; when an episode is legendary, it is presented as such, and perhaps with the admission that it is more fun to reconstruct legend than history. The sense of history allows an escape from the temptations of hyperreality. Napoleon, seated in his bathtub, discussing the sale of Louisiana, according to the memoirs of the period should spring up and spatter water on the others present; but the Museum explains that costumes are very expensive and apologizes for not attempting absolute verisimilitude. The waxworks refer to legends that have left their traces in the streets of the neighborhood: the colony, the aristocrats, the Creole beauties, the prostitutes, the pitiless swordsmen, the pirates, the riverboat gamblers, jazz, the Canadians, Spanish, French, English. New Orleans is not in the grip of a neurosis of a denied past; it passes out memories generously like a great lord; it doesn't have to pursue "the real thing."

Elsewhere, on the contrary, the frantic desire for the Almost Real arises only as a neurotic reaction to the vacuum of memories;

the Absolute Fake is offspring of the unhappy awareness of a present without depth.

The Monasteries of Salvation

The art patronage of California and Florida has shown that to be D'Annunzio (and to outstrip him) you don't have to be a crowned poet; you only have to have a lot of money, plus a sincere worship of all-consuming syncretism. And yet you can't help wondering whether, when America patronizes the past, it always does so in a spirit of gluttony and bricolage. So we had to run other checks, but our trip was undertaken in the name of the Absolute Fake, and thus we had to exclude examples of correct, philological art collections, where famous works are shown without any manipulation. Extreme instances had to be found, examples of the conjunction of archeology and falsification. And California in this respect is still the land of gold mines.

Eyes (and nerves) saturated with wax museums, Citizen Kane castles, and Madonna Inns, we approach the J. Paul Getty Museum in Malibu, on the Pacific coast below Santa Monica, in a spirit of profound mistrust. The beautiful and sensitive curator (wife of a university colleague in Los Angeles) who introduces me to the mysteries of the museum, sparing me the use of the earpiece and personal cassette supplied to visitors, is very reticent. She knows why I have come to the Getty Museum and where I have been recently; she is afraid of my sarcasm, as she shows me rooms filled with works by Raphael, Titian, Paolo Uccello, Veronese, Magnasco, Georges de la Tour, Poussin, even Alma-Tadema; and she is amazed at my bored manner as, after days of fake Last Suppers and Venuses de Milo, I cast absent glances on these drearily authentic pictures. She leads me through the wondrous collection of sculpture, Greek, Hellenistic, Roman, and takes me to the restoration workshop, where with scientific skill and philological scruple they chip away from the latest acquisitions even

31

noses added in the eighteenth century, because the Museum's philosophy is stern, learned, fiercely German; and J. Paul Getty has
proved in fact a cultivated patron, who wants to show the California public only works of unquestionable worth and authenticity.
But my Beatrice is shy and apologizes because to reach the inner
rooms we have to cross two large gardens and the airy peristyle.
We cross the Villa of the Papyruses of Herculaneum, totally reconstructed, with its colonnades, the Pompeiian wall-paintings, intact and dazzling, the snowy marble, the statue-population of the
garden where only plants that flourish along the bay of Naples are
growing. We have crossed something that is more than the Villa
of the Papyruses, because the Villa of the Papyruses is incomplete,
still buried, the supposition of an ancient Roman villa, whereas the
Malibu one is all there. J. Paul Getty's archeologists worked from
drawings, models of other Roman villas, learned conjectures, and
archeological syllogisms, and they have reconstructed the building
as it was or at least as it ought to have been. My guide is bewildered, because she knows that the most modern notions of mu-
seography insist that the container should be modern and aseptic,
and the number-one model is Wright's Guggenheim Museum. She
senses that the public, flung from the realer-than-real reconstruction to the authentic, could lose its bearings and consider the exterior real and the interior a great assemblage of modern copies.
In the decorative arts section, the Versailles rooms contain only
real and precious pieces, but here, too, the reconstruction is total,
even if the guidebook specifies what is antique and what is reconstruction, and the Régence Period Room is sheathed in the paneling from the Hôtel Herlaut, but the plaster cornice and the rosette
are reconstructed and the parquet, though also eighteenth-
century, was not part of the original room. The period commodes
also come from other residences, and are too numerous. And so
on. To be sure, in this reconstruction the visitor gets an idea of
the architecture of French rococo interiors far better than if he
saw the items displayed in separate cases, but the curators of the

Getty Museum are European-trained and fear that their work may be contaminated by the suspicion and confusion generated by experiments like the Hearst Castle.

For the rest, J. Paul Getty's declarations, quoted in the guide, are perceptive and coherent. If there is error, it is lucid error; there is nothing makeshift or ingenuous, but a precise philosophy of how the European past can be reexperienced on the coast of a California torn between memories of the pioneers and Disneyland, and hence a country with much future but no historical reminiscence.

How can a rich man, a lover of the arts, recall the emotions he felt one day in Herculaneum or in Versailles? And how can he help his compatriots understand what Europe is? It is easy to say: Put your objects all in a row with explanatory labels in a neutral setting. In Europe the neutral setting is called the Louvre, Castello Sforzesco, Uffizi, Tate Gallery (just a short walk from Westminster Abbey). It is easy to give a neutral setting to visitors who can breathe in the Past a few steps away, who reach the neutral setting after having walked, with emotion, among venerable stones. But in California, between the Pacific on one hand and Los Angeles on the other, with restaurants shaped like hats and hamburgers, and four-level freeways with ten thousand ramps, what do you do? You reconstruct the Villa of the Papyruses. You put yourself in the hands of the German archeologist, taking care he doesn't overdo; you place your busts of Hercules in a construction that reproduces a Roman temple; and if you have the money, you make sure that your marble comes from the original places of the model, that the workers are all from Naples, Carrara, Venice, and you also announce this. Kitsch? Perhaps. But in the Hearst Castle sense? Not exactly. In the sense of the Palace of Living Arts or the magic rooms of the Madonna Inn? The Venus de Milo with arms? Absolutely not.

The Palace of Living Arts and the Madonna Inn are the work of shrewd exploiters of the prestige of art. The Lyndon Johnson

Memorial is the work of a nouveau riche Texan who thought that his every act had become worthy of historiography and who raised a cenotaph to his laundry list. The Hearst Castle is the work of a too rich, too greedy rich man, starved not only for art but for the prestige that art can confer; and only the money at his disposal and his eclectic receptiveness kept him from making a total fake (but thus more authentic) like the castle of Ludwig of Bavaria, which is completely Gothic as Gothic was understood in the later nineteenth century.

The Getty Museum, on the contrary, is the work of one man and his collaborators who tried in their way to reconstruct a credible and "objective" past. If the Greek statues are not Greek, they are at least good Roman copies, and presented as such; if the tapestries based on authentic Raphael cartoons were woven today, they were studied so as to put the picture in a setting not unlike the one for which it was designed. The Cybele from the Mattei collection in Rome is placed in a temple of Cybele whose freshness, whose air of being just completed, upsets us, accustomed as we are to ancient, half-ruined temples; but the museum archeologists have made sure that it would look the way a little Roman temple must have looked when just finished; and for that matter we know very well that many classical statues, which fascinate us with their whiteness, were originally polychrome, and in the eyes, now blank, there was a painted pupil. The Getty Museum leaves the statues white (and in this sense is perhaps guilty of European-style archeological fetishism); but it supplies polychrome marbles for the walls of the temple, presented as a hypothetical model. We are tempted to think that Getty is more faithful to the past when he reconstructs the temple than when he displays the statue in its chill incompleteness and the unnatural isolation of the "correct" restoration.

In other words the Getty Museum, after the first reaction of mockery or puzzlement, raises a question: Who is right? How do you regain contact with the past? Archeological respect is only one of the possible solutions; other periods resolved the problem differently. Does the J. Paul Getty solution belong to the contemporary period? We try to think how a Roman patrician lived and what he was thinking when he built himself one of the villas that the Getty Museum reconstructs, in its need to reconstruct at home the grandeur of Greek civilization. The Roman yearned for impossible parthenons; from Hellenistic artists he ordered copies of the great statues of the Periclean age. He was a greedy shark who, after having helped bring down Greece, guaranteed its survival in the form of copies. Between the Roman patrician and the Greece of the fifth century there were, we might say, from five to seven hundred years. Between the Getty Museum and the remade Rome there are, roughly speaking, two thousand. The temporal gap is bridged by archeological knowledge; we can rely on the Getty team, their reconstruction is more faithful to Herculaneum than the Herculaneum reproduction was faithful to the Greek tradition. But the fact is that our journey into the Absolute Fake, begun in the spirit of irony and sophisticated repulsion, is now exposing us to some dramatic questions.

We leave the Getty Museum, we make a little hop of a few thousand miles, and we reach the Ringling Museum of Art in Florida. The Ringlings were not oil millionaires but circus owners. When they built themselves a palazzo, they made a Venetian fake that, all things considered, cost less than the Hearst castle and has an even greater abundance of fake certificates. But, in the same park on Sarasota Bay, they created an art museum that, when it comes to genuine works, can compare with the Getty: Caravaggio, Gaudenzio Ferrari, Piero di Cosimo, Rubens, El Greco, Cranach, Rembrandt, Veronese, Hals. It is smaller than the Louvre but bigger than the Frick. People who had money and spent it well.

But what houses the Museum? A vast, airy Renaissance villa, slightly out of kilter when it comes to proportions—dominated by a Michelangelo David—its colonnade filled with Etruscan statues (presumably authentic and snatched in periods when the tombs were less protected than they are today), a pleasant Italian garden. This garden is peopled with statues: It's like going to a party and finding old friends: Here is the Discobulus, over there's the Laocoön, hello Apollo Belvedere, how've you been? My God, always the same crowd.

Naturally, while the pictures inside are genuine, these statues are fakes. And the bronze plaques under each clearly say so. But what is the meaning of "fake" when applied to a plaster cast or a bronze recasting? We read one of the plaques, at random: "Dancer. Modern cast in bronze from a Greek original of the fifth century B.C. The original [or rather the Roman copy] is in the Museo Nazionale in Naples." So? The European museum has a Roman copy. But these are copies of sculpture, where if you observe certain technical criteria nothing is lost. Who has the heart to protest? And should we protest because the Giovanni da Bologna stands fairly close to the Laocoön, when in our own museums the same thing happens? Shall we protest, on the contrary, because the imitation of the Renaissance loggia, which is acceptable, is near the Grand Canal villa, which is crude? But what would happen to the visitor who, a thousand years hence, visited these mementoes, ignorant of a Europe long since vanished? Something like what happens to the visitor in today's Rome when he walks from the great insurance company's Palazzo in Piazza Venezia, past the Victor Emmanuel monument, down Mussolini's Via dei Fori Imperiali, to the Colosseum and then to the patches of the Servian walls trapped inside the Termini railroad station.

The condition for the amalgamation of fake and authentic is that there must have been a historic catastrophe, of the sort that has made the divine Acropolis of Athens as venerable as Pompeii, city of brothels and bakeries. And this brings us to the theme of the Last Beach, the apocalyptic philosophy that more or less explicitly rules these reconstructions: Europe is declining into barbarism and something has to be saved. This may not have been the reasoning of the Roman patrician, but it was that of the medieval art lover who accumulated classical reminiscences with incredible philological nonchalance and (see Gerbert d'Aurillac) mistook a manuscript of Statius for an armillary sphere, but could also have done the opposite (Huizinga says that the medieval man's sensitivity to works of art is the same that we would expect today from an astonished bourgeois). And we don't feel like waxing ironic on the piety mixed with accumulative instinct that led the Ringlings to purchase the entire theater of Asolo (wooden frame, stage, boxes, and gallery), which was housed in the villa of Caterina Cornaro from 1798 (and welcomed Eleonora Duse) but which was dismantled in 1930 and sold to a dealer in order to make room for a "more modern" hall. Now the theater is not far from the fake Venetian palazzo and houses artistic events of considerable distinction.

But to understand the Last Beach theme we must go back to California and to the Forest Lawn–Glendale cemetery. The founder's idea was that Forest Lawn, at its various sites, should be a place not of grief but of serenity, and there is nothing like Nature and Art for conveying this feeling. So Mr. Eaton, inventor of the new philosophy, peopled Forest Lawn with copies of the great masterpieces of the past, David and Moses, the St. George of Donatello, a marble reproduction of Raphael's Sistine Madonna, complementing it all with authentic declarations from Italian Government fine arts authorities, certifying that the Forest Lawn founders really did visit all the Italian museums to commission "authentic" copies of the real masterpieces of the Renaissance.

To see the Last Supper, admitted at fixed times as if for a theater performance, you have to take your seat, facing a curtain, with the Pietà on your left and the Medici Tombs sculptures on your right. Before the curtain rises, you have to hear a long speech that explains how in fact this crypt is the new Westminster Abbey and contains the graves of Gutzon Borglum, Jan Styka, Carrie Jacobs Bond, and Robert Andrews Millikan. Apart from mentioning the fact that the last-named won a Nobel Prize in physics, I won't

37

even try to say who the others are (but Mrs. Bond is the composer of "I Love You Truly"). If it hadn't been for Westminster Abbey, many characters we consider historic today would have remained insignificant barons: In the construction of Immortal Fame you need first of all a cosmic shamelessness.

Very well. Before revealing to the dewy eyes of the audience the stained-glass reproduction of the Last Supper, the Voice tells us what happened to Mr. Eaton when he went to Santa Maria delle Grazie and realized that the joint action of time and human wickedness (it was before the Second World War) would one day destroy Leonardo's masterpiece. Gripped by a sacred fever of preservation, Mr. Eaton contacts Signora Rosa Caselli-Moretti, descended of an ancient family of Perugian artisans, and commissions her to make a *glass* reproduction of Leonardo's masterpiece. Not the way it looks now in Santa Maria delle Grazie, but the way we suppose it must have looked when Leonardo painted it, or rather—better— the way Leonardo ought to have painted it if he had been less shiftless, spending three years and never managing to complete the picture. At this point the curtain rises. And I must say that, compared with the wax reproductions scattered all over California, this work by Signora Caselli-Moretti is a piece of honest craftsmanship and would not look out of place in a nineteenth-century European church. The artist also had the good sense to leave the face of Christ vague, sharing Leonardo's own fear in dealing with the icon of the Divine; and, from behind the glass, the cemetery management shines various lights that render every nuance of the sun (dawn, noon, dusk) in such a way as to demonstrate the mobility of the face of Jesus in the play of atmospheric variations.

All this machinery to reproduce the Past at Forest Lawn is exploited for profit. But the ideology proclaimed by Forest Lawn is the same as that of the Getty Museum, which charges no admission. It is the ideology of preservation, in the New World, of the treasures that the folly and negligence of the Old World are causing to disappear into the void. Naturally this ideology conceals something—the desire for profit, in the case of the cemetery; and in the case of Getty, the fact that it is the entrepreneurial colonization by the New World (of which J. Paul Getty's oil empire is part) that makes the Old World's condition critical. Just like the crocodile tears of the Roman patrician who reproduced the grandeurs of the very Greece that his country had humiliated and reduced to a colony. And so the Last Beach ideology develops its thirst for preservation of art from an imperialistic efficiency, but at the same time it is the bad conscience of this imperialistic efficiency, just as cultural anthropology is the bad conscience of the white man who thus pays his debt to the destroyed primitive cultures.

But, having said this, we must in fairness employ this American reality as a critical reagent for an examination of conscience regarding European taste. Can we be sure that the European tourist's pilgrimage to the *Pietà* of St. Peter's is less fetishistic than the American tourist's pilgrimage to the Pietà of Forest Lawn (here more accessible, tangible at close range)? Actually, in these museums the idea of the "multiple" is perfected. The Goethe Institut recently remade in Cologne Man Ray's spiked flatiron and his metronome with an eye; and since Duchamp's bicycle wheel survives only in a photograph, they reconstructed an identical one. In fact, once the fetishistic desire for the original is forgotten, these copies are perfect. And at this point isn't the enemy of the rights of art the engraver who defaces the plate to keep low the number of prints?

This is not an attempt to absolve the shrines of the Fake, but to call the European sanctuaries of the Genuine to assume their share of guilt.

The City of Robots

In Europe, when people wants to be amused, they go to a "house" of amusement (whether a cinema, theater, or casino); sometimes a "park" is created, which may seem a "city," but only metaphorically. In the United States, on the contrary, as everyone knows, there exist amusement cities. Las Vegas is one example; it is focused on gambling and entertainment, its architecture is totally artificial, and it has been studied by Robert Venturi as a completely new phenomenon in city planning, a "message" city, entirely made up of signs, not a city like the others, which communicate in order to function, but rather a city that functions in order to communicate. But Las Vegas is still a "real" city, and in a recent essay on Las Vegas, Giovanni Brino showed how, though born as a place for gambling, it is gradually being transformed into a residential city, a place of business, industry, conventions. The theme of our trip—on the contrary—is the Absolute Fake; and therefore we are interested only in absolutely fake cities. Disneyland (California) and Disney World (Florida) are obviously the chief examples, but if they existed alone they would represent a negligible exception. The fact is that the United States is filled with cities that imitate a city, just as wax museums imitate painting and the Venetian palazzos or Pompeiian villas imitate architecture. In particular there are the "ghost towns," the Western cities of a century and more ago. Some are reasonably authentic, and the restoration or preservation has been carried out on an extant, "archeological" urban complex; but more interesting are those born from nothing, out of pure imitative determination. They are "the real thing."

There is an embarrassment of riches to choose from: You can have fragments of cities, as at Stone Mountain near Atlanta, where you take a trip on a nineteenth-century train, witness an Indian raid, and see sheriffs at work, against the background of a fake Mount Rushmore. The Six Guns Territory, in Silver Springs, also has train and sheriffs, a shoot-out in the streets and French cancan in the saloon. There is a series of ranchos and Mexican missions in Arizona; Tombstone with its OK Corral, Old Tucson, Legend City near Phoenix. There is the Old South Bar-b-Q Ranch at Clewison, Florida, and so on. If you venture beyond the myth of the West, you have cities like the Magic Mountain in Valencia, California, or Santa Claus Village, Polynesian gardens, pirate islands, Astroworlds like the one in Kirby, Texas, and the "wild" territories of the various Marinelands, as well as ecological cities, which we will discuss elsewhere.

There are also the ship imitations. In Florida, for example, between Tampa and St. Petersburg, you can board the *Bounty*, anchored at the edge of a Tahitian village, faithfully reconstructed according to the drawings preserved by the Royal Society in London, but with an eye also on the old film with Charles Laughton and Clark Gable. Many of the nautical instruments are of the period, some of the sailors are waxworks, one officer's shoes are those worn by the actor who played the part, the historical information on the various panels is credible, the voices that pervade the atmosphere come from the sound track of the movie. But we'll stick to the Western myth and take as a sample city the Knott's Berry Farm of Buena Park, Los Angeles.

Here the whole trick seems to be exposed; the surrounding city context and the iron fencing (as well as the admission ticket) warn us that we are entering not a real city but a toy city. But as we begin walking down the first streets, the studied illusion takes over. First of all, there is the realism of the reconstruction: the dusty stables, the sagging shops, the offices of the sheriff and the telegraph agent, the jail, the saloon are life size and executed with absolute fidelity; the old carriages are covered with dust, the Chinese laundry is dimly lit, all the buildings are more or less practical, and the shops are open, because Berry Farm, like Disneyland, blends the reality of trade with the play of fiction. And if the dry-goods store is fake nineteenth-century and the shopgirl is dressed like a John Ford heroine, the candies, the peanuts, the pseudo-Indian handicrafts are real and are sold for real dollars, just as the soft drinks, advertised with antique posters, are real, and the customer finds himself participating in the fantasy because of his own authenticity as a consumer; in other words, he is in the role of the cowboy or the gold-prospector who comes into town to be fleeced. of all he has accumulated while out in the wilds.

Furthermore the levels of illusion are numerous, and this increases the hallucination—that is to say, the Chinese in the laundry or the prisoner in the jail are wax dummies, who exist, in realistic attitudes, in settings that are equally realistic, though you can't actually enter them; but you don't realize that the room in question is a glass display case, because it looks as if you could, if you chose, open the door or climb through the window; and then the next room, say, which is both the general store and the justice of the peace's office, looks like a display case but is actually practical, and the justice of the peace, with his black alpaca jacket and his pistols at his hips, is an actual person who sells you his merchandise. It should be added that extras walk about the streets and periodically stage a furious gun battle, and when you realize that the average American visitor is wearing blue jeans not very different from the cowboys', many of the visitors become confused with the extras, increasing the theatricality of the whole. For example, the village school, reconstructed with hyperrealistic detail, has behind the desk a schoolmarm wearing a bonnet and an ample checked skirt, but the children on the benches are little passing visitors, and I heard one tourist ask his wife if the children were real or "fake" (and you could sense his psychological readiness to consider them, at will, extras, dummies, or moving robots of the sort we will see in Disneyland).

Apparently ghost towns involve a different approach from that of wax museums or museums for copies of works of art. In the first nobody expects the wax Napoleon to be taken for real, but the hallucination serves to level the various historical periods and erase the distinction between historical reality and fantasy; in the case of the works of art what is culturally, if not psychologically, hallucinatory is the confusion between copy and original, and the fetishization of art as a sequence of famous subjects. In the ghost town, on the contrary, since the theatricality is explicit, the hallucination operates in making the visitors take part in the scene and thus become participants in that commercial fair that is apparently an element of the fiction but in fact represents the substantial aim of the whole imitative machine.

In an excellent essay on Disneyland as "degenerate utopia" ("a degenerate utopia is an ideology realized in the form of myth"), Louis Marin analyzed the structure of that nineteenth-century frontier city street that receives entering visitors and distributes them through the various sectors of the magic city. Disneyland's Main Street seems the first scene of the fiction whereas it is an extremely shrewd commercial reality. Main Street—like the whole city, for that matter—is presented as at once absolutely realistic and absolutely fantastic, and this is the advantage (in terms of artistic conception) of Disneyland over the other toy cities. The houses of Disneyland are full-size on the ground floor, and on a two-thirds scale on the floor above, so they give the impression of being inhabitable (and they are) but also of belonging to a fantastic past that we can grasp with our imagination. The Main Street façades are presented to us as toy houses and invite us to enter them, but their interior is always a disguised supermarket, where you buy obsessively, believing that you are still playing.

In this sense Disneyland is more hyperrealistic than the wax museum, precisely because the latter still tries to make us believe that what we are seeing reproduces reality absolutely, whereas Disneyland makes it clear that within its magic enclosure it is fantasy that is absolutely reproduced. The Palace of Living Arts presents its Venus de Milo as almost real, whereas Disneyland can permit itself to present its reconstructions as masterpieces of falsification, for what it sells is, indeed, goods, but genuine merchandise, not reproductions. What is falsified is our will to buy, which we take as real, and in this sense Disneyland is really the quintessence of consumer ideology.

But once the "total fake" is admitted, in order to be enjoyed it must seem totally real. So the Polynesian restaurant will have,

43

in addition to a fairly authentic menu, Tahitian waitresses in costume, appropriate vegetation, rock walls with little cascades, and once you are inside nothing must lead you to suspect that outside there is anything but Polynesia. If, between two trees, there appears a stretch of river that belongs to another sector, Adventureland, then that section of stream is so designed that it would not be unrealistic to see in Tahiti, beyond the garden hedge, a river like this. And if in the wax museums wax is not flesh, in Disneyland, when rocks are involved, they are rock, and water is water, and a baobab a baobab. When there is a fake—hippopotamus, dinosaur, sea serpent—it is not so much because it wouldn't be possible to have the real equivalent but because the public is meant to admire the perfection of the fake and its obedience to the program. In this sense Disneyland not only produces illusion, but—in confessing it—stimulates the desire for it: A real crocodile can be found in the zoo, and as a rule it is dozing or hiding, but Disneyland tells us that faked nature corresponds much more to our daydream demands. When, in the space of twenty-four hours, you go (as I did deliberately) from the fake New Orleans of Disneyland to the real one, and from the wild river of Adventureland to a trip on the Mississippi, where the captain of the paddle-wheel steamer says it is possible to see alligators on the banks of the river, and then you don't see any, you risk feeling homesick for Disneyland, where the wild animals don't have to be coaxed. Disneyland tells us that technology can give us more reality than nature can.

In this sense I believe the most typical phenomenon of this universe is not the more famous Fantasyland—an amusing carousel of fantastic journeys that take the visitor into the world of Peter Pan or Snow White, a wondrous machine whose fascination and lucid legitimacy it would be foolish to deny—but the Caribbean Pirates and the Haunted Mansion. The pirate show lasts a quarter of an hour (but you lose any sense of time, it could be ten minutes or thirty); you enter a series of caves, carried in boats over the surface of the water, you see first abandoned treasures, a captain's skeleton in a sumptuous bed of moldy brocade, pendent cobwebs, bodies of executed men devoured by ravens, while the skeleton addresses menacing admonitions to you. Then you navigate an inlet, passing through the crossfire of a galleon and the cannon of a fort, while the chief corsair shouts taunting challenges at the beleaguered garrison; then, as if along a river, you go by an invaded city which is being sacked, with the rape of the women, theft of jewels, torture of the mayor; the city burns like a match, drunken pirates sprawled on piles of kegs sing obscene songs; some, completely out of their heads, shoot at the visitors; the scene degenerates, everything collapses in flames, slowly the last songs die away, you emerge into the sunlight. Everything you have seen was on human scale, the vault of the caves became confused with that of the sky, the boundary of this underground world was that of the universe and it was impossible to glimpse its limits. The pirates moved, danced, slept, popped their eyes, sniggered, drank—really. You realize that they are robots, but you remain dumbfounded by their verisimilitude. And, in fact, the "Audio-Animatronic" technique represented a great source of pride for Walt Disney, who had finally managed to achieve his own dream and reconstruct a fantasy world more real than reality, breaking down the wall of the second dimension, creating not a movie, which is illusion, but total theater, and not with anthropomorphized animals, but with human beings. In fact, Disney's robots are masterpieces of electronics; each was devised by observing the expressions of a real actor, then building models, then developing skeletons of absolute precision, authentic computers in human form, to be dressed in "flesh" and "skin" made by craftsmen, whose command of realism is incredible. Each robot obeys a program, can synchronize the movements of mouth and eyes with the words and sounds of the audio, repeating ad infinitum all day long his established part (a sentence, one or two gestures) and the visitor, caught off guard by the succession of events, obliged to see several

45

things at once, to left and right and straight ahead, has no time to look back and observe that the robot he has just seen is already repeating his eternal scenario.

The "Audio-Animatronic" technique is used in many other parts of Disneyland and also enlivens a review of presidents of the United States, but in the pirates' cave, more than anywhere else, it demonstrates all its miraculous efficacy. Humans could do no better, and would cost more, but the important thing is precisely the fact that these are not humans and we know they're not. The pleasure of imitation, as the ancients knew, is one of the most innate in the human spirit; but here we not only enjoy a perfect imitation, we also enjoy the conviction that imitation has reached its apex and afterwards reality will always be inferior to it.

Similar criteria underlie the journey through the cellars of the Haunted Mansion, which looks at first like a rundown country house, somewhere between Edgar Allan Poe and the cartoons of Charles Addams; but inside, it conceals the most complete array of witchcraft surprises that anyone could desire. You pass through an abandoned graveyard, where skeletal hands raise gravestones from below, you cross a hill enlivened by a witches' sabbath complete with spirits and beldams; then you move through a room with a table all laid and a group of transparent ghosts in nineteenth-century costume dancing while diaphanous guests, occasionally vanishing into thin air, enjoy the banquet of a barbaric sovereign. You are grazed by cobwebs, reflected in crystals on whose surface a greenish figure appears, behind your back; you encounter moving candelabra. . . . In no instance are these the cheap tricks of some tunnel of love; the involvement (always tempered by the humor of the inventions) is total. As in certain horror films, detachment is impossible; you are not witnessing another's horror, you are inside the horror through complete synesthesia; and if there is an earthquake the movie theater must also tremble.

I would say that these two attractions sum up the Disneyland philosophy more than the equally perfect models of the pirate ship, the river boat, and the sailing ship *Columbia*, all obviously in working order. And more than the Future section, with the science-fiction emotions it arouses (such as a flight to Mars experienced from inside a spacecraft, with all the effects of deceleration, loss of gravity, dizzying movement away from the earth, and so on). More than the models of rockets and atomic submarines, which prompted Marin to observe that whereas the fake Western cities, the fake New Orleans, the fake jungle provide life-size duplicates of organic but historical or fantastic events, these are reduced-scale models of mechanical realities of today, and so, where something is incredible, the full-scale model prevails, and where it is credible, the reduction serves to make it attractive to the imagination. The Pirates and the Ghosts sum up all Disneyland, at least from the point of view of our trip, because they transform the whole city into an immense robot, the final realization of the dreams of the eighteenth-century mechanics who gave life to the Writer of Neuchâtel and the Chess-playing Turk of Baron von Kempelen.

Disneyland's precision and coherence are to some extent disturbed by the ambitions of Disney World in Florida. Built later, Disney World is a hundred fifty times larger than Disneyland, and proudly presents itself not as a toy city but as the model of an urban agglomerate of the future. The structures that make up California's Disneyland form here only a marginal part of an immense complex of construction covering an area twice the size of Manhattan. The great monorail that takes you from the entrance to the Magic Kingdom (the Disneyland part proper) passes artificial bays and lagoons, a Swiss village, a Polynesian village, golf courses and tennis courts, an immense hotel: an area dedicated, in other words, to organized vacationing. So you reach the Magic Kingdom, your eyes already dazzled by so much science fiction that the sight of the high medieval castle (far more Gothic than Disneyland: a Strasbourg Cathedral, let's say, compared to a San Miniato) no longer stirs the imagination. Tomorrow, with its violence, has made the colors fade from the stories of Yesterday. In this respect Disneyland is much shrewder; it must be visited without anything to remind us of the future surrounding it. Marin has observed that, to enter it, the essential condition is to abandon your car in an endless parking lot and reach the boundary of the dream city by special little trains. And for a Californian, leaving his car means leaving his own humanity, consigning himself to another power, abandoning his own will.

An allegory of the consumer society, a place of absolute iconism, Disneyland is also a place of total passivity. Its visitors must agree to behave like its robots. Access to each attraction is regulated by a maze of metal railings which discourages any individual initiative. The number of visitors obviously sets the pace of the line; the officials of the dream, properly dressed in the uniforms suited to each specific attraction, not only admit the visitor to the threshold of the chosen sector, but, in successive phases, regulate his every move ("Now wait here please, go up now, sit down please, wait before standing up," always in a polite tone, impersonal, imperious, over the microphone). If the visitor pays this price, he can have not only "the real thing" but the abundance of the reconstructed truth. Like the Hearst Castle, Disneyland also has no transitional spaces; there is always something to see, the great voids of modern architecture and city planning are unknown here. If America is the country of the Guggenheim Museum or the new skyscrapers of Manhattan, then Disneyland is a curious exception and American intellectuals are quite right to refuse to go there. But if America is what we have seen in the course of our trip, then Disneyland is its Sistine Chapel, and the hyperrealists of the art galleries are only the timid voyeurs of an immense and continuous "found object."

Ecology 1984 and Coca-Cola Made Flesh

Spongeorama, Sea World, Scripps Aquarium, Wild Animal Park, Jungle Gardens, Alligator Farm, Marineland: the coasts of California and Florida are rich in marine cities and artificial jungles where you can see free-ranging animals, trained dolphins, bicycling parrots, otters that drink martinis with an olive and take showers, elephants and camels that carry small visitors on their backs among the palm trees. The theme of hyperrealistic reproduction involves not only Art and History, but also Nature.

The zoo, to begin with. In San Diego each enclosure is the reconstruction, on a vast scale, of an original environment. The dominant theme of the San Diego zoo is the preservation of endangered species, and from this standpoint it is a superb achievement. The visitor has to walk for hours and hours so that bison or birds can always move in a space created to their measure. Of all existing zoos, this is unquestionably the one where the animal is most respected. But it is not clear whether this respect is meant to convince the animal or the human. The human being adapts to any sacrifice, even to not seeing the animals, if he knows that they are alive and in an authentic environment. This is the case with the extremely rare Australian koala, the zoo's symbol, who can live only in a wood entirely of eucalyptus, and so here he has his eucalyptus wood, where he happily hides amid the foliage as the visitors seek desperately to catch a glimpse of him through their binoculars. The invisible koala suggests a freedom that is easily granted to big animals, more visible and more conditioned. Since the temperature around him is artificially kept below zero, the polar bear gives the same impression of freedom; and since the rocks are dark and the water in which he is immersed is rather dirty, the fearsome grizzly also seems to feel at his ease. But ease can be demonstrated only through sociability and so the grizzly, whose name is Chester, waits for the microbus to come by at three-minute intervals and for the girl attendant to shout for Chester to say hello to the people. Then Chester stands up, waves his hand (which is a terrifying huge paw) to say hi. The girl throws him a cookie and we're off again, while Chester waits for the next bus.

This docility arouses some suspicions. Where does the truth of ecology lie? We could say that the suspicions are unfair, because of all possible zoos the San Diego is the most human, or rather, the most animal. But the San Diego zoo contains, *in nuce*, the philosophy that is rampant in such ecological preserves as Wild World or—the one we would choose as an example—Marine World Africa–USA in Redwood City, outside San Francisco. Here we can speak more legitimately of an Industry of the Fake because we find a Disneyland for animals, a corner of Africa made up of sandbars, native huts, palm trees, and rivers plied by rafts and *African Queens*, from which you can admire free-ranging zebras and rhinoceroses on the opposite shore; while in the central nucleus there is a cluster of amphitheaters, underground aquaria, submarine caves inhabited by sharks, glass cases with fierce and terribly poisonous snakes. The symbolic center of Marine World is the Ecology Theater, where you sit in a comfortable amphitheater (and if you don't sit, the polite but implacable hostess will make you, because everything must proceed in a smooth and orderly fashion, and you can't sit where you choose, but if possible next to the latest to be seated, so that the line can move properly and everybody takes his place without pointless search), you face a natural area arranged like a stage. Here there are three girls, with long blond hair and a hippie appearance; one plays very sweet folk songs on the guitar, the other two show us, in succession, a lion cub, a little leopard, and a Bengal tiger only six months old. The animals are on leashes, but even if they weren't they wouldn't seem dangerous because of their tender age and also because, thanks perhaps to a few poppy seeds in their food, they are somewhat sleepy. One of the girls explains that the animals, traditionally ferocious, are actually quite good when they are in a pleasant and friendly environment, and she invites the children in the audience to come up on stage and pet them. The emotion of petting a Bengal tiger isn't an everyday occurrence and the public is spurting ecological goodness from every pore. From the pedagogical point of view, the thing has a certain effect on the young people, and surely it will teach them not to kill fierce animals, assuming that in their later life they happen to encounter any. But to achieve this "natural peace" (as an indirect allegory of social peace) great efforts had to be made: the training of the animals, the construction of an artificial environment that seems natural, the preparation of the hostesses who educate the public. So the final essence of this apologue on the goodness of nature is Universal Taming.

The oscillation between a promise of uncontaminated nature and a guarantee of negotiated tranquillity is constant: In the marine amphitheater where the trained whales perform, these animals are billed as "killer whales," and probably they are very dangerous when they're hungry. Once we are convinced that they are dangerous, it is very satisfying to see them so obedient to orders, diving, racing, leaping into the air, until they actually snatch the fish from the trainer's hand and reply, with almost human moans, to the questions they are asked. The same thing happens in another amphitheater with elephants and apes, and even if this is a normal part of any circus repertory, I must say I have never seen elephants so docile and intelligent. So with its killer whales and its dolphins, its strokable tigers and its elephants that gently sit on the belly of the blond trainer without hurting her, Marine World presents itself as a reduced-scale model of the Golden Age, where the struggle for survival no longer exists, and men and animals interact without conflict. Only, if the Golden Age is to be achieved, animals have to be willing to respect a contract: In return they will be given food, which will relieve them from having to hunt, and humans will love them and defend them against civilization. Marine World seems to be saying that if there is food for all then savage revolt is no longer necessary. But to have food we must accept the *pax* offered by the conqueror. Which, when you think about it, is yet another variation on the theme of the "white man's burden." As in the African stories of Edgar Wallace, it will be Commissioner Sanders who establishes peace along the great river, provided Bozambo doesn't think of organizing an illicit powwow with the other chiefs. In which case the chief will be deposed and hanged.

Strangely, in this ecological theater the visitor isn't on the side of the human master, but on the side of the animals; like them, he has to follow the established routes, sit down at the given moment, buy the straw hats, the lollipops, and the slides that celebrate wild and harmless freedom. The animals earn happiness by being humanized, the visitors by being animalized.

In the humanization of animals is concealed one of the most clever resources of the Absolute Fake industry, and for this reason the Marinelands must be compared with the wax museums that reconstruct the last day of Marie Antoinette. In the latter all is sign but aspires to seem reality. In the Marinelands all is reality but aspires to appear sign. The killer whales perform a square dance and answer the trainers' questions not because they have acquired linguistic ability, but because they have been trained through conditioned reflexes, and we interpret the stimulus-response relationship as a relationship of meaning. Thus in the entertainment industry when there is a sign it seems there isn't one, and when there isn't one we believe that there is. The condition of pleasure is that something be faked. And the Marinelands are more disturbing than other amusement places because here Nature has almost been regained, and yet it is erased by artifice precisely so that it can be presented as uncontaminated nature.

This said, it would be secondhand Frankfurt-school moralism to prolong the criticism. These places are enjoyable. If they existed in our Italian civilization of bird killers, they would represent praiseworthy didactic occasions; love of nature is a constant of the most industrialized nation in the world, like a remorse, just as the love of European art is a passion perennially frustrated. I would like to say that the first, most immediate level of communication that these Wild Worlds achieve is positive; what disturbs us is the allegorical level superimposed on the literal one, the implied promise of a *1984* already achieved at the animal level. What disturbs us is not an evil plan; there is none. It is a symbolic threat. We know that the Good Savage, if he still exists in the equatorial forests, kills crocodiles and hippopotamuses, and if they want to survive the hippopotamuses and the crocodiles must submit to the falsification industry: This leaves us upset. And without alternatives.

The trip through the Wild Worlds has revealed subtle links between the worship of Nature and the worship of Art and History. We have seen that to understand the past, even locally, we must have before our eyes something that resembles as closely as possible the original model. There can be no discussion of the White House or Cape Kennedy unless we have in front of us a reconstruction of the White House or a scale-model of the Cape Kennedy rockets. Knowledge can only be iconic, and iconism can only be absolute. The same thing happens with nature; not only far-off Africa but even the Mississippi must be re-experienced, at Disneyland, as a reconstruction of the Mississippi. It is as if in Rome there were a park that reproduced in smaller scale the hills of the Chianti region. But the parallel is unfair. For the distance between Los Angeles and New Orleans is equal to that between Rome and Khartoum, and it is the spatial, as well as the temporal, distance that drives this country to construct not only imitations of the past and of exotic lands but also imitations of itself.

The problem now, however, is something else. Accustomed to realizing the Distant (in space and in time) through almost "carnal" reproduction, how will the average American realize the relationship with the supernatural?

If you follow the Sunday morning religious programs on TV you come to understand that God can be experienced only as nature, flesh, energy, tangible image. And since no preacher dares show us God in the form of a bearded dummy, or as a Disneyland robot, God can only be found in the form of natural force, joy, healing, youth, health, economic increment (which, let Max Weber teach us, is at once the essence of the Protestant ethic and of the spirit of capitalism).

Oral Roberts is a prophet who looks like a boxer; in the heart of Oklahoma he has created Oral Roberts University, a science-fiction city with computerized teaching equipment, where a "prayer tower" looking something like a TV transmitter sends out through the starry spaces the requests for divine aid that arrive there, accompanied by cash offerings, from all over the world, via Telex, as in the grand hotels. Oral Roberts has the healthy appearance of a retired boxer who isn't above putting on the gloves and trading a few punches every morning, followed by a brisk shower and a Scotch. His broadcast is presented like a religious music hall (Broadway in Heavenly Jerusalem) with interracial singers praising the Lord as they come tap dancing down the stairs, one hand stretched forward, the other behind, singing "ba ba doop" to the tune of "Joshua Fit the Battle of Jericho," or words like "The Lord is my comfort." Oral Roberts sits on the staircase (the reference is to Ziegfeld and not to Odessa) and converses with Mrs. Roberts while reading the letters of distressed faithful. Their problems don't involve matters of conscience (divorce, embezzlement of workers' wages, Pentagon contracts) but rather matters of digestion, of incurable diseases. Oral Roberts is famous because he possesses healing power, the touch that cures. He can't touch over TV, but he constantly suggests an idea of the divine as energy (his usual metaphor is "electric charge"), he orders the devil to take his hands off the postulant, he clenches his fists to convey an idea of vitality and power. God must be perceived in a tactile way, as health and optimism. Oral Roberts sees heaven not as the Mystic Rose but as Marineland. God is a good hippopotamus. A rhinoceros fighting his Armageddon. Go 'way, devil, or God will have you by the balls.

We switch channels. Now a middle-aged Dark Lady is holding forth, on a program about miracles. Believing in miracles means as a rule believing in the cancer that vanishes after the doctors have given up all hope. The miracle is not the Transubstantiation, it is the disappearance of something natural but bad. The Dark Lady, heavily made up and smiling like the wife of a CIA director visiting General Pinochet, interviews four doctors with an array of very convincing degrees and titles. Seated in her garden scented with roses, they try desperately to save their professional dignity. "Dr. Gzrgnibtz, I'm not here to defend God, who doesn't need my help, but tell me: Haven't you ever seen a person who seemed doomed to die and then suddenly recovered?" The doctor is evasive. "Medicine can't explain everything. Sometimes there are psychosomatic factors. Every doctor has seen people with advanced cancers, and two months later they were riding a bicycle." "What did I tell you? It's a remission that can only come from God!" The doctor ventures a last defense of reason: "Science doesn't have all the answers. It can't explain everything. We don't know everything. . . ." The Dark Lady rocks with almost sensual laughter. "What did I tell you? That's the Truth! You've said something very profound, Doctor! We can't know everything! There's your demonstration of the power of God, the supernatural power of God! The supernatural power of God doesn't need any defending. I know! I know! Thank you, dear friends, our time is up!" The Dark Lady didn't even try, as a Catholic bishop would have done, to discover if the healed person had prayed, nor does she wonder why God exercised his power on that man and not on his unfortunate neighbor in the next bed. In the Technicolor rose garden something that "seems" a miracle has taken place, as a wax face seems physically a historic character. Through a play of mirrors and background music, once again the fake seems real. The doctor performs the same function as the certificate from the Italian fine arts authorities in the museums of copies: The copy is authentic.

But if the supernatural can assume only physical forms, such is also the inescapable fate of the Survival of the Soul. This is what the California museums say. Forest Lawn is a concentration of historical memories, Michelangelo reproductions, *Wunderkammern* where you can admire the reproduction of the British crown jewels, the life-size doors of the Florentine Baptistery, the Thinker of Rodin, the Foot of Pasquino, and other assorted bijouterie, all served up with music by Strauss (Johann). The various Forest Lawn cemeteries avoid the individual cenotaph; the art masterpieces of all time belong to the collective heritage. The graves at the Hollywood Forest Lawn are hidden beneath discreet bronze plaques in the grass of the lawns; and in Glendale the crypts are very restrained, with nonstop Muzak and reproductions of nineteenth-century statues of nude girls: Hebes, Venuses, Disarmed Virgins, Pauline Borgheses, a few Sacred Hearts. Forest Lawn's philosophy is described by its founder, Mr. Eaton, on great carved plaques that appear in every cemetery. The idea is very simple: Death is a new life, cemeteries mustn't be places of sadness or a disorganized jumble of funerary statues. They must contain reproductions of the most beautiful artworks of all time, reminders of history (great mosaics of American history, mementoes — fake — of the Revolutionary War), and they must be a place with trees and peaceful little churches where lovers can come and stroll hand in hand (and they do, dammit), where couples can marry (a large sign at the entrance to Forest Lawn–Glendale announces the availability of marriage ceremonies), where the devout can meditate, reassured of the continuity of life. So the great California cemeteries (undeniably more pleasant than ours in Italy) are immense imitations of a natural and aesthetic life that continues after death. Eternity is guaranteed by the presence (in copies) of Michelangelo and Donatello. The eternity of art becomes a metaphor for the eternity of the soul, the vitality of trees and flowers becomes a metonymy of the vitality of the body that is victoriously consumed underground to give new lymph to life. The industry of the Absolute Fake gives a semblance of truth to the myth of immortality through the play of imitations and copies, and it achieves the presence of the divine in the presence of the natural — but the natural is "cultivated" as in the Marinelands.

Immediately outside these enclosures, the amusement industry deals with a new theme: the Beyond as terror, diabolical presence, and nature as the Enemy. While the cemeteries and the wax museums sing of the eternity of Artistic Grace, and the Marinelands raise a paean to the Goodness of the Wild Animal, popular movies, in the vein of *The Exorcist*, tell of a supernatural that is ferocious, diabolical, and hostile. The number-one hit movie, *Jaws*, was about a fierce and insatiable monster animal that devours adults and children after having torn them apart. The shark in *Jaws* is a hyperrealistic model in plastic, "real" and controllable like the audioanimatronic robots of Disneyland. But he is an ideal relative of the killer whales in Marineland. For their part, the devils that invade films like *The Exorcist* are evil relatives of the healing divinity of Oral Roberts; and they reveal themselves through physical means, such as greenish vomit and hoarse voices. And the earthquakes or tidal waves of the disaster movies are the brothers of that Nature that in the California cemeteries seems reconciled with life and death in the form of privet, freshly mown lawns, pines stirring in a gentle breeze. But as Good Nature must be perceived physically also in the form of string music, Evil Nature must be felt in the form of physical jolts through the synesthetic participation of "Sensurround," which shakes the audience in their seats. Everything must be tactile for this widespread and secondary America that has no notion of the Museum of Modern Art and the rebellion of Edward Kienholz, who remakes wax museums but puts on his dummies disturbing heads in the form of clocks or surrealist diving helmets. This is the America of Linus, for whom happiness must assume the form of a warm puppy or a security blanket, the America of Schroeder, who brings Beethoven to life not so much through a simplified score played on a toy piano as through the realistic bust in marble (or rubber). Where Good, Art, Fairytale, and History, unable to become flesh, must at least become Plastic.

The ideology of this America wants to establish reassurance through Imitation. But profit defeats ideology, because the consumers want to be thrilled not only by the guarantee of the Good but also by the shudder of the Bad. And so at Disneyland, along with Mickey Mouse and the kindly Bears, there must also be, in tactile evidence, Metaphysical Evil (the Haunted Mansion) and

Historical Evil (the Pirates), and in the waxwork museums, alongside the Venuses de Milo, we must find the graverobbers, Dracula, Frankenstein, the Wolf Man, Jack the Ripper, the Phantom of the Opera. Alongside the Good Whale there is the restless, plastic form of the Bad Shark. Both at the same level of credibility, both at the same level of fakery. Thus, on entering his cathedrals of iconic reassurance, the visitor will remain uncertain whether his final destiny is hell or heaven, and so will consume new promises.

1975

2

THE RETURN
OF THE
MIDDLE
AGES

Dreaming
of the
Middle Ages

Are there any connections between the Heroic Fantasy of Frank Frazetta, the new satanism, Excalibur, the Avalon sagas, and Jacques Le Goff? If they met aboard some unidentified flying object near Montaillou, would Darth Vader, Jacques Fournier, and Parsifal speak the same language? If so, would it be a galactic pidgin or the Latin of the Gospel according to St. Luke Skywalker?

Indeed, it seems that people like the Middle Ages. A few minutes in an American bookstore allow you to discover many interesting specimens of this neomedieval wave. Let me quote only a few titles of paperbacks you find in the course of a nonsystematic browse: *A World Called Camelot, The Return of the King, The Sword Is Forged, The Lure of the Basilisk, Dragonquest, Dragonflight, The Dome in the Forest, The Last Defender of Camelot, The Dragon Hoard, Dr. Who and the Crusaders, Magic Quest, Camber the Heretic*, plus scattered items ranging from Celtic sagas, witchcraft, enchanted castles, and haunted dungeons to swords in the stone, unicorns, and explicitly neomedieval space operas.

If one does not trust "literature," one should at least trust pop culture. In a drugstore recently I picked up, at random, a series of comic books offering the following smorgasbord: *Conan the King*, *The Savage Sword of Conan the Barbarian*, *Camelot 3000*, *The Sword and the Atom* (these last two displaying a complex intertwining of Dark Ages and laser beams), *The Elektra Saga*, *Crystar the Crystal Warrior*, *Elric of Melibone*. . . .

I could go on. But there is no special reason for amazement at the avalanche of pseudo-medieval pulp in paperbacks, midway between Nazi nostalgia and occultism. A country able to produce Dianetics can do a lot in terms of wash-and-wear sorcery and Holy Grail frappé. It would be small wonder if the next porn hit stars Marilyn Chambers as La Princesse Lointaine (if Americans have succeeded in transforming Rostand's *Chanteclair* into the *Fantastiks*, why not imagine the Princess of Tripoli offering the keys of her chastity belt to a bearded Burt Reynolds?). Not to mention such postmodern neomedieval Manhattan new castles as the Citicorp Center and Trump Tower, curious instances of a new feudalism, with their courts open to peasants and merchants and the well-protected high-level apartments reserved for the lords.

American cultivated masochism has abundantly agonized about such wonders as the Hearst Castle and the exterior of the Cloisters (the interior being more philologically inspired). But this is beside the point.

The chronicles of the New Middle Ages also tell of thousands of readers discovering Barbara Tuchman. The director of the Metropolitan Museum has decided to exhibit as "real" fakes all the forgeries that his public previously admired as the real thing, and the crowds queueing at the museum, a few years ago, for the exhibition of medieval Irish art are a clear symptom of a new taste.

America, having come to grips with 1776, is devouring the Real Past. Canned philology perhaps, but philology all the same. The Americans want and really like responsible historical reconstruction (perhaps because only after a text has been rigorously reconstructed can it be irresponsibly deconstructed). Like many

Europeans, many Americans also took the film *Excalibur* as the real Middle Ages; but many, many others are looking for something more real.

What's happening on the other side of the Atlantic Ocean? In Great Britain and France the nineteenth century was the age of the historical novel, of Walter Scott and Victor Hugo, and there is a fate which links the historical novel to medieval topics. This trend never died, and the shelves of every bookstore in London or Paris are full of interesting examples of medieval novels or romances. On the other hand, Italians have never scored remarkable achievements in this field. The relationship between Italian literature and the Middle Ages has always been unfortunate. Such names as Guerrazzi, Cantù, Grossi, and D'Azeglio sound unfamiliar to foreign ears, and rightly so. With perhaps the sole exception of D'Azeglio's *Ettore Fieramosca*, the medieval stuff produced in Italy during the last century was clumsy, boring, and bombastic. Our national novel of that time, Manzoni's *The Betrothed*, did not dog the footsteps of grand knights and emperors; it was set in the seventeenth century and told a story of oppressed peasants in a period of national frustration. Thus Italian critics have been surprised that during the last decade many Italian novels inspired by the Middle Ages have appeared, some of them winning an unexpectedly large audience. I will refrain from listing all the round tables and symposia that have recently been devoted to this problem, as the topic of "the return of the Middle Ages" has become obsessive. Other countries, even though they are more accustomed to this kind of revival, are also debating the same question, and we should try to provide some answer.

Thus we are at present witnessing, both in Europe and America, a period of renewed interest in the Middle Ages, with a curious oscillation between fantastic neomedievalism and responsible philological examination. Undoubtedly what counts is the second aspect of the phenomenon, and one must wonder why Americans are more or less experiencing the same obsession as Europeans and why both are devouring the reconstructions of Duby, Le Roy Ladurie, and Le Goff as if they were a new form of narrative. Who could have suspected, a decade ago, that people were ready to swallow the registers of a medieval parish in Poitou as if they were the chronicle of an Agatha Christie vicarage?

We are dreaming the Middle Ages, some say. But in fact both Americans and Europeans are inheritors of the Western legacy, and all the problems of the Western world emerged in the Middle Ages: Modern languages, merchant cities, capitalistic economy (along with banks, checks, and prime rate) are inventions of medieval society. In the Middle Ages we witness the rise of modern armies, of the modern concept of the national state, as well as the idea of a supernatural federation (under the banner of a German Emperor elected by a Diet that functioned like an electoral convention); the struggle between the poor and the rich, the concept of heresy or ideological deviation, even our contemporary notion of love as a devastating unhappy happiness. I could add the conflict between church and state, trade unions (albeit in a corporative mode), the technological transformation of labor. At the beginning of the present millennium came the widespread introduction of windmills, there was the invention of horseshoes, of the shoulder harness for horses and oxen, of stirrups, and the modern type of rudder hinged to the stern below the surface of the water (without which invention the discovery of America would not have been possible). The compass came into use, and there was the final acceptance of Arab mathematics, hence the rise of modern ways of computing and double-entry bookkeeping. At the end of the era, if we agree that the era stops conventionally in 1492, came gunpowder and the Gutenberg galaxy.

We are still living under the banner of medieval technology. For instance, eyeglasses were a medieval invention, as important as the mechanical loom or the steam engine. At that time, an intellectual who became farsighted at the age of forty (bear in mind the difficulty of reading unreadable manuscripts by torchlight in dark rooms beneath shadowy vaults) was unable to produce actively after the age of fifty. With the introduction of eyeglasses intellectual productivity increased enormously and the following centuries could better exploit these human resources.

None of the aforementioned ideas and realities was born in classical antiquity. From ancient Greece and Rome we acquired a certain idea of tragedy (but our theater is based on a medieval model) and an ideal of beauty, as well as our basic philosophical concepts. But from the Middle Ages we learned how to use them. The Middle Ages are the root of all our contemporary "hot" problems, and it is not surprising that we go back to that period every time we ask ourselves about our origin. All the questions debated during the sessions of the Common Market originate from the situation of medieval Europe.

Thus looking at the Middle Ages means looking at our infancy, in the same way that a doctor, to understand our present state of health, asks us about our childhood, or in the same way that the psychoanalyst, to understand our present neuroses, makes a careful investigation of the primal scene.

Our return to the Middle Ages is a quest for our roots and, since we want to come back to the real roots, we are looking for "reliable Middle Ages," not for romance and fantasy, though frequently this wish is misunderstood and, moved by a vague impulse, we indulge in a sort of escapism à la Tolkien.

But is dreaming of the Middle Ages really a typical contemporary or postmodern temptation? If it is true—and it is—that the Middle Ages turned us into Western animals, it is equally true that people started dreaming of the Middle Ages from the very beginning of the modern era.

A Continuous Return

Modern ages have revisited the Middle Ages from the moment when, according to historical handbooks, they came to an end.

The modern era begins with some astounding achievements of the human spirit: the discovery of America, the liberation of Granada (with the consequent destruction of the Arab scientific legacy which would have anticipated the Renaissance and the rise of modern science), and the beginning of the second Diaspora with the exile of the Jews from Spain (pogroms were invented earlier, by the Crusaders; Western civilization has a complex pedigree).

Immediately after the official ending of the Middle Ages, Europe was ravaged by a pervasive medieval nostalgia. In Italy the great poets of the Renaissance, from Pulci to Boiardo and Ariosto, returned to the themes of the Knights saga. Teofilo Folengo wrote *Baldus*, a poem conceived in an incredible *latin de cuisine*; Torquato Tasso, the great poet of Italian Mannerism, celebrated the glories of the Crusaders. In Spain, Cervantes told the story of a man unable to reconcile the intrusion of reality with his love for medieval literature. Shakespeare borrowed and reshaped a lot from medieval narrative.

At the flowering of the English Renaissance John Dee or Robert Fludd rediscovered symbols and emblems of medieval Jewish mysticism. Even in the baroque period, when modern science seemed dominated by the new paradigms of Galileo or Newton, the Church of the Counter-Reformation worked silently to improve or to pollute the philosophy of the Schoolmen, while in France Mabillon rediscovered the treasuries of medieval manuscripts. As a semiotician I cannot forget that one of the most outstanding achievements in the theory of signs was due to an innovating follower of Aquinas, John of Saint Thomas or, as they call him now, Jean Poinsot. During the Age of Reason, while the circle of the French *Encyclopédie* was seemingly fighting the final battle against the remnants of the Dark Ages, these Dark Ages started charming the aristocrats, with the Gothic novel and early Ossianic Romanticism. Geographically close, even though psychologically far from the Castle of Otranto, Ludovico Antonio Muratori collected in his *Rerum Italicarum Scriptores* the ancient chronicles of medieval grandeur. Soon Chateaubriand was to celebrate the rise of Gothic cathedrals under the trees of the Celtic forest, while thanks to Walter Scott, Victor Hugo, and the restorations of Viollet-le-Duc, the whole nineteenth century would dream of its own Middle Ages, thus avenging the enlightened gesture of Napoleon, who cut the tympanum of Notre Dame to allow his imperial cortège to enter the cathedral.

Oddly enough one could see, from the Confessional of the Black Penitents, Fulton's steamboat sailing triumphantly; and I do not exactly know whether the spinning jenny and the power loom were neo-Gothic machinery or whether the Nightmare Abbey of Gregory the Monk was a factory for the concoction of Gothic dreams. The Italian Risorgimento was a period of abundant medieval *repêchage*, not to mention Italian opera, full as it is of troubadours; and finally there was the German neomedieval vertigo of the castle of Ludwig of Bavaria and Wagner's parsifalization of the universe.

What would Ruskin, Morris, and the pre-Raphaelites have said if they had been told that the rediscovery of the Middle Ages would be the work of the twentieth-century mass media?

Classicism and Medievalism

At this point we must bring up at least two questions. First, what distinguishes this permanent rediscovery of the Middle Ages from the equally permanent return to the classical heritage? Second, did the many Middle Ages (too many) always fit the same archetype?

As for the first question, we can oppose the model of philological reconstruction to that of utilitarian bricolage.

In the case of the remains of classical antiquity we reconstruct them but, once we have rebuilt them, we don't dwell in them, we only contemplate them as an ideal model and a masterpiece of faithful restoration. On the contrary, the Middle Ages have never been reconstructed from scratch: We have always mended or patched them up, as something in which we still live. We have cobbled up the bank as well as the cathedral, the state as well as the church. We no longer dwell in the Parthenon, but we still walk or pray in the naves of the cathedral. Even when we live with Aristotle or Plato, we deal with them in the same terms suggested by our medieval ancestors. When one scrapes away the medieval incrustations from Aristotle and renews him, this reread Aristotle will adorn the shelves of academic libraries but will still not connect with our everyday life.

Since the Middle Ages have always been messed up in order to meet the vital requirements of different periods, it was impossible for them to be always messed about in the same way. So I'll try to outline at least ten types of Middle Ages, to warn readers that every time one speaks of a dream of the Middle Ages, one should first ask which Middle Ages one is dreaming of.

Ten Little Middle Ages

1. The Middle Ages as a *pretext*. This is the Middle Ages of opera or of Torquato Tasso. There is no real interest in the historical background; the Middle Ages are taken as a sort of mythological stage on which to place contemporary characters. Under this heading we can include also the so-called cloak-and-dagger novels (or *les romans de cape et d'épée*). There is a difference between historical novels and cloak-and-dagger stuff. The former choose a particular historical period so as to gain a better understanding not only of that period but (through it) of our present time, seen as the end result of those remote historical events. The characters of the novel need not be "really historical" (that is, people who really existed); it is enough for them (albeit fictional) to be representative of their period. Lady Rowena and Pierre Bezukhov are inventions of novels, but they tell us something "true" about the English Middle Ages and about Russia at the time of Napoleon. On the contrary in the cloak-and-dagger novel the fic-

tional characters must move among "real" historical figures who will support their credibility. Think of Dumas and of the crucial narrative role played by such characters as Richelieu and Louis XIII. Notwithstanding the presence of "real" characters, the psychology of d'Artagnan has nothing to do with the psychology of his century, and he could have blustered through the same adventures during the French Revolution. Thus in historical novels fictional characters help one to understand the past (and the past is not taken as a pretext), while in cloak-and-dagger novels the past (taken as a pretext) helps one to enjoy the fictional characters.

2. The Middle Ages as the site of an *ironical revisitation*, in order to speculate about our infancy, of course, but also about the illusion of our senility. Ariosto and Cervantes revisit the Middle Ages in the same way that Sergio Leone and the other masters of the "spaghetti Western" revisit nineteenth-century America, as heroic fantasy, something already fashioned by the early Hollywood studios. In the same sense, Rabelais was playing upon his fantastically revisited Sorbonne, but he no longer believed in the Paris he was telling of, as the characters in Monty Python movies do not believe in the grotesque period they inhabit.

3. The Middle Ages as a *barbaric* age, a land of elementary and outlaw feelings. These are the Middle Ages of Frazetta's fantasies, but, at a different level of complexity and obsession, they are also the Middle Ages of early Bergman. The same elementary passions could exist equally on the Phoenician coasts or in the desert of Gilgamesh. These ages are Dark par excellence, and Wagner's *Ring* itself belongs to this dramatic sunset of reason. With only a slight distortion, one is asked to celebrate, on this earth of virile, brute force, the glories of a new Aryanism. It is a shaggy medievalism, and the shaggier its heroes, the more profoundly ideological its superficial naïveté.

4. The Middle Ages of *Romanticism*, with their stormy castles and their ghosts. Germane to the eastern cruelty of *Vathek*, these Middle Ages return in some contemporary space-operas, where it

is enough to put computers in the dungeon to transform it into a starship.

5. The Middle Ages of the *philosophia perennis* or of neo-Thomism, which loom not only behind Maritain and the pastoral and dogmatic views of Pius XII or John Paul II but can also be perceived, as a transparent source of inspiration, behind many kinds of formal and logical thinking in contemporary secular philosophers. Recently, in my *Semiotics and the Philosophy of Language*, I studied the medieval theory of definition as it was imposed by Porphyry's *Isagoge* and I showed to what extent it was affected by certain logical quirks. My purpose was to demonstrate how these quirks continue to affect many contemporary theories of meaning that, frequently without acknowledging it, are still in debt to the Porphyrian line of thought. In this sense, the perennial vigor of the Middle Ages is not derived necessarily from religious assumptions, and there is a lot of hidden medievalism in some speculative and systematic approaches of our time, such as structuralism.

6. The Middle Ages of *national identities*, so powerful again during the last century, when the medieval model was taken as a political utopia, a celebration of past grandeur, to be opposed to the miseries of national enslavement and foreign domination.

7. The Middle Ages of *Decadentism*. Think, obviously, of the Pre-Raphaelite Brotherhood, think of Ruskin, but think also of Huysmans' *À rebours* and of the ecstasies of Des Esseintes. The typical Italian version of this decadent Middle Ages is found in the neomedievalism of Giosuè Carducci and Gabriele D'Annunzio (though the former was not a fin-de-siècle decadent). At first an invention of intellectuals, it was then organically inserted into the project of nationalistic restoration and produced, in architecture and the visual arts, a lot of fakes, sometimes interesting and sometimes pathetic, in Italian cities.

8. The Middle Ages of *philological reconstruction*, which goes from Mabillon through Muratori up to the best of Gilson, to the rediscovery of the *Acta Danicorum Philosophorum* and to the *Annales* school. This philological attitude can be applied either to great

historical events or to the imperceptibility of underlying social and technological structures, and to the forms of everyday life. Fortunately in this case no one would speak of "medieval fashion." Not fully free from the curiosity of the mass media, these Middle Ages help us, nevertheless, to criticize all the other Middle Ages that at one time or another arouse our enthusiasm. These Middle Ages lack sublimity, thank God, and thus look more "human."

9. The Middle Ages of so-called *Tradition*, or of occult philosophy (or *la pensée sapientielle*), an eternal and rather eclectic ramshackle structure, swarming with Knights Templars, Rosicrucians, alchemists, Masonic initiates, neo-Kabbalists, drunk on reactionary poisons sipped from the Grail, ready to hail every neofascist Will to Power, eager to accept as a visual ersatz for their improbable visions all the paraphernalia of the Middle Ages number 3, mixing up René Guénon and Conan the Barbarian, Avalon and the Kingdom of Prester John. Antiscientific by definition, these Middle Ages keep going under the banner of the mystical weddings of the micro- with the macrocosm, and as a result they convince their adepts that everything is the same as anything else and that the whole world is born to convey, in any of its aspects and events, the same Message. Fortunately the message got lost, which makes its Quest fascinating for the happy few who stand prooftight, philology-resistant, bravely ignorant of the Popperian call for the good habit of falsification. To synthesize the way of Traditional thought, let me mention two basic cognitive models, one epistemological and one logical, that the Traditional way of thinking usually, and irresponsibly, turns upside down: The model of *post hoc ergo propter hoc* is reversed into *propter hoc ergo ante hoc*, and the logical model of the *modus ponens* is reversed into what I call *modus indisponens* (to translate this Latin-Italian pun let me call it the "upsetting mode"). A good instance of *propter hoc ergo ante hoc* is given by an argument that one can find in many of the most famous discourses about the *Pimander:* It is well known that the *Corpus Hermeticum* was written in the first centuries of the Christian era but the adepts of the Tradition firmly maintain (even after

71

the decisive demonstration of Casaubon) that it was written at the time of Moses or of Pythagoras and, in any case, before Plato. Now the argument runs as follows: Since the *Corpus Hermeticum* contains ideas that "later" circulated within the Platonic milieu, this proves that it was written before Plato. As for the *modus indisponens*, it works (?) as follows:

If p then q, but k then w,

and can be exemplified by the following argument: "If a = b, then b = a." But the *Corpus Hermeticum* says that *sicut inferius sic superius*; therefore, the Holy Grail is none other than the *Lapis Philosophorum*. I know that all this is not real Middle Ages and that our old doctors debating their *quaestiones quodlibetales* at the Faculty of Arts were more rigorous than Henry Corbin or Gilbert Durand; but the thinking of the Tradition usually proceeds under the banner of a permanent Arthurian Land, continually revisited for enjoying intemporal ecstasies.

10. Last, very last, but not least, the *expectation of the Millennium*. These Middle Ages which have haunted every sect fired by enthusiasm still accompany us and will continue to do so, until midnight of the Day After. Source of many insanities, they remain however as a permanent warning. Sometimes it is not so medieval to think that perhaps the end is coming and the Antichrist, in plainclothes, is knocking at the door.

Which One?

So, before rejoicing or grieving over a return of the Middle Ages, we have the moral and cultural duty of spelling out what kind of Middle Ages we are talking about. To say openly which of the above ten types we are referring to means to say who we are and what we dream of, if we are simply practicing a more or less honest form of divertissement, if we are wondering about our basic problems or if we are supporting, perhaps without realizing it, some new reactionary plot.

Living
in the New
Middle Ages

In any case, there is one sense in which we dream of the Middle Ages so that our era can be defined as a new Middle Ages. I wrote an essay on this subject more than ten years ago, and though some aspects of our time to which I referred then have partly changed, I believe that it is worth reprinting here some of the reflections I expressed then.

First of all, when we say that our age is neomedieval, we have to establish to which notion of the Middle Ages we are referring. To begin with, we must realize that the term defines two, quite distinct, historical periods: one that runs from the fall of the Roman empire in the West to the year 1000, a period of crisis, decadence, violent adjustments of peoples and clashes of cultures, and another that extends from the year 1000 to what in our schooldays was called Humanism, and it is no accident that many foreign historians consider this already a period of full bloom; they even talk of three Renaissances, the Carolingian, another in the eleventh and twelfth centuries, and the third one, the Renaissance proper.

Assuming that the Middle Ages can be synthesized in a kind
of abstract model, to which of the two does our own era correspond? Any thought of strict correspondence, item by item, would
be ingenuous, not least because we live in an enormously speeded-
up period where what happens in five of our years can sometimes
correspond to what happened then in five centuries. Secondly, the
center of the world has expanded to cover the whole planet; now-
adays civilizations and cultures and various phases of development
live together, and in ordinary terminology we are led to talk about
the "medieval condition" of the people of Bengal while we see
New York as a flourishing Babylon. So the parallel, if we make it,
must be established between certain moments and situations of
our planetary civilization and various moments of a historical process that stretches from the fifth to the thirteenth century A.D. To
be sure, comparing a precise historical moment (today) with a period of almost a thousand years sounds like an insipid game, and
it would be insipid if that were what it is. But here we are trying
to formulate a "hypothesis of the Middle Ages" (as if we were
setting out to fabricate a Middle Ages and were deciding what
ingredients are required to make one that is efficient and credible).

What is required to make a good Middle Ages? First of all, a
great peace that is breaking down, a great international power that
has unified the world in language, customs, ideologies, religions,
art, and technology, and then at a certain point, thanks to its own
ungovernable complexity, collapses. It collapses because the "barbarians" are pressing at its borders; these barbarians are not necessarily uncultivated, but they are bringing new customs, new views
of the world. These barbarians may burst in with violence, because
they want to seize a wealth that has been denied them, or they
may steal into the social and cultural body of the reigning Pax,
spreading new faiths and new perspectives of life. At the beginning
of its fall, the Roman empire is not undermined by the Christian
ethic; it has already undermined itself by syncretically welcoming
Alexandrian culture and the Oriental cult of Mithra or Astarte,
toying with magic, new sexual ethics, various hopes and images of

salvation. It has received new racial components, it has perforce eliminated many strict class divisions, reduced the difference between citizens and noncitizens, patricians and plebeians; it has retained its division of wealth but has watered down the distinctions among social roles, nor could it do otherwise. It has witnessed phenomena of rapid acculturations, has raised to government men of races that two hundred years earlier would have been considered inferior, has relaxed the dogmata of many theologies. In the same period the government can worship the classical gods, the soldiers can worship Mithra, and the slaves, Jesus. Instinctively the faith that, in a remote way, seems most lethal to the system is persecuted, but as a rule a great repressive tolerance allows everything to be accepted.

The collapse of the Great Pax (at once military, civil, social, and cultural) initiates a period of economic crisis and power vacuum, but it is only a justifiable anticlerical reaction that has sanctioned seeing the Dark Ages as being so "dark." In fact, even the early Middle Ages (perhaps more than the Middle Ages after the year 1000) were a period of incredible intellectual vitality, of impassioned dialogue among barbarian civilizations, Roman heritage, and Christian-Eastern elements, a time of journeys and encounters, when Irish monks crossed Europe spreading ideas, encouraging reading, promoting foolishness of every description. In short, this is where modern Western man came to maturity, and it is in this sense that a model of the Middle Ages can help us understand what is happening in our own day. At the collapse of a great Pax, crisis and insecurity ensue, different civilizations clash, and slowly the image of a new man is outlined. It will come clear only afterwards, but the basic elements are already there, bubbling in a dramatic cauldron. Boethius, who popularizes Pythagoras and rereads Aristotle, is not repeating from memory the lesson of the past but is inventing a new way of culture, and, pretending to be the last of the Romans, he is actually setting up the first Study Center of the barbarian courts.

It is a commonplace of present-day historiography that we are

75

living through the crisis of the Pax Americana. It would be childish to fix in a precise image the "new barbarians," also because the word "barbarian" has always had a negative, misleading connotation for our ears. It would be hard to say whether they are the Chinese or the peoples of the Third World or the young protest generation or the Puerto Rican immigrants who are turning New York into a Spanish-speaking city. For that matter, who were the barbarians in the centuries of the decline of the empire: the Huns, the Goths, or the Asiatic and African peoples, who involved the hub of the empire in their trade and their religions? The only specific thing that was disappearing was the Roman, just as the Liberal is disappearing today, the Anglophone entrepreneur whose folk epic was *Robinson Crusoe* and whose Virgil was Max Weber.

In the homes of suburbia the average crew-cut executive still personifies the Roman of ancient virtues; but in the '60's and '70's his son let his hair grow in Indian style, wore a Mexican poncho, played the sitar, read Buddhist texts or Leninist pamphlets, and often succeeded (as in the late empire) in reconciling a dizzying variety of influences—such as Hesse, the zodiac, alchemy, the thoughts of Mao, marijuana, and urban guerrilla techniques. The generation of the '80's seems to be returning to the model of its fathers. But this phenomenon concerns the upper middle class, not the kids we see break-dancing.

Some years ago an Italian geographer, Giuseppe Sacco, discussed the medievalization of the city. A series of minorities, rejecting integration, form clans, and each clan picks a neighborhood that becomes its own center, often inaccessible: We are close to the medieval *contrada* (Sacco teaches in Siena). The clan spirit dominates also the well-to-do classes who, pursuing the myth of nature, withdraw from the city to the garden suburbs with their own shopping malls, bringing other types of microsocieties into existence.

Sacco also discusses the theme of the Vietnamization of territories, theaters of permanent tension because of the breakdown of the consensus. Among the replies of authority is the tendency to decentralize the great universities (a kind of student defoliation) to avoid dangerous mass agglomerations. In this framework of permanent civil war, marked by the clash of opposing minorities, without a center, the cities will tend more and more to become what we already find in certain Latin American localities, inured to guerrilla warfare, where "the fragmentation of the social body is appropriately symbolized by the fact that the doorman of an apartment is customarily armed with a submachine gun. In these same cities public buildings look like fortresses, and some, the presidential residences, for instance, are surrounded by a kind of earthwork to protect them against bazooka attack."*

Naturally our medieval parallel must be articulated so as not to fear symmetrically opposed images. For while in the other Middle Ages decline in population was strictly linked with abandonment of the cities and famine in the country, difficulty of communication, decay of the Roman roads and postal system, lack of central control, today what seems to be happening (with regard to and preceding the crisis of central powers) is the opposite phenomenon: excess of population interacts with excess of communication and transportation, making the cities uninhabitable not through destruction and abandonment but through a paroxysm of activity. The ivy that slowly undermined the great, crumbling buildings is replaced by air pollution and the accumulation of garbage that disfigures and stifles the big restored buildings. The city is filled with immigrants, but is drained of its old inhabitants, who use it to work in then run off to the fortified suburbs. Manhattan is approaching the point where nearly all its inhabitants will be non-white, as Turin will be almost completely inhabited by southern Italians, while on the surrounding hills and in the plains patrician castles spring up, bound by good neighbor protocol, reciprocal

---

*"Città e società verso il nuovo medioevo," in U. Eco et al., *Il nuovo medioevo* (Milan: Bompiani, 1973).

distrust, and the great ceremonial occasions for meeting. The big city, today no longer invaded by belligerent barbarians or devastated by fires, suffers from water shortages, blackouts, gridlocks.

The early Middle Ages are characterized also by a marked technological decline and by the impoverishment of the rural areas. Iron is scarce, and a peasant who drops his only sickle into the well has to wait for the miraculous intervention of a saint to recover it (as legends confirm), otherwise he's done for. The frightening decrease in population begins to be reversed only after the year 1000 thanks to the introduction of the cultivation of beans, lentils, and other pulses, with high nutritional value, otherwise Europe would have died of constitutional weakness (the relationship between beans and cultural renaissance is crucial). Today the parallel is inverted, has come full circle: immense technological development causes gridlocks and malfunctions and the vastly expanded alimentary industry has converted to the production of poisonous and carcinogenic foods.

For that matter the consumer society at its maximum level does not produce perfect objects, but rather little machines that are highly perishable (if you want a good knife, buy it in Africa; in the United States it will break on second use). And the technological society is tending to become a society of used and useless objects, whereas in the countryside we see deforestation, abandonment of cultivation, pollution of water, atmosphere, and vegetation, the extinction of animal species, and so on. If not beans, at least an injection of genuine elements is becoming increasingly urgent.

It seems improbable, but the fact is that in his lifetime a man had few occasions to see his neighboring city and many occasions to go to Santiago de Compostela or to Jerusalem. Medieval Europe was furrowed by pilgrimage routes (listed in handy tourist guides that mentioned the abbatial churches the way they list motels and Hiltons today) as our skies are furrowed by air routes that make it easier to travel from Rome to New York than to Rome from Spoleto.

It could be objected that the seminomad medieval society was a society of unsafe journeys; setting out meant making your will (think of the departure of old Anne Vercos in Claudel's *L'Annonce faite à Marie*), and traveling meant encountering bandits, vagabond hordes, and wild animals. But the concept of the modern journey as a masterpiece of comfort and safety has long since come to grief, and boarding a jet through the various electronic checkpoints and searches to avoid hijacking restores perfectly the ancient sense of adventurous insecurity, presumably destined to increase.

"Insecurity" is a key word: This feeling must be inserted into the picture of chiliastic anxieties: The world is about to end, a final catastrophe will close the millennium. The famous terrors of the year 1000 are only legendary—this has now been demonstrated—but throughout the tenth century there was a sneaking fear of the end, and this has also been demonstrated (except that toward the end of the millennium the psychosis was already past). As for our own time, the recurrent themes of atomic and ecological catastrophe suffice to indicate vigorous apocalyptic currents. As a utopian corrective, in the past there was the idea of the *renovatio imperii*; today there is the fairly adjustable idea of "revolution"—both with solid, real prospects, but with a final shift as far as the original objective is concerned (it is not the empire that will be renewed, but there will be a rebirth of the communes and the rise of national monarchies that will control insecurity). But insecurity is not only "historical," it is psychological, it is one with the man-landscape/man-society relationship. In the Middle Ages a wanderer in the woods at night saw them peopled with maleficent presences; one did not lightly venture beyond the town; men went armed. This condition is close to that of the white middle-class inhabitant of New York, who doesn't set foot in Central Park after five in the afternoon or who makes sure not to get off the subway in Harlem by mistake, nor does he take the subway alone after midnight (or even before, in the case of women). Meanwhile, as the police on all sides begin to repress robbery through indiscrim-

79

inate massacre of good guys and bad, the practice of revolutionary
theft and kidnapping the ambassador is established, just as a cardinal and his entourage used to be captured by some Robin Hood
and traded for a couple of merry companions of the forest destined for the gallows or the wheel. Final touch to this collective
insecurity: the fact that, now as then, and contrary to the usage
established by modern liberal nations, war is no longer declared
and you never know if there is a state of belligerence or not. For
that matter, if you go to Leghorn, Verona, or Malta, you will
realize that the troops of the empire are garrisoned in the various
national territories as a constant presidium, multilingual forces with
admirals continually tempted to use their units to make war (or
politics) on their own.

In these broad territories in the grip of insecurities, bands of
outcasts roam, mystics, adventurers. In the general crisis of the
universities and the plan of uncoordinated student grants, the students are turning into *vagantes*, and they look always and only to
unofficial masters, rejecting their "natural educators." And, further, we have on the one hand actual mendicant orders, who live
off public charity in the search for a mystical happiness (drugs or
divine grace, it makes little difference, particularly because various
non-Christian religions appear connected with chemical happiness). The local citizens refuse to accept them and persecute them.
As in the Middle Ages the borderline between the mystic and the
thief is often minimal, and Manson is simply a monk who has
gone too far, like his ancestors, in satanic rites. When a powerful
man offends the legitimate government, it implicates him, as Philip
the Fair did with the Templars, in sex scandals. Mystical stimula-
tion and diabolical rite are very close, and Gilles de Rais, burned
alive for having devoured too many children, was a companion-in-
arms of Joan of Arc, a warrior as charismatic as Che. Other credos
akin to those of the mendicant orders are asserted, in a different
key, by politicized groups whose moralism has monastic roots, with

its recall to poverty, to austerity of behavior, and to "the service of the people."

If the parallels seem untidy, think of the enormous difference, under the apparently religious cover, that obtained among lax, contemplative monks, who in the privacy of their monasteries carried on outrageously, and the active, populist Franciscans, the doctrinaire and intransigent Dominicans, all voluntarily and diversely withdrawn from the social context, which was despised as decadent, diabolical, the source of neurosis and alienation. These societies of reformers, divided between a furious practical activity in the service of the outcasts and a violent theological debate, were riven by reciprocal accusations of heresy and a constant to-and-fro of excommunications. Each group manufactures its dissidents and its heresiarchs, the attacks that Franciscans and Dominicans made on each other are not very different from those of Trotskyites and Stalinists—nor is this the politically cynical index of an aimless disorder, but on the contrary, it is the index of a society where new forces are seeking new images of collective life and discover that they cannot be imposed except through the struggle against the established "systems," exercising a conscious and severe intolerance in theory and practice.

When we come to cultural and artistic parallels the scene proves far more complex. On the one hand we find a fairly perfect correspondence between two ages that, in different ways but with identical educational utopias and with equal ideological camouflage of their paternalistic aim to control minds, try to bridge the gap between learned culture and popular culture through visual communication. In both periods the select élite debates written texts with alphabetic mentality, but then translates into images the essential data or knowledge and the fundamental structure of the ruling ideology. The Middle Ages are the civilization of vision, where the cathedral is the great book in stone, and is indeed the advertisement, the TV screen, the mystic comic strip that must narrate and explain everything, the nations of the earth, the arts and crafts, the days of the year, the seasons of sowing and reaping, the mysteries of the faith, the episodes of sacred and profane history, and the lives of the saints (great models of behavior, as superstars and pop singers are today, an élite without political power, but with great charismatic power).

Alongside this massive popular-culture enterprise there proceeds the work of composition and collage that learned culture is carrying out on the flotsam of past culture. Take one of the magic boxes of Cornell or Arman, a collage of Ernst, a useless machine of Munari or Tinguely, and you will find yourself in a landscape that has nothing to do with Raphael or Canova but has a lot to do with medieval aesthetic taste. In poetry there are centos and riddles, the kennings of the Irish, acrostics, verbal compounds of multiple quotations that recall Pound and Sanguineti, the lunatic etymological games of Virgil of Bigorre and Isidore of Seville, who immediately suggest Joyce (as Joyce knew), the poetry treatises and their temporal exercises of composition, which read like a script for Godard, and especially the taste for collecting and listing. Which then became concrete in the treasure-rooms of princes or cathedrals, where they preserved indiscriminately a thorn from the cross of Jesus, an egg found inside another egg, a unicorn's horn, St. Joseph's engagement ring, the skull of St. John at the age of twelve [sic].

And over all reigned a total lack of distinction between aesthetic objects and mechanical objects (a robot in the form of a cock, artistically engraved, was given by Harun al Rashid to Charlemagne, a kinetic jewel if ever there was one); and there was no difference between the object of "creation" and the object of curiosity, or between the work of the artisan and that of the artist, between the "multiple" and the unique piece, and, least of all, between the curious trouvaille (the art nouveau lamp and a whale's tooth) and the work of art. All was ruled by a taste for gaudy color and a notion of light as a physical element of pleasure. It is of no importance that, in the past, golden vases were encrusted with topazes set to reflect the rays of the sun coming through the stained glass of a church, and now there is the multimedia orgy of any Electric Circus, with strobe lights and water effects.

Huizinga said that to understand medieval aesthetic taste you have to think of the sort of indiscriminate reaction an astonished bourgeois feels when viewing a curious and precious object. Huizinga was thinking in terms of post-Romantic aesthetic sensibility; today we would find this sort of reaction is the same as that of a young person seeing a poster of a dinosaur or motorcycle or a magic transistorized box in which luminous beams rotate, a cross between a technological model and a science-fiction promise, with some elements of barbarian jewelry.

An art not systematic but additive and compositive, ours and that of the Middle Ages: Today as then the sophisticated elitist experiment coexists with the great enterprise of popularization (the relationship between illuminated manuscript and cathedral is the same as that between MOMA and Hollywood), with interchanges and borrowings, reciprocal and continuous; and the evident Byzantinism, the mad taste for collecting, lists, assemblage, amassing of disparate things is due to the need to dismantle and reconsider the flotsam of a previous world, harmonious perhaps, but by now obsolete.

Nothing more closely resembles a monastery (lost in the countryside, walled, flanked by alien, barbarian hordes, inhabited by monks who have nothing to do with the world and devote themselves to their private researches) than an American university campus. Sometimes the prince summons one of those monks and makes him a royal counselor, sends him as envoy to Cathay; and he moves from the cloister to secular life with indifference, becoming a man of power and trying to rule the world with the same aseptic perfection with which he collected his Greek texts. Whether his name is Gerbert de Aurillac or McNamara, Bernard of Clairvaux or Kissinger, he can be a man of peace or a man of war (like Eisenhower, who wins some battles and then retires to a monastery, becoming president of a university, only to return to the service of the empire when the crowd calls him as its charismatic hero).

But it is doubtful that these monastic centers will have the task of recording, preserving, and transmitting the wealth of past culture, perhaps through complicated electronic devices that will recall it a piece at a time, stimulating its reconstruction without ever revealing its secrets fully. The other Middle Ages produced, at the end, the Renaissance, which took delight in archeology; but actually the Middle Ages did not carry out any systematic preservation; rather it performed a heedless destruction and a disordered preservation: It lost essential manuscripts and saved others that were quite negligible; it scratched away marvelous poems to write riddles or prayers in their place, it falsified sacred texts, interpolating other passages and, in doing so, wrote "its own" books. The Middle Ages invented communal society without possessing any precise information on the Greek *polis*, it reached China thinking to find men with one foot or with their mouths in their bellies, it may have arrived in America before Columbus, using the astronomy of Ptolemy and the geography of Eratosthenes.

Our own Middle Ages, it has been said, will be an age of "permanent transition" for which new methods of adjustment will have to be employed. The problem will not so much be that of preserving the past scientifically as of developing hypotheses for the exploitation of disorder, entering into the logic of conflictuality. There will be born—it is already coming into existence—a culture of constant readjustment, fed on utopia. This is how medieval man invented the university, with the same carefree attitude that the vagabond clerks today assume in destroying it, and perhaps transforming it. The Middle Ages preserved in its way the heritage of the past but not through hibernation, rather through a constant retranslation and reuse; it was an immense work of bricolage, balanced among nostalgia, hope, and despair.

Under its apparent immobility and dogmatism, this was paradoxically a moment of "cultural revolution." Naturally the whole process is characterized by plaques and massacres, intolerance and death. Nobody says that the Middle Ages offer a completely jolly prospect. As the Chinese said, to curse someone: "May you live in an interesting period."

3
THE GODS
OF THE
UNDERWORLD

The Sacred
Is Not Just
a Fashion

In 1938, coming from the pleasant town of Smallville, there arrived in the city of Metropolis Clark Kent, alias Superman; and by now everybody knows everything about him. But even in those far-off days of neotechnological capitalism, when in Chicago they were compiling the *International Encyclopedia of Unified Science* and considered the propositions of the metaphysical philosophers meaningless, there was nothing mysterious about Superman. The boy's ability to fly like a plane and lift ocean liners as if they were twigs could be scientifically explained. He came from Krypton, where, as is well known, gravity is different, and so it was normal for him to have superpowers. Even his extraordinary memory derived from the fact that, again thanks to gravity, he developed better than other boys his age a talent for speed reading, which for that matter was already being taught in the universities.

There was nothing mystical about the Superman of history.

As we enter the 1980's, the movie *Superman* is quite a different matter. First of all, it is no accident that he should have an onerous father like Marlon Brando, whose story takes up almost

half the film, or that his father should impart to the child about
to leave for Earth a Knowledge of which we know nothing, con-
cretized in stalagmites of diamond, a material about as symbolic
as anything imaginable. Or that he should give his son a highly
trinitarian viaticum, put him in a spacecraft in the form of a cra-
dle, which navigates through space like the comet of the Magi. Or
that the adult Superman, possessed by ill-tempered voices like a
Joan of Arc in skirts, should have problems worthy of the Mount
of Olives and Tabor-like visions. He is the Son of Man.

So Clark Kent would arrive on Earth to fulfill the hopes of a
generation that enjoys Tolkien's *Silmarillion* and deciphers a theo-
gony that obliges them to memorize the children of Ilúvatar and
the Quendi and the Atani and the flowery meadows of Valinor
and the wounds of Melkor: all things that, if they had had to be
studied in school, would have driven the same generation to occupy the university or high school in protest against notionism.

So the reincarnation of Superman would seem to be the pop
version of a series of more complex and profound phenomena that
apparently reveal a trend: the return to religious thought. All Is-
lamic countries are returning to a theocratic view of social and
political life, masses of American lemmings rush towards suicide
in the name of an unearthly happiness, neomillenarian and glos-
solalic movements invade the Italian provinces, Catholic Action is
on the rise, the prestige of the papal throne is renewed. And along
with these manifestations of "positive" religiosity there is the new
religiosity of the ex-atheists, disappointed revolutionaries who fall
on the traditional classics, astrologers, mystics, macrobioticians,
visionary poets, the neo-fantastic (sociological science fiction no
more, but new Arthurian cycles), and finally not the texts of Marx
and Lenin but dark works by the unfashionable great, dejected
Mitteleuropeans perhaps, suicides unquestionably, who never published anything in their lifetime, who managed to concoct only
one manuscript and that not complete, long misunderstood because they wrote in the language of some minority, all a hand-to-

hand struggle with the mystery of death and of evil, writers who felt only profound contempt for human efforts and the modern world.

On the basis of these elements, these undeniable trends, the mass media, however, seem to confect a scenario that repeats the pattern suggested by Feuerbach to explain the birth of religion. Man somehow feels he is infinite, or rather that he is capable of desiring in an unlimited fashion; he desires everything, we might say. But he realizes that he is incapable of achieving what he desires, and therefore he must prefigure an Other (who possesses to an optimum degree what he most desires), to whom he delegates the job of bridging the gap between what is desired and what can be done.

In other words, the mass media indicate the symptoms of a crisis in the optimistic ideologies of progress: both the positivistic-technological, which wanted to build a better world with the help of science, and the materialistic-historical, which wanted to build a perfect society through revolution. On the other hand, the media tend to mythicize the fact that these two crises (which in many ways are the same) are translated into politico-social, economic terms, such as reassertion of law and order, or in other words, conservative restraint (compare Fellini's parable of the orchestra conductor). The mass media expound the same problem through other allegories and underline the phenomena of the return to religiosity. In this sense, while they seem to act as thermometer, reporting a rise in temperature, they are actually part of the fuel that keeps the furnace going.

In fact, it is a bit ingenuous to speak of a return of institutional religious forms. They had never disappeared. Take certain young Catholics' associations: In a climate of public opinion where everyone was talking about the complete Marxification of the young, it was most difficult for non-Marxists to assert themselves as an organized force with a certain appeal. Similarly the success of the new Pope's paternal image looks more like the spontaneous process of reinforcement of images of authority at a time of institutional crisis than like a new religious phenomenon. After all, believers continue to believe, and nonbelievers adapt and become Christian Democrats if the Christian Democrats offer a steady job in Town Hall, but flirt with the "historic compromise" if it looks like the Communist Party can get them a job in the regional government.

But in discussing these phenomena it is important to distinguish between institutional religion and the sense of the sacred. A recent book edited by Franco Ferrarrotti, *Forme del sacro in un'epoca di crisi* (Forms of the Sacred in a Period of Crisis), again brings up this important distinction: the fact that frequenting the sacraments was becoming less popular never meant that the sense of the sacred was threatened. The forms of personal religiosity, which became concrete in the post–Vatican II movements, marked the very decade in which the newspapers were making people believe that society had become entirely secular. And the neomillenarian movements have grown steadily in both Americas and develop strikingly today in Italy for reasons involving the clash between advanced industrial society and disadvantaged proletariat. Finally, a role is played in this story of the sacred also by atheist neomillenarianism, that is to say terrorism, which repeats in violent forms a mystical scenario, requiring suffering testimony, martyrdom, purifying bloodbath. In a word, all these phenomena are real, but they are not part of the script, now fashionable, of the new post-68' traditionalism. At most they cover, when they are made picturesquely evident, the truly new facts that concern instead conservative political action.

The theme of the recourse to the sacred becomes interesting, in my view, when it refers to a certain atheist sacrality not presented as the answer of traditional religious thought (to the disappointment of the left), but rather as the autonomous product of a crisis in secular thinking. This phenomenon also, however, is not something recent, and its roots must be sought in the past. The interesting thing is that it follows, in atheistic forms, the modes that typified religious thought.

The fact is that the ideas of God that have peopled human history belong to two types. On the one hand there is a personal God who is the fullness of being ("I am he who is") and therefore sums up in himself all the virtues mankind does not have, and he is the God of omnipotence and victory, the Lord of Hosts. But this same God is often shown in an opposite way: as he who is not. Not because he cannot be named, not because he cannot be described with any of the categories we use to designate the things that are. This God who is not passes through the very history of Christianity: He hides himself, is ineffable, can be drawn upon only through negative theology, is the sum of what cannot be said of him; in speaking of him we celebrate our ignorance and he is named at most as vortex, abyss, desert, solitude, silence, absence.

This is the God that the sense of the sacred feeds upon, ignoring the institutionalized churches, as Rudolf Otto described it more than fifty years ago in his famous *Das Heilige (The Idea of the Holy)*. The sacred appears to us as "numen," as "tremendum," it is the sense that there is something not produced by man and towards which the human being feels at once attraction and repulsion. It produces a sense of terror, an irresistible fascination, a feeling of inferiority and a desire for expiation and suffering. In the historical religions this confused sentiment has taken the form, in turn, of divinities more or less terrifying. But in the secular universe it has assumed, for at least a hundred years, other forms. The awesome and the fascinating no longer wear the anthropomorphic guise of the most perfect being but take on that of a Void in whose regard our aspirations are doomed to defeat.

A religiosity of the Unconscious, of the Vortex, of the Lack of Center, of Difference, of the *béance* has spread through modern thought as the subterranean counterpoint to the uncertainty of the nineteenth-century ideology of progress and the cyclic play of economic crisis. This secularized and infinitely absent God has accompanied contemporary thought under various names, and burst forth in the renascence of psychoanalysis, in the rediscovery of Nietzsche and Heidegger, in the new anti-metaphysics of Absence and Difference. During the period of political optimism a sharp break was created between these ways of conceiving the sacred, that is to say the unknowable, and the ideologies of political omnipotence: With the crisis both of Marxist optimism and that of liberal optimism this religiosity of the void in which we are steeped has invaded even the thought of the so-called Left.

But if this is the case, then the return to the sacred long preceded the orphan syndrome of the disillusioned, who were becoming paranoid because they discovered that the Chinese were neither infallible nor totally good. The "betrayal" by the Chinese, if anything, gave the final (very exterior) blow to those who for some time had been feeling that beneath the world of rational truths proposed by science (both capitalist and proletarian) there were hidden rifts, black holes. But these same people lacked the strength to conduct a lucid, skeptical criticism, with a sense of humor and irreverence towards the authorities.

In the coming years it will be worthwhile to ponder these new negative theologies, the liturgies they inspire, their effect on revolutionary thought. And to see to what extent they, too, remain susceptible to the criticism of Feuerbach, for one thing. In other words, to see if through these cultural phenomena a new Middle Ages is to take shape, a time of secular mystics, more inclined to monastic withdrawal than to civic participation. We should see how much, as antidote or as antistrophe, the old techniques of reason may apply, the arts of the Trivium, logic, dialectic, rhetoric. As we suspect that anyone who goes on stubbornly practicing them will be accused of impiety.

1979

The Suicides
of the Temple

The strangest thing about the story of the People's Temple suicides is the media reaction, both in America and in Europe. Their reaction is: "Inconceivable, an inconceivable event." In other words, it seems inconceivable that a person long considered respectable, like Jim Jones (all those who knew him over these past years, who contributed to his charitable activities or exploited him for garnering votes, have unanimously defined him as an altruistic preacher, a fascinating personality, a convinced integrationist, a good democrat, or as we Italians would say, an "antifascist"), could then go mad, turn into a bloodthirsty autocrat, a kind of Bokassa who stole the savings of his faithful followers, used drugs, indulged in the most promiscuous sex, hetero and homo, and commended the slaughter of those who attempted to escape his rule. It seems incredible that so many nice people followed him blindly, and to the point of suicide. It seems incredible that a neo-Christian sect, gentle, mystical-communist in its inspiration, should end up transformed into a gang of killers, driving its escapees to seek police protection against the menace of murder. It seems incredible that respectable pensioners, students, blacks eager for social integration, should abandon beautiful, pleasant California, all green lawns and spring breezes, to go and bury themselves in the equatorial jungle, teeming with piranhas and poisonous snakes. It is incredible that the families of the brainwashed young could not make the government intervene strongly, and that only at the end poor Congressman Ryan started an inquiry, which cost him his life. All, all incredible, in other words, unheard of, what's the world coming to, what next?

We remain stunned not by Jim Jones but by the unconscious hypocrisy of "normal" people. Normal people try desperately to repress a reality that has been before their eyes for at least two thousand years. For the story of the People's Temple is old, a matter of flux and reflux, of eternal returns. Refusal to remember these things leads us then to see in terrorist phenomena the hand of the CIA or the Czechs. If only evil really did come always from across the border. The trouble is that it comes not from horizontal distances but from vertical. Certain answers, that is, must be sought from Freud and Lacan, not from the secret services.

What's more, American politicians and journalists didn't even have to go and read the sacred texts on the history of millenarian sects or the classics of psychoanalysis. The story of the People's Temple is told in one of the latest books of that sly operator Harold Robbins (sly because he always concocts his novels with bits of reality, whether it's the story of Hefner or Porfirio Rubirosa or some Arab magnate). The book in question is *Dreams Die First*. There is the Reverend Sam (who happens to bear a very close resemblance to the Reverend Sun Myung Moon), who has founded a laboratory to which the young initiates bring all their money; he then invests it in shrewd financial speculations. Sam preaches peace and harmony, introduces his young people to the most complete sexual promiscuity, sets up a mystical retreat in the jungle, where he imposes rigid discipline, initiation through drugs, with torture and persecution for those attempting escape, until finally the borderlines between worship, criminality, and rites à la Manson family become very faint. This is the Robbins novel. But Robbins invents nothing, not even at the level of fictional translation of real-life events.

Some decades ahead of him, in *The Dain Curse*, the great Dashiell Hammett portrays a Holy Grail cult, naturally set in California—where else?—which begins by enrolling rich members and taking their money: The cult is not at all violent, even if the initiations (here, too) involve drugs and sleight of hand (among other things, the staging recalls that of the Eleusinian mysteries). The prophet, according to Hammett, was an impressive man: When he looked at you, you felt all confused. Then he went crazy and believed he could do and achieve anything. . . . He dreamed of convincing the whole world of his divinity. . . . He was a madman who would see no limit to his power.

You can almost think you are hearing the interviews published during the past few days in the *New York Times:* He was a wonderfully sweet and kind person, a magnetic personality, he made you feel you belonged to a community. And the lawyer Mark Lane tries to clarify how Jones was seized with paranoia, by thirst for absolute power. And if we now reread the book, *The Family*, that Ed Sanders wrote about Charles Manson's California cult and its degeneration, we find everything already there.

So why do these things happen, and why in California? The second half of the question is fairly ingenuous. There are certain reasons why California is specially fertile in producing cults, but the basic scenario is far older. In brief, Jones's cult, the People's Temple, had all the characteristics of the millenarian movements throughout Western history from the first centuries of Christianity down to the present. (And I speak only of these because there would be no room to talk about Jewish millenarianism or analagous cults in the Orient, or various corybantisms in the classical age, or similar manifestations on the African continent, found, unchanged, today in Brazil.)

The Christian series probably begins in the third century A.D.

with the extreme wing of the Donatists, the Circoncellions, who went around armed with clubs, attacking the imperial troops, assassinating their sworn enemies, those loyal to the Church of Rome. They blinded their theological adversaries with mixtures of lime and vinegar; thirsting for martyrdom, they would stop wayfarers and threaten death if they refused to martyr them; they organized sumptuous funeral banquets and then killed themselves by jumping off cliffs. In the wake of the various interpretations of the Apocalypse, tense with expectation of the millennium, the various medieval movements arose, the fraticelli and the apostolics of Gherardo Segarelli, from which was born the revolt of Fra Dolcino, the brothers of the free spirit, the swindlers suspected of satanism, the various Catharist groups who sometimes committed suicide by starving themselves (the "endura"). In the twelfth century, Tanchelm, endowed with impressive charisma, had his followers give him all their wealth and he scoured Flanders; Eudes de l'Etoile dragged his followers through the forests of Brittany until they all ended on the pyre; during the Crusades the bands of Tafurs, all hairy and dirty, took to sacking, cannibalism, the massacre of the Jews; insuperable in battle, these Tafurs were feared by the Saracens; later the sixteenth-century Revolutionary of the Upper Rhine fiercely pursued the massacre of ecclesiastics; in the thirteenth century flagellant movements spread (the Crucifers, Brothers of the Cross, the secret Flagellants of Thuringia), moving from one village to another, lashing themselves until they bled. The Reformation period witnessed the mystical communism of the city of Münster, where followers of Thomas Münzer, under John of Leyden, set up a theocratic state, sustained by violence and persecution. Believers had to renounce all worldly goods, were forced into sexual promiscuity, while the leader increasingly assumed divine and imperial attributes, and any recalcitrants were locked in church for days and days until they were all prostrate, bowing before the will of the prophet; then finally everything was purified in an immense massacre in which all the faithful lost their lives.

It could be observed that suicide is not the rule in all these movements, but violent death—bloodbath, destruction on the pyre—certainly is. And it is easy to understand why the theme of suicide (for that matter present among the Circoncellions) seems to become popular only today; the reason is that for those past movements the desire for martyrdom, death, and purification was satisfied by the authorities in power. You have only to read a masterpiece of our Italian medieval literature, the story of Fra Michele the Minorite, to see how the promise of the stake had a sure, uplifting fascination for the martyr, who could moreover hold others responsible for that death which he nevertheless so ardently desired. Naturally in today's California, where even a mass murderer like Manson lives quietly in prison and applies for parole, where, in other words, authority refuses to administer death, the desire for martyrdom must take on more active forms: *Do it yourself*, in short.

The historical parallels are endless (the eighteenth-century camisards, for example, the Cevenne prophets in the seventeenth, the Convulsionarians of San Medardo, down to the various Shakers, Pentecostals, and Glossolalics now invading Italy and in many places absorbed into the Catholic Church). But if you simply compare the characteristics of the Jim Jones cult with a synthetic model of the various millenarian cults (overlooking the various differences) you will find some constant elements. The cult is born in a moment of crisis (spiritual, social, economic), attracting on the one hand the truly poor and on the other some "rich" with a self-punishing syndrome; it announces the end of the world and the coming of the Antichrist (Jones expected a fascist coup d'état and nuclear holocaust). It starts with a program of common ownership of property and convinces the initiates that they are the elect. As such they become more at home with their bodies, and after a strict phase they progress to practices of extreme sexual freedom. The leader, endowed with charisma, subjects everyone to his own psychological power and, for the common good, exploits both the material donations and the willingness of the faithful to be mystically possessed. Not infrequently drugs or forms of self-hypnosis are employed to create a psychological cohesion for the group. The leader proceeds through successive stages of divinization. The group goes from self-flagellation to violence against the unfaithful and then to violence against themselves, in their desire for martyrdom. On the one hand, a persecution delirium rages, and on the other the group's oddness actually unleashes genuine persecution, which accuses the group of crimes it hasn't even committed.

In Jones's case, the liberal attitude of American society drove him to invent a plot (the congressman coming to destroy them) and then the self-destructive occasion. Obviously, the theme of the flight through the forest is also present. In other words the church of the People's Temple is only one of many examples of a revival of the millenarian cults in which at the end (after a start justified by situations of social crisis, pauperism, injustice, protest against authority and the immorality of the times), the elect are overwhelmed by the temptation, gnostic in origin, which asserts that to free themselves from the rule of the angels, lords of the cosmos, they have to pass through all the forms of perversion and cross the swamp of evil.

So then, why today? Why in the United States to such an extent, why in California? If millenarianism is born out of social insecurity and explodes in moments of historical crisis, in other countries it can take on socially positive forms (revolution, conquest, struggle against the tyrant, even nonviolent pursuit of martyrdom, as for the early Christians; and in all these cases it is supported by solid theory, which allows the social justification of one's own sacrifice); or it can imitate the historically positive forms, while rejecting social justification (as happens with the Red Brigades). In America, where there is now no central object against which to join battle as there was during the war in Vietnam, where the society allows even aliens to receive unemployment compensation, but where loneliness and the mechanization of life drive people to drugs or to talking to themselves in the street, the search for the alternative cult becomes frantic. California is a paradise cut off from the world, where all is allowed and all is inspired by an obligatory model of "happiness" (there isn't even the filth of New York or Detroit; you are condemned to be happy). Any promise of community life, of a "new deal," of regeneration is therefore good. It can come through jogging, satanic cults, new Christianities. The threat of the "fault" which will one day tear California from the mainland and cast her adrift exerts a mythical pressure on minds made unstable by all the artificiality. Why not Jones and the good death he promises?

The truth is that, in this sense, there is no difference between the destructive madness of the Khmers, who wipe out the populations of cities and create a mystical republic of revolutionaries dedicated to death, and the destructive madness of someone who contributes a hundred thousand dollars to the prophet. America takes a negative view of Chinese austerity, of the sense of permanent campaign among the Cubans, the sinister madness of the Cambodians. But then when it finds itself facing the appearance of the same desire for millenarian renewal, and sees it distorted in the asocial form of mass suicide, it cannot understand that the promise to reach Saturn one day is not enough. And so it says something "inconceivable" has happened.

1978

Whose Side
Are the
Orixà On?

This evening, in São Paulo, some friends are taking me to the city's extreme outskirts, in the direction of the international airport. About an hour by car, to the Afro-Brazilian rites. We come to a big building rather high up above an expanse of poor houses, not quite a *favela*: The favela is farther on, you can glimpse the faint lights in the distance. The building is well-made, it looks like a parish hall. It's a *terreiro*, or house, or tent of Candomblé. A tourist, or even a Brazilian who has never visited it (and there are many, the majority, at least from the middle class upwards), would start talking excitedly of macumba.

We introduce ourselves; an old black man purifies us with some incense. On entering, I expect to find a hall like certain Umbanda tents I have already visited, a triumph of religious kitsch, complicated by syncretistic forebearance: altars crammed with statues of the Sacred Heart, the Madonna, native Indian gods, red devils of the sort seen only in the productions of Lindsay Kemp. Instead, this hall has an almost Protestant severity, with few decorations. At the end, the benches for the noninitiate worshipers; to the side, beside the drummers' platform, the sumptuous seats for the Ogà. The Ogà are people of some social standing, often intellectuals, who are not necessarily believers, but in any case respect the cult; they are assigned the honorary function of advisers and guarantors of the house, and they are selected on the indication of a higher divinity. The great novelist Jorge Amado occupies such a position in a terreiro of Bahia, selected by Iansà, a Nigerian deity, mistress of war and of the winds. The French ethnologist Roger Bastide, who studied these cults, was chosen by decree of Oxossi, a Yoruban deity, patron of hunters. On the side opposite the drums are the seats for guests, where we are shown by the *pai-de-santo*, the Babalorixà, the equivalent (more or less) of the pastor of this church. An impressive, white-haired mestizo, of great dignity. He knows who his guests are; he makes some shrewd remarks about the risk that these rationalist intellectuals may commit the sin of disbelief.

But in this church that can welcome so generously the African gods and the Christian pantheon, tolerance is the rule; this place is the very essence of syncretism. In fact, on the rear wall I see three images that amaze me: the polychrome statue of a naked Indio wearing a feather crown, and another statue of an old black slave dressed in white, seated, smoking a pipe. I recognize them: They are a *caboclo* and a *preto velho*, spirits of those who have crossed over, who play an important role in the Umbanda rites, but not in the Candomblé, which establishes relations only with the higher divinities, the Orixà of African mythology. What are these two doing here, on either side of the great Crucifix? The pai-de-santo explains to me that it is a tribute: The Candomblé doesn't "use" them, but would never think of denying their presence and their power.

It is the same thing with the Exù. In the Umbanda he is often seen as a devil (they sell little metal statues of him, with very long horns and tail, and the trident; or statues of wood or colored terracotta, enormous, repulsively kitsch, like the lascivious devil in a Folies Bergère spectacle); the Candomblé doesn't consider him a devil, but a sort of median spirit, a degenerate Mercury, messenger of higher spirits, in good as in evil. It doesn't honor him, doesn't await his possession, but at the beginning of the rite the pai-de-santo will hasten to purify the room with an enormous cigar (waved rather like a thurible), asking the Exù politely, in fact, to keep out and not to disturb the ceremony. As if to say: Jesus and the devil aren't our thing, but it's best to maintain a good-neighborly relationship.

What does the Candomblé honor? The Orixà, the higher divinities of the African religions, the Nago-Yoruba of Sudan, or the Bantu Angolan and Congolese, those that came with the first slaves to Brazil and never afterwards abandoned them. The great Ologun, father of all the gods, who is not depicted, and also Oxalà, whom popular syncretism identifies with Jesus Christ and, in particular, with Our Lord of Bonfim, worshiped in Bahia. And then the others, of whom more below.

As I find myself talking with an obviously cultured pai-de-santo, I immediately ask him some awkward questions, making it clear that my curiosity is of a theological and philosophical nature. Are these Orixà persons, for example, or forces? Natural forces, the priest explains, cosmic vibrations, water, wind, leaves, rainbow. Then why are their statues seen everywhere, and why are they identified with Saint George or Saint Sebastian? The pai-de-santo smiles, then goes on to speak to me of the deep roots of this cult, to be discerned also in Judaism, and in even more ancient religions; he tells me that the Candomblé accepts the Mosaic law, and he smiles again when I mention the rites of black magic, the notorious macumba, which is, in fact, the maleficent variation of the Candomblé and in the Umbanda rite becomes the Quimbanda, where the Exù and his mate, the lascivious Pomba-Gira, possess human bodies in trance—the rites, in other words, that are performed also before soccer games, where roosters are killed so that the members of the opposing team will fall ill or die. He smiles like a theologian of the Gregorian University asked to express an opinion about the miracle of San Gennaro or weeping statues of the Madonna. He will say nothing against popular belief, but nothing in its favor, either. He smiles; the populace is what it is. But what about the Umbanda then? A recent cult, born in the 1930's, combining African religions, Catholicism, occultism, and Allan Kardec spiritualism: a product of French positivism. People who believe in reincarnation, where the initiates in trance are possessed by spirits (and by pretos velhos and caboclos) and then start prophesying and giving advice to the faithful. The Umbanda is the conservative, spiritualist version of the Afro-Brazilian rite, and has firmly asserted that it respects with absolute devotion the established order. Whereas the Candomblé (the pai-de-santo doesn't tell me this, but I know it) originated in the black slaves' search for their own cultural identity; it is an act of revolt, or rather of proud, voluntary ghettoization, religious and cultural, and in fact it was long persecuted; in Pernambuco they tell of a police chief who as late as the '30's collected the severed ears and hands of those damned fetishists he arrested.

The story of the development of the various cults is confused (there is a library of hundreds of volumes); I am not trying here to clear up an obscure chapter of Brazilian ethnology: I am only listing some suspicions. The Rui Barbosa law of 1888 (a law considered golden) abolishes slavery but does not confer a "regenerated" social status on the slave. Indeed, in 1890, in a weak attempt to abolish slavery as a stigma, all the archives of the slave trade are ordered burned. A hypocritical move, because it prevents the slaves from ever reconstructing their history, their origin; they become formally free, but with no past. So it is easy to understand why, towards the end of the last century, the cults become official, intensify, emerge into the open; in the absence of family "roots," the blacks try to regain their cultural identity by means of religion. And yet it is curious that in a period of positivism, inflamed by European spiritualistic theories, it is the white intellectuals who influence the black people's cults, causing them gradually to absorb the principles of nineteenth-century spiritualism. These phenomena occurred also in European history; when forms of revolutionary millenarianism existed, the action of the official churches tended always to transform them into phenomena of more learned millenarianism, based on hope and not on violence. Thus we might think that the Candomblé rites remain as nuclei of "hard" millenarianism in the midst of the more edulcorated Umbanda rites. But I cannot talk about this with the pai-de-santo. I will receive my answer, an ambiguous one, when I come out into the garden to visit the houses of the divinities.

While a swarm of girls, most of them black, in ritual Bahian dress, comes gaily crowding in for the final preparations, a gentleman all in white, from cap to shoes, because it is the month of Oxalà, symbolized by this color, welcomes us and shows us around, speaking Italian. By now he speaks it badly; he came here from Italy after the war (always regard with suspicion those who arrived here immediately after the war; in fact he speaks about his adventures as a soldier in East Africa and about Marshal Graziani). He's had many ups and downs, tried all the religions, and now found peace: "If they were to tell me that the world is going to end right here [he points his finger in front of himself], I would shift only a bit in the other direction."

The Orixà's houses, arranged around the vast garden like the chapels of some Holy Mountain in Italy, display on the outside the image of the Catholic saint syncretized with his Orixà counterpart. The interiors are a symphony of crude and violent colors, provided by the flowers, the statues, by the hues of the recently cooked foods offered to the gods: white for Oxalà, blue and pink for Yemanjà, red and white for Xangò, yellow and gold for Ogùn, and so on. Only the initiated can enter; otherwise you kneel, kiss the threshold, touching your forehead and the back of your ear with one hand. But then, I ask, is Yemanjà, goddess of waters and/or procreation, Our Lady of the Conception or not? And is or is not Xangò Saint Jerome? And why did I see Ogùn syncretized as Saint Anthony in Bahia and as Saint George in Rio, whereas here Saint George appears, radiant in his blue and green cloak, ready to spear the dragon, in the house of Oxossi? I think I know the answer, because it was given to me years ago by the sacristan of a Catholic church in Bahia: You know how ingenuous the poor are, he said; to make them pray to Saint George you have to tell them he's the same as Oxossi. But now my guide gives me the opposite reply: You know how the poor are; to make them acknowledge the reality and power of Oxossi you have to let them believe he's Saint George. No doubt about it: The Candomblé is an old and wise religion.

But now the rite is beginning. The pai-de-santo performs his propitiatory fumigations, the drums begin their obsessive rhythm, while a cantor intones the *pontos*, ritual strophes which are sung in chorus by the initiated. The initiated are mostly women; the *filha-de-santo* is the trained medium who during the dance will be visited by an Orixà. For some time there have been also male initiates, but the medium's gift seems a privilege reserved for women. A few weeks later, in Bahia, I visited a terreiro four hundred years old, where I was received by the *mae-de-santo* or Ialorixà, venerable and grave as an abbess; women of this kind have always dominated the cultural and social life of Salvador, capital of Bahia; and writers like Jorge Amado speak of them with affection and deference. Here some of the women are white. They point out a blonde to me: a German psychologist; she dances rhythmically, her blank eyes staring into space. Slowly she begins to sweat, in the eager hope of going into a trance. She does not succeed, to the very end; she is not yet ripe for the embrace of the gods. When all the other daughters of the saint are off in ecstasy, I see her still wriggling at the back, almost weeping, distraught, trying to lose control, following the music of the atabaques, the sacred drums that have the power to summon the Orixà. And meanwhile, one by one, many of the initiated make the physical and mystical leap; you see them suddenly stiffen, their eyes glazed, their movements automatic. Depending on which Orixà visits them, their movements celebrate his nature and powers: soft gestures of the hands, waved, palms down, at the sides, as if swimming, for those possessed by Yemanjà; slow bent movements, those of Oxalà, and so on (in the Umbanda, when the Exù arrives, the possessed move in nervous, evil jerks). Those who have received Oxalà will be covered with special veils, because their fortune has been great and exceptional.

In our party there is a fifteen-year-old European girl with her parents. They told her beforehand that if she wanted to come she would have to follow everything with close attention and respect, but with detachment, exchanging opinions with the others, not allowing herself to become involved. For if Pythagoras was right, music can make us do what it wants; on other occasions I have seen visiting nonbelievers, particularly susceptible, fall into a trance like ripe fruit. Now the girl is sweating; she feels nausea, wants to go outside. There she is immediately joined by the Italian in white, who speaks to her parents and says to leave her in the house for a few weeks; the girl clearly has mediumistic qualities, she has reacted positively to Ogùn, she must be cultivated. The girl wants to leave; her parents are frightened. She has grazed the mystery of the strange relationships between the body, the forces of nature, and the techniques of casting spells. Now she is embarrassed, believes she was the victim of a fraud: When she goes back to school she will learn about Dionysiac rites and perhaps never realize that for a moment she, too, was a maenad.

The rite is over, we take our leave of the pai-de-santo. I ask him which Orixà's son I am. He looks into my eyes, examines the palms of my hands, and says: "Oxalà." I tease one of my friends, who is the son merely of Xangò.

Two days later, in Rio, other friends take me to another Candomblé terreiro. This is in a poorer neighborhood, the faith is on a more popular level. The house in São Paulo seemed a Protestant church, but this one seems a Mediterranean shrine. The costumes are more African. Those visited by Oxalà will receive at the end some splendid masks that I thought existed only in the comics of Tim Tyler; they are great trappings of straw, which sheath the whole body. It is a procession of vegetal ghosts, whom the celebrants lead by the hand, like blind men, groping in their catatonic movements, dictated by the god.

Here the *comida dos santos*, the ritual foods offered to the Orixà, are excellent Bahian cusine, displayed outdoors on great leaves, like immense corbeilles of tribal delicacies; and at the end of the rite we, too, are to eat them. The pai-de-santo is an odd sort, dressed like Orson Welles as Cagliostro, with a young face of a rather flaccid beauty (he is white and blond); he smiles with priestly affection at the faithful, who kiss his hands. With few movements, a suburban John Travolta, he signals the start of the various phases of the dancing. Later he will abandon his vestments and reappear in jeans, to suggest a faster pace for the drums, a freer movement for the initiate about to go into trance. He allows us to witness only the beginning and the end; he apparently doesn't want us present when the initiates go into trance, which is always the most violent moment. Is it out of respect for us, or for the faithful? He takes us into his house, offers us a supper of *fejoada*.

On the wall there are strange, brightly colored pictures, somewhere between Indian and Chinese, with surreal subjects, like those seen in America in the magazines of pseudo-Oriental underground groups. The pictures are his; he is a painter. We talk about ethics and theology. He doesn't have the theological severity of the other evening's pai-de-santo; his religiosity is more indulgent, pragmatic. He denies that good and evil exist: All is good. I say to him: "But if he [I nod towards my friend] wants to kill me and comes to ask your advice, you surely must tell him that it is evil to kill me!" "I don't know," he replies, with a vague smile, "maybe for him it's a good thing, I don't know. I will explain to him only that it is better not to kill you." He displays a tender pride in his charisma. He tells of the love he feels for his people, the serenity that comes from contact with the Orixà. He won't commit himself as to their cosmic nature, their relation to the saints. There are no differences; it is enough to be serene. The Candomblé theology changes from one terreiro to another. I ask him who my Orixà is. Again he fights shy, these things are hard to say, they can change with the circumstances; he doesn't believe in this ability to judge; if I really insist, just looking at me like this, off-hand, he would say I'm a son of Oxalà. I don't tell him I received the same answer two nights ago. I still want to catch him out.

My friend, the one supposed to kill me, plays the politically concerned Brazilian. He speaks to the pai-de-santo of the contradictions of the country, the injustices, asks him if his religion could also drive men to revolt. The Babalorixà says evasively that these are problems he doesn't want to discuss, then he smiles again with excessive sweetness, as when he assured me my friend wouldn't kill me, and he murmurs something like: "But if it were necessary, it could . . ."

What does he mean? That for the present it isn't necessary? That the Candomblé is still a religion of the oppressed, and would be ready to inspire them to revolt? Doesn't he trust us? He dismisses us at four in the morning, as the trance is fading in the contorted limbs of the sons and daughters of the saint. Dawn is breaking. He presents us with some of his works of art. He looks like the manager of a dance hall in a working-class neighborhood. He has asked nothing of us; he has only given us presents and invited us to a supper.

I still have one question, which I didn't ask even his São Paulo colleague. I have realized, and not only in these two cases, that the Candomblé (not to mention the Umbanda) is attracting more and more whites. I've encountered a doctor, a lawyer, and many proletarians and subproletarians. Originally, an ancient assertion of racial autonomy, establishing for blacks a space impenetrable by the religion of the Europeans, these rites are becoming more and more a generalized offer of hope, consolation, communal life. They are dangerously close to the practices of carnival and soccer, even if more faithful to ancient traditions, less consumeristic, able to reach more deeply the personality of the adepts—wiser, I would say, truer, bound more to elementary pulsations, to the mysteries of the body and of nature. But still they represent one of the many ways the disinherited masses are képt on their reservation, while at their expense the generals industrialize the country, offering it to the exploitation of foreign capital. The question I didn't ask the two pai-de-santos is this: Whose side are the Orixà on?

As a son of Oxalà, would I have been entitled to ask it?

1979

Striking at
the Heart
of the State

The anxious waiting for another communiqué from the Red Brigades about the fate of Aldo Moro and the heated debates about how to behave when it comes have led the press to contradictory reactions. Some papers refused to print the first communiqué, but they couldn't avoid publicizing it with banner headlines; others did print it, but in type so small that only those with 20-20 vision could read it (unacceptable discrimination). As for its content, here again the reaction was embarrassed, because all were unconsciously awaiting a text full of "Ach so!"s or words with five consonants in a row, thus immediately betraying the hand of the German terrorist or the Czechoslovakian agent; instead they were confronted with a long, political argument.

For argument it was, and this fact eluded no one; and the more alert also realized that the argument was addressed not to the "enemy" but to potential friends, to demonstrate that the Red Brigades are not a bunch of desperados lashing out at random, but must be seen as the vanguard of a movement justified in the context of the international situation.

If this is how things stand, you cannot react by simply declaring that the communiqué is raving, delirious, vain, mad. It must be analyzed calmly, attentively; that is the only way to ascertain where the communiqué, which commences from fairly lucid premises, reveals the fatal theoretical and practical weakness of the Red Brigades.

We must have the courage to say that the "raving" message contains a highly acceptable premise and translates, even if in a fairly sketchy way, a thesis that all European and American culture, from the students of '68 to the theoreticians of the *Monthly Review*, as well as the left-wing parties, has constantly repeated. So if there is "paranoia," it lies not in the premises but, as we shall see, in the practical conclusions drawn from them.

I don't think it's a good idea to smile at the bogey of the so-called SIM or Stato Imperialistico delle Multinazionali (the Imperialist State of the Multinationals). The way it is depicted here may have a B-film quality; still no one can refuse to see that international planetary policy is no longer determined by individual governments but, in fact, by a network of productive interests (it could also be called the network of the multinationals), which decides local politics, wars and peaces, and—again—establishes the relations between the capitalistic world and China, Russia, and the Third World.

If anything, what's interesting is that the Red Brigades have abandoned their Disney-like mythology, in which on one side there was a wicked individual capitalist named Uncle Scrooge and on the other the Beagle Boys, a cheating rabble, true, but with a certain charge of crazy amiability because they stole, to the tunes of proletarian confiscation, from the stingy, egotistical capitalist.

The Beagle game had previously been played by the Tupamaros of Uruguay, who were convinced that the Brazilian and Argentinian Scrooges would become irritated and would turn Uruguay into a second Vietnam, while the citizens, impelled to sympathize with the Beagles, would become so many Vietcong. The game didn't work, because Brazil didn't make a move and the multinationals, which had to produce and sell in the Cono Sur, fostered Perón's return to Argentina, divided the revolutionary or guerrilla forces, allowed Perón and his descendants to sink into the shit up to their necks, and at that point the more quick-witted Montoneros fled to Spain and the more idealistic paid with their lives.

It is precisely because the power of the multinationals exists (have we forgotten about Chile?) that the idea of a Che Guevara–type revolution has become impossible. The Russians had their revolution while all the European states were engaged in a world war; the long march was organized in China while the rest of the world had other things on its mind. . . . But when you live in a universe where a system of productive interests exploits the atomic stalemate to impose a peace useful to all sides and to send through the heavens satellites that spy on one another in turn, at this point national revolution can no longer be waged; everything is decided elsewhere.

The historic compromise on the one hand and terrorism on the other represent two answers (obviously antithetical) to this situation. The confused idea that motivates terrorism is a very modern principle and a very capitalistic one (for which classical Marxism found itself unprepared), a principle of systems theory. The great systems are headless, they have no protagonists and they do not live on individual egoism, either. Therefore they cannot be struck by killing the king; they are struck when they are made unstable through acts of harassment, exploiting their own logic: if there exists a completely automated factory, it will not be upset by the death of the owner but rather by erroneous bits of information inserted here and there, making work hard for the computers that run the place.

Modern terrorism pretends (or believes) that it has pondered Marx; but in fact, even if indirectly, it has pondered Norbert Wiener on the one hand and science fiction on the other. The problem is that it hasn't pondered enough—nor has it studied in sufficient depth—cybernetics. The proof is that in all their previous propaganda the Red Brigades still spoke of "striking at the heart of the state," cultivating on the one hand the nineteenth-century notion of the state and, on the other, the idea that the adversary has a heart or a head, as in the battles of a bygone age, when if you could strike the king, riding at the head of his troops, the enemy army was demoralized and destroyed.

In their latest pamphlet the Red Brigades abandon the idea of heart, of state, of wicked capitalist, of "murdering" cabinet minister. Now the adversary is the system of the multinationals, who use Moro as their pawn or, at least, as a recipient of information.

What is the error in the (theoretical and practical) reasoning that, at this point, the Red Brigades are committing, especially when they appeal, against multinational capital, to multinational terrorism?

First ingenuousness. Once they have grasped the idea of the great systems, they promptly mythologize it, insisting that the multinationals have "secret plans," which Moro would be one of the few to know. In reality, the great systems have no secrets, and how they operate is well known. If multinational equilibrium advises against the formation of a left-wing government in Italy, it is childish to think that they would send Moro a form letter telling him how to defeat the working class. It would suffice (this is an invention) to stir up something in South Africa, upset the diamond market in Amsterdam, influence the course of the dollar, and thus cause a lira crisis.

Second ingenuousness. Terrorism is not the enemy of the great systems; on the contrary, it is their natural counterweight, accepted, programmed.

The multinationals' system cannot live in a world war economy (and an atomic world war at that); but it also knows that it cannot reduce the natural drives of biological aggression or the impatience of peoples or groups. That is why it accepts little local wars, which are then disciplined and reduced by shrewd international inter entions; and likewise it accepts terrorism. A factory here, a factory there, in upheaval because of sabotage: The system can still go ahead. A plane is hijacked from time to time: The airlines lose money for a week, but to make up for that the newspapers and TV networks make money. Furthermore, terrorism gives police forces and armies a raison d'être, because if you keep them idle they start demanding fulfillment in some broader conflict. Finally, terrorism serves to justify disciplined interventions where an excess of democracy makes the situation less governable.

The "national" capitalist, on the order of Uncle Scrooge, fears rebellion, robbery, and revolution, which could steal the means of production from him. Modern capitalism, which invests in numerous countries, always has a fairly wide space for maneuver and can bear terrorist attack in one isolated point, or in two points, or three.

As it is headless and heartless, the system displays an incredible capacity for healing and stabilizing. Wherever it is struck, that place will always be peripheral. If the president of the German manufacturers association loses his life, such incidents are statistically acceptable, like highway deaths. For the rest (and this has been amply described), they proceed to medievalize their territory, with fortified castles and great residential complexes with private guards and photoelectric cells.

The only serious trouble would be a terrorist uprising spread over the entire world territory, a mass terrorism (such as the Red Brigades seem to invoke); but the multinationals' system "knows" (insofar as a system can "know") that this hypothesis is to be rejected. The multinationals system doesn't send children down in the mines: the terrorist is someone who has nothing to lose but his chains, but the system manages things in such a way that, except for the inevitable outsiders, everybody has something to lose in a situation of generalized terrorism. It knows that when terrorism, beyond some picturesque feat, begins to make the everyday life of the masses too uneasy, the masses stand firm against terrorism.

What is it that, on the contrary, the multinationals' system

117

looks askance at, as we have seen lately? The fact that, all of a sudden, in Spain, Italy, France, and elsewhere, parties come into power that have workers' organizations behind them. No matter how "corruptible" these parties may be, the day that mass organizations stick their noses into the international management of capital, there could be trouble. It's not that the multinationals would die if Marchais took Giscard's place, but everything would become more difficult.

There is the specious concern that if the Communists came to power they would learn the secrets of NATO (open secrets, anyway): The real concern of the multinationals' system (and I say this quite coldly, having no sympathy for the historical compromise as it is proposed today) is that control by the popular parties might disturb a management of power.

Terrorism, on the contrary, is a much lesser concern, because it's a biological consequence of the multinationals, just as a day of fever is the reasonable price of an effective vaccine.

If the Red Brigades are right in their analysis of a world government by the multinationals, then they must recognize that they, the Red Brigades, are the natural and programmed counterweight. They must recognize that they are acting out a script already written by their presumed enemies. Instead, after having discovered, however crudely, an important principle of the logic of systems, the Red Brigades reply with a nineteenth-century *feuilleton* featuring avengers and executioners, good and efficient as the Count of Monte Cristo. It would be laughable, if this novel weren't written in blood.

The conflict is between great powers, not between demons and heroes. Unhappy, therefore, is the nation that finds the "heroes" underfoot, especially if they still think in religious terms and involve the population in their bloody ascent to an uninhabited paradise.

1978

Why Are They
Laughing in
Those Cages?

In February 1979 I sent an article to *La Repubblica* of Milan. Or rather, not an article but a little story, the kind that are technically called uchronias, science fiction, that is, or reverse utopias, on the order of "what would have happened if Caesar hadn't been stabbed." Since it was fiction and not political opinion, it ended up in the culture section. Every author is more or less fond of the things he writes, and he is fonder of some than of others; I was very proud of that story, but I must say that I received no interesting reactions of the kind I have received for many other things written with less commitment. The fact is that, except for fans of the genre, few people believe that uchronias (or utopias) are a serious way of reflecting on the present.

In that story I imagined that things in Italy, and in the world, had gone differently after World War II, and that Italy during the past decades had been at war with a Turkish fascist empire. I amused myself by imagining the various political alliances that would result, and above all, I saw the founders of the Red Brigades praised in Parliament, their officers leading commando groups, decorated with gold medals, and I pictured the heroic Red Brigades fighting off the Turkish invader, eulogized by Giorgio Amendola, while Paul VI sadly reflected on how much calmer Italy would have been if, after 1945, we had had thirty years of peace.

What was the meaning of that story? That democratic culture had too easily branded as reactionary certain theories of animal behavior according to which there exists in the species (in all species) a quotient of violence that must somehow manifest itself. Wars, which, not without reason, though with evil glee, the Futurists praised as "the world's only hygiene," are important safety valves, which serve to release and sublimate this violence. If there are no wars (and personally I would rather there be as few as possible) we have to accept the idea that a society will somehow express the quotient of violence it harbors.

But the moral of the story was something else: namely, that provided this violence is released, it is irrelevant whether its release takes the form of attacks on banks, murders for questions of honor, campaigns for the burning of heretics, acts of satanism, collective suicides as in Guyana, nationalistic outbursts, or revolutionary utopias for the salvation of the proletariat. The final moral was that, if the founders of the Red Brigades had been offered a splendid nationalist or colonialist myth, say the slaughter of the Jews, they would have fallen in behind it and not behind the dream of striking at the heart of the bourgeois state.

These reflections are apposite now, as, on the one hand, the trial of Moro's presumed assassins is in progress and, on the other hand, we witness the grotesque ritual of the Anglo-Argentine war.

What is so frightening about the war over the Falklands? Not the fact that General Galtieri sought an external enemy in order to allay internal tensions; that is normal dictatorial technique, and everybody must do his job, however filthy it may be. Nor the fact that Britain should react in a manner closer to Francis Drake than to postmodern, because noblesse oblige, and each is prisoner of his own history and his own national myths.

What is frightening is the fact that the Montoneros, Firmenich, the revolutionary Peronistas, all those who moved European democratic public opinion when they were languishing in the generals' prisons and who were actually excused when they engaged in small-scale terrorism (of course, people said, they live under a dictatorship), all these full-time revolutionaries are today enthusiastically on the side of the government, dazzled by the nationalistic invitation to die for the sacred borders of the fatherland.

It sounds exactly like my story: If the Argentinian generals had invented a nice war ten years ago, these heroes would never have committed acts of terrorism, but would have got themselves killed, dagger clenched in their teeth, hurling hand grenades against the white rajah James Brooke—perhaps crying out "Mompracem!"—new tiger-cubs of the pampas. Chile refuses to fall in line behind Argentina, because Pinochet is smart and needs American support, but look: Cuba agrees at once. Castro must be more familiar with Errol Flynn than with Marx.

I see many analogies between the Red Brigades snickering during the Moro trial and the Montoneros now crying "Viva Galtieri!" Just as I see many analogies with what has happened in a country as allergic to ideologies as the United States, where violence, in order to erupt, needs other pretexts, like the worship of Satan. I understand the indignation and the horror of Giampaolo Pansa, who in yesterday's *Repubblica* couldn't understand how the Red Brigades could be so jolly, and how the thought of the murder victim did not weigh on them. But if we reread the reports of the investigation and trial of Charles Manson and his "family" after the stabbing of Sharon Tate, it is the same script, the same psychology, the same lack of remorse, the same sense of having done something that gave meaning to a life that, all things considered, was too boring and peaceful. And it is the same jollity of those hundreds of poor people who drank poison and administered it to their children, to follow the mystical suicide of a preacher who, not long before, had been ready to sacrifice himself for far more acceptable causes.

This also explains the "repentant" terrorists. How is it possible to repent after arrest, and repent profoundly, turning in your companions, whereas you didn't repent at the moment when you were firing a couple of bullets into the nape of a helpless man? Why, because there was the impulse to kill and, once that was satisfied, the game was over; so why not repent? Ideology has nothing to do with it: It was a pretext.

I am fully aware that this kind of talk risks sounding reactionary. The problem is to know, to understand, that not all sacrifices, not all bloodshed, is carried out for fun. But it is a difficult matter of rational discriminations; and to articulate them, you must first of all be unrelentingly suspicious of the mystique of sacrifice and blood. I don't mean to suggest that there is no difference between those whom society recognizes as heroes and those whom society recognizes as bloodthirsty madmen, even if the difference is much less than our schoolbooks would have us believe. I don't want to suggest that all ideologies and all ideals are transitory pretexts for impulses of violence that spring from the depths of the species. Perhaps there is a distinction, a very simple one.

Real heroes, those who sacrifice themselves for the collective good, and whom society recognizes as such (maybe some time later, whereas at the time they are branded as irresponsible outlaws), are always people who act *reluctantly*. They die, but they would rather not die; they kill, but they would rather not kill; and in fact afterwards they refuse to boast of having killed in a condition of necessity.

Real heroes are always impelled by circumstances; they never choose because, if they could, they would choose not to be heroes. For example—Salvo D'Acquisto, or one of the many partisans who fled to the mountains, was captured and tortured, and never talked, in order to lessen the tribute of blood, not to encourage it.

The real hero is always a hero by mistake; he dreams of being an honest coward like everybody else. If it had been possible, he would have settled the matter otherwise, and without bloodshed. He doesn't boast of his own death or of others'. But he doesn't repent. He suffers and keeps his mouth shut; if anything, others then exploit him, making him a myth, while he, the man worthy of esteem, was only a poor creature who reacted with dignity and courage in an event bigger than he was.

But we know at once and without hesitation that we must be wary of those who set out, fired (and firing), moved by an ideal of purification through blood, their own and others', but more often, others'. We must not let it amaze us, or shock us too much. But we mustn't ignore the existence of these phenomena, either.

If we don't accept and recognize, bravely, the inevitability of this behavior (studying techniques to confine it, prevent it, offering other, less bloody safety valves), we run the risk of being idealists and moralists as much as those whose bloodthirsty madness we so reprove. To recognize violence as a biological force is true materialism (historical or dialectical, it matters little) and the Left has been wrong not to study biology and ethology sufficiently.

1982

On the Crisis
of the Crisis
of Reason

In a weekly magazine recently I happened to read an interview with a famous novelist (I won't mention his name because, on the one hand, the phrase was only attributed to him, and on the other I am reconstructing it from memory, and I don't want to attribute to someone a thing he may not have said; but if he didn't say it, others are saying the same thing); he declared that reason can no longer explain the world in which we live and we now have to rely on other instruments.

Unfortunately, the interview failed to specify what those other instruments are, leaving the reader free to imagine: feeling, delirium, poetry, mystical silence, a sardine can opener, the high jump, sex, intravenous injections of sympathetic ink. Even more unfortunately, each of these imagined instruments could, indeed, be the opposite of reason, but each opposition would imply a different definition of reason.

For example, the book that originated this debate* seems to

---

*Aldo Gargani, ed., *Crisi della ragione* (Turin: Einaudi, 1979).

speak of a crisis in what is called a "classical" model of reason, as Aldo Gargani explains with great clarity in the introduction. But the alternatives that Gargani proposes in other philosophical contexts go under the name of reason or rational activity or at least reasonable activity, as he admits. Among the other essays in the book (to mention only a few), Ginzburg's opposes deductive reasoning with a hypothetical conjectural reasoning, judged valid by Hippocrates, by Aristotle, and by Peirce; Veca's essay offers a persuasive series of rules for reasonable conjecture; Viano proposes a prudent definition of rationality as justification of special beliefs, to make them understood by all.

Here are some good definitions of the nonclassical rational position, which allows us to remain within reality and not delegate the job of reason to delirium or track and field events. The problem is not to kill reason, but to render bad reasons harmless, and to dissociate the notion of reason from that of truth. But the name for this honorable job is not "hymn to crisis." It has been called, since the time of Kant, "critique." The recognition of limits.

Confronted by a shibboleth like that of the crisis of reason, we feel that, to start with, we must define not so much reason as the concept of crisis. And the indiscriminate use of that concept is a case of editorial cramps. Crisis sells well. During the last few decades we have witnessed the sale (on newsstands, in bookshops, by subscription, door-to-door) of the crisis of religion, of Marxism, of representation, the sign, philosophy, ethics, Freudianism, presence, the subject (I omit other crises that I don't understand professionally even if I endure them, such as that of the lira, of housing, the family, institutions, oil). Whence the well-known quip: "God is dead, Marxism is undergoing a crisis, and I don't feel so hot myself."

Let us consider something pleasant, like the crisis of representation. Even assuming that whoever speaks of it has a definition of representation (which is often not the case), if I rightly understand what they're saying—namely that we are unable to construct and exchange images of the world that are certainly apt to convey the form, if there is one, of this world—it seems to me that the definition of this crisis began with Parmenides, continued with Gorgias, caused Descartes no small amount of concern, made things awkward for everyone thanks to Berkeley and Hume, and so on, down to phenomenology. If Lacan is interesting it's because he resumes Parmenides. Those who rediscover the crisis of representation today seem to have charmingly vague ideas about the continuity of this discussion (I am reminded of another joke, the one about the student asked to discuss the death of Caesar: "What? Dead? I didn't even know he was sick!").

But even admitting the considerable age of the crisis, I still don't understand what the hell it means. I cross the street on a red light, the cop blows his whistle, and then fines *me* (not someone else). How can all this happen if the idea of the subject is in a state of crisis, along with the sign and reciprocal representation? I begin to suspect this is not the point. But then what was having the crisis? Can we clear it up? Or is it the notion of crisis itself that is in critical condition? Or are you subjecting me to a series of terrorist actions? I protest.

Back to reason, that is, to the definition of. As we move through the forest of the different and age-old philosophical definitions, we can (with the crudeness of one allowed only a few hundred words) outline five basic meanings:

1. Reason is that type of natural knowledge, characteristic of man, opposed on the one hand to mere instinctive reactions, and on the other to intuitive knowledge (such as mystical illuminations, faith, subjective experiences not communicable through language, and so on). In this case we speak of reason to say that man is capable of producing abstractions and of speaking through abstractions. This notion does not seem to me to be undergoing a crisis; man is made in this way, beyond any doubt. At most we must decide to what extent this proceeding by abstractions is good compared to other ways of thinking, because undoubtedly the per-

son who has mystical visions also thinks. But speaking of the crisis of reason is itself formulating an abstraction, using our rational capacities to cast doubt on the goodness of a certain type of exercise of these same capacities.

2. Reason is a special faculty of knowing the Absolute by direct view; it is the self-knowledge of the idealistic ego; it is the intuition of prime principles which both the cosmos and the human mind obey, and even the divine mind. This concept is undergoing a crisis, no question about that. It has given us far too many headaches. If somebody comes and tells us he has a direct view of the Absolute and tries to impose it on us, we kick him. But don't call it crisis of reason. It's that man's crisis.

3. Reason is a system of universal principles that precede man's abstractive capacity. At most man may recognize them, perhaps with difficulty and after long reflection. This is Platonism, no matter what name it's given. It is an illustrious position, and its crisis is considerable, from Kant on (and even earlier). This is the notorious classical reason. You come across it even in mathematics or contemporary logic. Its crisis is obvious but not universally accepted. What does it mean, to say that the sum of the inner angles of a triangle must always add up to one hundred and eighty degrees because this is a necessary truth? At most one should discuss the difference between universal truth, evident truth, and postulated truth. If I posit Euclidean geometry, it is necessary truth that the sum of the interior angles equals one hundred and eighty degrees. As a rule we aspire to the freedom to change the postulates in special situations. If someone grants me that freedom, I grant him permission to use the notion of necessary truth. Obviously, it is over decisions of this sort that the battle for definition number 5 is waged, as we will see below.

4. Reason is a faculty of judging and discerning (good and evil, true and false). This is Cartesian common sense. If you insist on the natural origin of this faculty, you return to something close to definition number 3. This notion today is surely undergoing a

crisis, but in an ambiguous way. I would call it a crisis of excess: This innocent naturalness has been shifted from reason to other "faculties," such as Desire, Need, Instinct. Instead of insisting on the crisis of this notion (surely fairly dangerous and "ideological"), I would find it more useful to create a crisis for the certainty of its surrogates. In this respect, the new Cartesianism of the irrational, so to speak, seems to me far more upsetting.

To say that these four definitions of reason are in a state of crisis is like saying, after Galileo and Copernicus, that the earth moves around the sun. It may be necessary to add that the sun is motionless only in relation to the earth, but the first affirmation is now watertight and the idea that the sun moves around the earth is surely undergoing a crisis (but why repeat it?).

5. Thus we come to the fifth definition. Which is also in a state of crisis, but a different crisis from the others. It is not so much undergoing a crisis as it is *critical*, because in a sense it is the only definition that allows us to recognize a "rational" or "reasonable" way of constantly creating a crisis in both reason and classical rationalism and in the anthropological notions of rationality and, in the final analysis, its own conclusions.

The fifth definition is very modern, but also very ancient. If you reread Aristotle carefully you can derive it also from his writings, with some prudence. Reread Kant (and rereading always means reading with reference to our problems, explicitly subjecting the original picture to criticisms and precautions); Kant still works pretty well, too, in this regard.

As I was saying, in this fifth meaning, rationality is exercised through the very fact that we are expressing propositions regarding the world, and even before making sure that these propositions are "true," we have to make sure that others can understand them. So we have to work out some rules for common speech, logical rules which are also linguistic rules. Which is not to assert that when we speak we have to say always and only one thing, without ambiguity or multiple meanings. On the contrary, it is rather rational and reasonable to recognize that there exist also discourses (in dreams, in poetry, in the expression of desires and passions) that mean several things at once, contradictory among themselves.

But precisely because it is fortunately obvious that our speech is also open and has multiple meanings, every so often, and in certain matters, we have to work out agreed norms of speech, for specific situations where we all decide to adopt the same criteria for using words and for linking them in propositions which can then be debated. Can I reasonably assert that human beings love food? Yes, even if there are dyspeptics, ascetics, and anorexics. We must simply agree and establish that, in this area of problems, statistical evidence can be held reasonable.

Is stylistic evidence valid in establishing what is the "right" meaning of the *Iliad*, or whether Bo Derek is more desirable than Sigourney Weaver? No, the rules change. And who doesn't agree with this criterion? I won't say it's irrational, but allow me to look at it with suspicion. If possible, I avoid it.

Don't ask me what I must do if it sneaks in; it will be reasonable to decide *in what way* when the situation arises. Both the laws of logic and those of rhetoric (in the sense of a technique of argument) belong to this type of reasonableness. Fields must be established in which the former are preferable to the latter.

A logical friend said to me: "I renounce all certitudes, except the first mention." What's rational about this attitude? For the layman, I will explain in a few words. The *modus ponens* is the rule of reasoning (and hence the rule for a comprehensible and agreed discourse) whereby if I assert *if p then q*, and acknowledge that *p* is true, then *q* can only follow. In other words, if I agree to define all French citizens as Europeans (and we agree on this meaning postulate), then if Monsieur Ali Hassan is a French citizen everyone must recognize that he is European.

The *modus ponens* does not apply in poetry, or dreams, or the language of the unconscious in general. We must only decide where it has to apply, that is, begin a discourse after deciding whether or not we accept the *modus ponens*. And naturally we must agree on the premise, because someone may want to define as French citizens only those born in France of French parents with white skin.

Sometimes, when it comes to the definition of premises, the meaning-postulates that we want to accept, infinite conflicts can develop. It is then reasonable not to insist on the *modus ponens*, until all agree on the premise. But afterwards, it seems reasonable to obey the *modus ponens*, if it has been assumed as valid. And it will be rational not to refer to the *modus ponens* in those cases where we can suspect that no result of reciprocal comprehensibility will be achieved (it is impossible to analyze according to the *modus ponens* the proposition of Catullus *odi et amo*, unless we redefine the notion of hatred and love — but to redefine them in a rational way we would have to reason according to the *modus ponens* . . .).

In any case, if someone uses the *modus ponens* to demonstrate to me that the *modus ponens* is an eternal, rational law (classical, to be sensed and accepted), I will consider it rational to call his claim irrational. However, it seems to me reasonable to reason according to the *modus ponens* in many instances, for example, in playing cards: If I have established that four aces beat four tens, if you then have four aces, I have to admit that you have won. The point is to establish that we can also change the game, by mutual consent.

What I continue to consider irrational is somebody's insistence that, for instance, Desire always wins out over the *modus ponens* (which could also be possible); but then to impose on me his own notions of Desire and to confute my confutation, he tries to catch me in contradiction by using the *modus ponens*. I feel a Desire to bash him one.

I attribute the spread of such irrational behavior to the great number of publications that play with metaphorical irresponsibility on the crises of reason. But let me make it clear that the problem affects us not only at the level of learned debate, but also in daily behavior and political life. And so, a qualified *Viva!* to the *modus ponens*.

1980

4

REPORTS
FROM THE
GLOBAL
VILLAGE

Towards a
Semiological
Guerrilla
Warfare

Not long ago, if you wanted to seize political power in a country, you had merely to control the army and the police. Today it is only in the most backward countries that fascist generals, in carrying out a coup d'état, still use tanks. If a country has reached a high level of industrialization the whole scene changes. The day after the fall of Khrushchev, the editors of *Pravda, Izvestiia*, the heads of the radio and television were replaced; the army wasn't called out. Today a country belongs to the person who controls communications.

I'm not saying anything new; by now not only students of communication but also the general public is aware that we are living in the Age of Communication. As Professor McLuhan has suggested, information is no longer an instrument for producing economic merchandise, but has itself become the chief merchandise. Communication has been transformed into heavy industry. When economic power passes from the hands of those who control the means of production to those who not only control information media but can also control the means of production, the problem of alienation also alters its meaning. Faced by the prospect of a communications network that expands to embrace the universe, every citizen of the world becomes a member of a new proletariat. But no revolutionary manifesto could rally this proletariat with the words: "Workers of the world, unite!" Because, even if the communications media, as means of production, were to change masters, the situation of subjection would not change. We can legitimately suspect that the communications media would be alienating even if they belonged to the community.

What makes the newspaper something to fear is not (or, at least, is not only) the economic and political power that runs it. The newspaper was already defined as a medium for conditioning public opinion when the first gazettes came into being. When someone every day has to write as much news as his space allows, and it has to appear readable to an audience of diverse tastes, social class, education, throughout a country, the writer's freedom is already finished: The contents of the message will not depend on the author but on the technical and sociological characteristics of the medium.

For some time the severest critics of mass culture have been aware of all this, and they agree: "The mass media do not transmit ideologies; they are themselves an ideology." This position, which I defined as "apocalyptic" in a previous book of mine, implies this further argument: It doesn't matter what you say via the channels of mass communication; when the recipient is surrounded by a series of communications which reach him via various channels at the same time, in a given form, the nature of all this disparate information is of scant significance. The important thing is the gradual, uniform bombardment of information, where the different contents are leveled and lose their differences.

You will have observed that this is also the familiar position expressed by Marshall McLuhan in his *Understanding Media*. But, for the so-called apocalyptics, McLuhan's conviction was translated into a tragic consequence: Liberated from the contents of communication, the addressee of the messages of the mass media receives only a global ideological lesson, the call to narcotic passiveness. When the mass media triumph, the human being dies.

But Marshall McLuhan, on the contrary, setting out from the same premises, concludes that, when the mass media triumph, the Gutenbergian human being dies, and a new man is born, accustomed to perceive the world in another way. We don't know if this man will be better or worse, but we know he is new. Where the apocalyptics saw the end of the world, McLuhan sees the beginning of a new phase of history. This is exactly what happens when a prim vegetarian argues with a user of LSD: The former sees the drug as the end of reason, the latter as the beginning of a new sensitivity. Both agree on the chemical composition of psychedelics.

But the communications scholar must ask himself this question: Is the chemical composition of every communicative act the same?

Naturally there are educators who display a simpler optimism, derived from the Enlightenment; they have firm faith in the power of the message's contents. They are confident that they can effect a transformation of consciousness by transforming television programs, increasing the amount of truth-in-advertising spots, the precision of the news in the columns of the newspaper.

Both to them and to those who believe that "the medium is the message," I would like to recall an image we have seen in many cartoons and comic strips, a slightly obsolete image, rather racist, but a splendidly suitable example in this situation. It is the image of the cannibal chief who is wearing an alarm clock as a necklace. I don't believe that cannibals so adorned exist any longer, but we can translate the original into various other experiences of our everyday lives. The world of communications, for example, is full of cannibals who transform an instrument for measuring time into an "op" jewel.

If this is so, then it is not true that the medium is the message; it may be that the invention of the clock, accustoming us to think of time in the form of space divided into regular parts, changed some people's way of perception, but there are undoubtedly others for whom the clock message has a different meaning.

But if this is so, it is still equally untrue that acting on the form and contents of the message can convert the person receiving it. For the receiver of the message seems to have a residual freedom: the freedom to read it in a *different* way. I say "different" and not "mistaken." A brief look at the mechanics of communication can tell us something more precise on this subject.

The communication chain assumes a Source that, through a Transmitter, emits a Signal via a Channel. At the end of the Channel the Signal, through a Receiver, is transformed into a Message for the Addressee. Since the Signal, while traveling through the Channel, can be disturbed by Noise, one must make the Message *redundant*, so that the information is transmitted clearly. But the other fundamental requirement of this chain is a Code, shared by the Source and the Addressee. A Code is an established system of probabilities, and only on the basis of the Code can we decide whether the elements of the message are intentional (desired by the Source) or the result of Noise. It seems to me very important to bear in mind the various links in this chain, because when they are overlooked there are misunderstandings that prevent us from observing the phenomenon with attention. For example, many of Marshall McLuhan's theses on the nature of the media stem from the fact that he uses the term "media" broadly, for phenomena that can be at times reduced to the Channel, and at other times to the Code, or to the form of the message. Through criteria of economy, the alphabet reduces the possibilities of the sound-making organs but, in doing so, provides a Code for communicating experience; the street provides me with a Channel along which it is possible to send any communication. To say that the alphabet and the street are "media" is lumping a Code together with a Channel. To say that Euclidian geometry and a suit of clothes are media is lumping together a Code (the elements of Euclid are a way of formalizing experience and making it communicable) and a Message (a given suit, through codes of dress—conventions accepted by society—communicates an attitude of mine towards my fellows). To say that light is a medium is a refusal to realize that there are at least three definitions of "light." Light can be a Signal of information (I use electricity to transmit impulses that, in Morse code, mean particular messages); light can be a Message (if my girlfriend puts a light in the window, it means her husband has gone out); and light can be a Channel (if I have the light on in my room I can read the message-book). In each of these cases the impact of a phenomenon on the social body varies according to the role it plays in the communication chain.

But, to stay with the example of light, in each of these three cases the meaning of the message changes according to the code with which I interpret it. The fact that light, when I use Morse code to transmit luminous signals, is a signal—and that this signal is light and not something else—has, on the Addressee, far less impact than the fact that the Addressee knows Morse code. If, for example, in the second of my hypothetical cases, my girlfriend uses light as a signal to transmit in Morse code the message "my husband is home" but I continue to refer to our previously established code, whereby "light" means "husband absent," my behavior (with all the ensuing unpleasant consequences) is determined not by the form of the message or its contents according to the Emitting Source but by the code I am using. It is the code used that gives the light-signal a specific content. The move from the Gutenberg Galaxy to the New Village of Total Communication will not prevent the eternal drama of infidelity and jealousy from exploding for me, my girlfriend, and her husband.

And so the communication chain outlined above will have to be modified as follows: The Receiver transforms the Signal into Message, but this message is still the empty form to which the Addressee can attribute various meanings depending on the Code he applies to it.

If I write the phrase "no more," you who interpret it accord-

139

ing to the English-language code will read it in the sense that seems most obvious to you; but I assure you that, read by an Italian, the same words would mean "not blackberries," or else "No, I prefer blackberries"; and further, if, instead of a botanical frame of reference, my Italian reader used a legal one, he would take the words to mean "No, respites," or, in an erotic frame of reference, as a reply: "No, brunettes" to the question "Do gentlemen prefer blondes?"

Naturally, in normal communication, between one human being and another, for purposes connected with everyday life, such misunderstandings are few; the codes are established in advance. But there are extreme cases, and first among them is that of aesthetic communication, where the message is deliberately ambiguous precisely to foster the use of different codes by those who, in different times and places, will encounter the work of art.

If in everyday communication ambiguity is excluded, in aesthetic communication it is deliberate; and in mass communication ambiguity, even if ignored, is always present. We have mass communication when the Source is one, central, structured according to the methods of industrial organization; the Channel is a technological invention that affects the very form of the signal; and the Addressees are the total number (or, anyway, a very large number) of the human beings in various parts of the globe. American scholars have realized what a Technicolor love movie, conceived for ladies in the suburbs, means when it is shown in a Third World village. In countries like Italy, where the TV message is developed by a centralized industrial Source and reaches simultaneously a northern industrial city and a remote rural village of the South, social settings divided by centuries of history, this phenomenon occurs daily.

But paradoxical reflection also is enough to convince us on this score. The American magazine *Eros* published famous photographs of a white woman and a black man, naked, kissing; if those images had been broadcast over a popular TV channel, I presume that the significance attributed to the message by the governor of

Alabama would be different from that of Allen Ginsberg. For a California hippie, for a Greenwich Village radical, the image would have meant the promise of a new community; for a Klansman, the message would have signified a terrible threat of rape.

The mass communication universe is full of these discordant interpretations; I would say that variability of interpretation is the constant law of mass communications. The messages set out from the Source and arrive in distinct sociological situations, where different codes operate. For a Milanese bank clerk a TV ad for a refrigerator represents a stimulus to buy, but for an unemployed peasant in Calabria the same image means the confirmation of a world of prosperity that doesn't belong to him and that he must conquer. This is why I believe TV advertising in depressed countries functions as a revolutionary message.

The problem of mass communications is that until now this variability of interpretation has been random. Nobody regulates the way in which the addressee uses the message—except in a few rare cases. And here, even if we shift the problem, even if we say "the medium is not the message" but rather "the message depends on the code," we do not solve the problem of the communications era. If the apocalyptic says, "The medium does not transmit ideologies: It itself is ideology; television is the form of communication that takes on the ideology of advanced industrial society," we could now only reply: "The medium transmits those ideologies which the addressee receives according to codes originating in his social situation, in his previous education, and in the psychological tendencies of the moment." In this case the phenomenon of mass communication would remain unchanged: There exists an extremely powerful instrument that none of us will ever manage to regulate; there exist means of communication that, unlike means of production, are not controllable either by private will or by the community. In confronting them, all of us, from the head of CBS to the president of the United States, from Martin Heidegger to the poorest fellah of the Nile delta, all of us are the *proletariat.*

141

And yet I believe it is wrong to consider the battle of man against the technological universe of communication as a strategic affair. It is a matter of tactics.

As a rule, politicians, educators, communications scientists believe that to control the power of the media you must control two communicating moments of the chain: the Source and the Channel. In this way they believe they can control the message. Alas, they control only an empty form that each addressee will fill with the meanings provided by his own cultural models. The strategic solution is summed up in the sentence "We must occupy the chair of the Minister of Information" or even "We must occupy the chair of the publisher of *The New York Times*." I will not deny that this strategic view can produce excellent results for someone aiming at political and economic success, but I begin to fear it produces very skimpy results for anyone hoping to restore to human beings a certain freedom in the face of the total phenomenon of Communication.

So for the strategic solution it will be necessary, tomorrow, to employ a guerrilla solution. What must be occupied, in every part of the world, is the first chair in front of every TV set (and naturally, the chair of the group leader in front of every movie screen, every transistor, every page of newspaper). If you want a less paradoxical formulation, I will put it like this: The battle for the survival of man as a responsible being in the Communications Era is not to be won where the communication originates, but where it arrives. I mention guerrilla warfare because a paradoxical and difficult fate lies in store for us—I mean for us scholars and technicians of communication. Precisely when the communication systems envisage a single industrialized source and a single message that will reach an audience scattered all over the world, we should be capable of imagining systems of complementary communication that allow us to reach every individual human group, every individual member of the universal audience, to discuss the arriving message in the light of the codes at the destination, comparing them with the codes at the source.

A political party that knows how to set up a grass-roots action that will reach all the groups that follow TV and can bring them to discuss the message they receive can change the meaning that the Source had attributed to this message. An educational organization that succeeds in making a given audience discuss the message it is receiving could reverse the meaning of that message. Or else show that the message can be interpreted in different ways.

Mind you: I am not proposing a new and more terrible form of control of public opinion. I am proposing an action to urge the audience to control the message and its multiple possibilities of interpretation.

The idea that we must ask the scholars and educators of tomorrow to abandon the TV studios or the offices of the newspapers, to fight a door-to-door guerrilla battle like provos of Critical Reception can be frightening, and can also seem utopian. But if the Communications Era proceeds in the direction that today seems to us the most probable, this will be the only salvation for free people. The methods of this cultural guerrilla have to be worked out. Probably in the interrelation of the various communications media, one medium can be employed to communicate a series of opinions on another medium. To some extent this is what a newspaper does when it criticizes a TV program. But who can assure us that the newspaper article will be read in the way we wish? Will we have to have recourse to another medium to teach people how to read the newspaper in a critical fashion?

Certain phenomena of "mass dissent" (hippies, beatniks, new Bohemias, student movements) today seem to us negative replies to the industrial society: The society of Technological Communication is rejected in order to look for alternative forms, using the means of the technological society (television, press, record companies . . .). So there is no leaving the circle; you are trapped in it willy-nilly. Revolutions are often resolved in more picturesque forms of integration.

But it could be that these nonindustrial forms of communication (from the love-in to the rally of students seated on the grass of the campus) can become the forms of a future communications guerrilla warfare—a manifestation complementary to the manifestations of Technological Communication, the constant correction of perspectives, the checking of codes, the ever renewed interpretations of mass messages. The universe of Technological Communication would then be patrolled by groups of communications guerrillas, who would restore a critical dimension to passive reception. The threat that "the medium is the message" could then become, for both medium and message, the return to individual responsibility. To the anonymous divinity of Technological Communication our answer could be: "Not Thy, but *our* will be done."

1967

The Multiplication
of the Media

A month ago the TV gave us a chance to see again a classic we remembered with admiration, affection, and respect; I refer to Kubrick's *2001*. After this revisitation, I talked with a number of friends, and their opinion was unanimous: They were disappointed.

That film, which had stunned us only a few years ago with its extraordinary technical and figurative invention, its metaphysical breadth, now seemed to repeat wearily things we had seen a thousand times before. The drama of the paranoid computer still maintains its tension, though it no longer seems amazing; the beginning with the monkeys is still a fine piece of cinema, but those non-aerodynamic spaceships have long lain in the toybox of our now-grown children, reproduced in plastic (the spaceships, I believe, not our children); the final images are kitsch (a lot of pseudo-philosophical vagueness in which anyone can put the allegory he wants), and the rest is discographic, music and sleeves.

And yet we considered Kubrick an innovator of genius. But that is the point: The mass media are genealogical, and they have no memory (two characteristics that ought to be incompatible).

The mass media are genealogical because, in them, every new invention sets off a chain reaction of inventions, produces a sort of common language. They have no memory because, when the chain of imitations has been produced, no one can remember who started it, and the head of the clan is confused with the latest great grandson. Furthermore, the media learn; and thus the spaceships of *Star Wars*, shamelessly descended from Kubrick's, are more complex and plausible than their ancestor, and now the ancestor seems to be their imitator.

It would be interesting to enquire why this process does not occur in the traditional arts, to ask why we can still understand that Caravaggio is better than the Caravaggeschi, and that *Dallas* cannot be confused with Balzac. It could be said that in the mass media it is not invention that dominates but technical execution, which can be imitated and perfected. But that isn't the whole story. For example, Wenders's film *Hammett* is technically much more sophisticated than Huston's classic *The Maltese Falcon*, and yet we follow the former only with interest and the latter with religious devotion. So a system or a horizon of expectations operates in us, the audience. When Wenders is as old as Huston will we perhaps see his work again with the same emotion? I'm not up to handling here so many and such formidable questions. But I believe that in *The Maltese Falcon* we will always enjoy a certain ingenuousness that in Wenders is already lost. Wenders's film, unlike the *Falcon*, already moves in a universe where these relationships have inevitably mingled, where it is hard to say that the Beatles are alien to the great musical tradition of the West, where comic strips enter museums via pop art but museums' art enters comic strips via the far from ingenuous culture of men like Crepax, Pratt, Moebius, and Drouillet. And for two evenings in a row the kids pack into a Palasport, but on the first night it's the Bee Gees and the next it's John Cage or a performer of Satie; and the third evening they would go (and, alas, can go no more) to hear Cathy Berberian singing a program of Monteverdi, Offenbach, and—in fact—the

Beatles, but sung like Purcell. And Berberian added to the Beatles' music nothing that it was not already quoting, and only in part without knowing, without wanting to.

Our relationship with mass-produced goods has changed and also with the products of "high" art. Differences have been reduced, or erased; but along with the differences, temporal relationships have been distorted, the lines of reproduction, the befores and the afters. The philologist is still aware of them, but not the ordinary consumer. We have achieved what the enlightened and enlightenment culture of the '60's was demanding, that there should not be, on the one hand, products for helot masses and, on the other, difficult products for the cultivated, refined public. The distances have been reduced, the critics are puzzled. Traditional criticism complains that the new techniques of enquiry analyze Manzoni and Donald Duck with the same precision and can no longer tell them apart (and it's a cheap lie, contrary to all the printed evidence) without realizing (through lack of attention) that it is, on the contrary, the development of the arts itself, today, that tries to obliterate this distinction. To begin with, a person of scant culture today can read Manzoni (how much he understands is another question) but he cannot read the comic strips of *Metal Hurlant* (which are sometimes as hermetic, specious, and boring as the bad experimenters for the "happy few" in previous decades could be). And this situation tells us that when such shifts of horizon occur, they don't have to mean things are going better or worse: Things have simply changed, and even value judgments must be formed according to different parameters.

What's interesting is that, instinctively, high school kids know these things better than some seventy-year-old pedagogue (I refer to arterial, not necessarily calendar age). The high school teacher is convinced that the boy is not studying because he reads *Batman*, and perhaps the boy isn't studying because he reads (along with *Batman* and Moebius—and the difference between them is the same as that between Barbara Cartland and Ivy Compton-Burnett) Hesse's

147

Siddharta, but as if it were a gloss to Pirsig's book *Zen and the Art of Motorcycle Maintenance*. It is clear at this point that the school must also review its manuals (if it ever had any) on how to read. And on what is poetry and what is nonpoetry.

But the schools (and society, and not only the young) must learn new instructions on how to react to the mass media. Everything that was said in the '60's and '70's must be re-examined. Then we were all (perhaps rightly) victims of a model of the mass media based on that of the relationship with authority: a centralized transmitter, with precise political and pedagogical plans, controlled by Authority (economic or political), the messages sent through recognizable technological channels (waves, wires, devices identifiable as a screen, whether movie or TV, radio, magazine page) to the addressees, victims of ideological indoctrination. We would only have to teach the addressees to "read" the messages, to criticize them, and perhaps we would attain the age of intellectual freedom, of critical awareness. . . . This was another dream of '68.

What radio and television are today, we know—incontrollable plurality of messages that each individual uses to make up his own composition with the remote-control switch. The consumer's freedom may not have increased, but surely the way to teach him to be free and controlled has changed. And, for the rest, two new phenomena have slowly progressed: the multiplication of the media and the media squared.

What is a mass medium today? A TV program? That, too, surely. But let's try to imagine a not imaginary situation. A firm produces polo shirts with an alligator on them and it advertises them (a traditional phenomenon). A generation begins to wear the polo shirts. Each consumer of the polo shirt advertises, via the alligator on his chest, this brand of polo shirt (just as every owner of a Toyota is an advertiser, unpaid and paying, of the Toyota line and the model he drives). A TV broadcast, to be faithful to reality, shows some young people wearing the alligator polo shirt. The young (and the old) see the TV broadcast and buy more alligator polo shirts because they have "the young look."

Where is the mass medium? Is it the newspaper advertisement, is it the TV broadcast, is it the polo shirt? Here we have not one but two, three, perhaps more mass media, acting through different channels. The media have multiplied, but some of them act as media of media, or in other words media squared. And at this point who is sending the message? The manufacturer of the polo shirt? its wearer? the person who talks about it on the TV screen? Who is the producer of ideology? Because it's a question of ideology: You have only to analyze the implications of the phenomenon, what the polo-shirt manufacturer wants to say, and what its wearer wants to say, and the person who talks about it. But according to the channel under consideration, in a certain sense the meaning of the message changes, and perhaps also its ideological weight. There is no longer Authority, all on its own (and how consoling it was!). Shall we perhaps identify with Authority the designer who had the idea of inventing a new polo-shirt design, or the manufacturer (perhaps in the provinces) who decided to sell it, and to sell it on a wide scale, to make money, as is only right, and to avoid having to fire his employees? Or those who legitimately agree to wear it, and to advertise an image of youth and heedlessness, or happiness? Or the TV director, who to characterize a generation has one of his young actors wear the polo shirt? Or the singer, who, to cover his expenses, agrees to sponsor the polo shirt? All are in it, and all are outside it: Power is elusive, and there is no longer any telling where the "plan" comes from. Because there is, of course, a plan, but it is no longer intentional, and therefore it cannot be criticized with the traditional criticism of intentions. All the professors of theory of communications, trained by the texts of twenty years ago (this includes me), should be pensioned off.

Where are the mass media? In the festival, the procession, the conference organized by the Culture Commissioner on Immanuel Kant, which now finds a thousand young people seated on the floor to hear the stern philosopher who has taken as his motto the admonition of Heraclitus: "Why do you want to pull me in every direction, ye unread? Not for you did I write, but for those who can understand me." Where are the mass media? What is more private than a telephone call? But what happens when someone hands over to an investigating magistrate the tape of a private phone call—a call made to be taped and delivered to the magistrate, and then leaked by someone in the government to the newspapers, so the newspapers will talk about it, thus compromising the investigation? Who produced the message (and its ideology)? The idiot who spoke, unawares, over the phone? Or the one who delivered it? The magistrate, the newspaper, the reader who failed to understand the game and who, in passing the message on to others, assured its success?

Once upon a time there were the mass media, and they were wicked, of course, and there was a guilty party. Then there were the virtuous voices that accused the criminals. And Art (ah, what luck!) offered alternatives, for those who were not prisoners of the mass media.

Well, it's all over. We have to start again from the beginning, asking one another what's going on.

1983

Culture as
Show Business

The years 1979 and 1980 were a time when, as some ripened novelties were already being theorized, the first puzzled questions were beginning to be asked about other novelties even newer, forgive the expression. The riper novelties concerned an evident shift in the concept of spectacle: a phenomenon of the '70's. Slowly, the crowds, and not only the young, had emerged from the confinement of the theaters. First there was street-corner theater, with its Brechtian flavor, and then its younger sibling, the street fair, and then happenings, then, the celebrations: theater as party, and parties as theater. . . . All subjects on which, as I was saying, a vast theoretical literature now exists; and theoretical literature, as is well known, either kills or at least makes "respectable" spontaneous developments—which are then no longer spontaneous. Now that festivities have come under municipal management, involving all the less marginal strata of an entire city (and thus entertainment has slipped through the fingers of those who, in fact, were improvising at the margin), we will not be so snobbish as to say they have lost their flavor, but they have unquestionably become a "genre," like the detective novel, the classical tragedy, the symphony, or square dancing. And in the face of all these new aesthetics, sociologies, and semiotics of the *festa*, there is nothing further to be said.

The upsetting innovation, on the other hand, came about with the appearance of something that has been labeled, with or without innuendo, "culture as show business."

The wording is ambiguous—as if theater and festival, or the village band playing in the square, were not culture. But despite decades and decades of cultural anthropology (which has taught us that even defecatory positions are part of a community's material culture), we still tend to speak of culture only with reference to "high" culture (literature, philosophy, classical music, gallery art, and stage theater), so the phrase "culture as show business" is meant to denote something quite specific—and to denote it in the light of an ideology (however unspecific) of culture with a capital C. In other words, the premise is that show business is amusement, faintly culpable, whereas a lecture, a Beethoven symphony, a philosophical discussion are boring experiences (and therefore "serious"). The son who gets a bad grade at school is strictly forbidden by his parent to go to a rock concert, but may attend a cultural event (which, on the contrary, will supposedly be good for him).

Another characteristic of the "serious" cultural event is that the audience must not participate. It sits and listens, or watches; in this sense a spectacle (or what was once a spectacle in the "bad" sense) can become "serious" when the public takes no active part but simply attends passively. So it is possible that the audience of Greek comedy watched while spitting out fruit pits and taunting the actors; but today, in a dutifully archeologized amphitheater, the same comedy is more culture than entertainment, and people keep quiet (and, it is hoped, are bored).

Now in the last year some disturbing events have taken place. Cultural centers, which for years have been organizing debates, lectures, round tables, found themselves faced by a *third phase*. The first phase was the normal procedure up until '68: Someone spoke, the audience, in reasonable numbers, listened, with a few polite questions at the end, and everybody was back home in the space of two hours. The second phase was '68: Somebody tried to speak, an unruly audience contested his right to take the floor in an authoritarian manner, somebody else in the audience spoke in his place (just as authoritarian, but we realized that only gradually), in the end some sort of motion was made and carried, then everybody home. The third phase, on the other hand, proceeds like this: Somebody speaks, the huge audience is unbelievably crammed in, seated on the floor, packed into the adjacent rooms, sometimes even on the front steps; they allow the speaker to go on for an hour, for two, three hours, they participate in the debate for another two hours, and they never want to go home.

The third phase can be dismissed in a very highbrow, academic fashion. Bored by politics, the new (but also the old) generation now wants to hear "the truth"; High Culture, in fact, returns in triumph. But even the most rigid academic must feel a certain malaise, because these new masses (and I believe we can call them "masses," even if they are not the same masses that attend sports events or rock concerts) go to cultural events, listen, and with alert attention, speak up, with observations ranging from the acute and learned insight to the howl of the soul, but they behave as if they were at a show. They don't spit out apricot pits or strip naked, but clearly they come partly for the collective occasion, or in other words (to use an expression somewhat overworked, but worth recycling, I believe, for these experiences), *to be together.*

I could cite countless examples (ranging from open-air symphony concerts to debates on epistemology—all occasions where you no longer see the old, familiar crowd), but the one that most struck me (also because I was involved) was the series of lectures or encounters with philosophers organized by the municipal library of Cattolica. People have talked about it a great deal. It is surprising that a small city of a few thousand inhabitants should organize, in the off season, evenings devoted to philosophy (an ancient ghost, about to be eliminated even from upper school curricula). There was further amazement when it turned out that as many as a thousand people came to some of these meetings. And it was still more amazing to learn that the meetings lasted up to four hours, and that the questions came not only from those who already knew everything and wanted to conduct a learned argument with the speaker but also from those who asked the philosopher his thoughts about drugs, love, death, happiness—to such a degree that some speakers had to ward off the questions and remind the questioners that a philosopher is not an oracle and mustn't be too charismatized (who would ever have said this ten years ago?). But the amazement is bound to increase when certain quantitative and geographical calculations are made. I am speaking of my own experience. Obviously Cattolica by itself didn't suffice to supply so many "clients." And, in fact, many came from out of town, from Romagna, the Marches, even farther away. I realized that many came from Bologna, the city where I teach three days a week. Why should anyone come from Bologna to Cattolica to hear me talk for less than forty-five minutes, when they can come as much as they like to the University during the year, where admission is free (whereas a trip from Bologna to Cattolica, what with gas, tolls, dinner in a restaurant, comes to more than a theater ticket)? The answer is simple: They didn't come to hear me. They came to experience the *event*: to hear also the others, to take part in a collective happening.

A show? I would feel no hesitation or embarrassment or bitterness in saying yes. There have been many historical periods in which a philosophical or legal debate was also a show: In Paris, in the Middle Ages, people went to follow the discussions of the *quaestiones quodlibetales*, not only to hear what the philosopher had to say, but to witness a competition, a debate, an agonistic happening. And don't tell me that the Athenians packed their amphitheaters to hear a tragic trilogy plus a satyr play just in order to remain quietly seated to the end. They went to experience an event, where the presence of the others also counted, and the food and drink booths, and the ritual that was part of the general character of a "cultural" festival—as people went to Lincoln Center to see *Einstein on the Beach*, whose action lasts just over five hours and which was conceived in such a way that the audience could stand up, go out, have something to drink and argue a bit, then come back in, then go out again. Entering and leaving is not obligatory. I presume people who go to the stadiums to hear Beethoven follow the symphony from beginning to end, but what counts is the collective rituality—as if that which used to be High Culture can be reaccepted and placed in a new dynamics provided it also permits encounters, experiences in common. If a conservative objects that, absorbed in this way, capital-C Culture doesn't give anything, because the necessary concentration is missing, he is told (if his interlocutor is polite, but there are more curt alternatives) that there is no knowing how much used to be absorbed by the normal client of a lecture or concert, who would doze off only to wake with a start at the concluding applause. The conservative would have no objection to anyone's carrying Plato to the beach, even if he had to read the philosopher among a thousand noises; and he would praise the good will of this cultivated and enterprising bather; but he doesn't want that same reader to go with his friends to hear a debate on Plato instead of going to the disco. Perhaps it is hard to make him understand that turning something into a show does not perforce mean distraction, frivolity, loss of intensity. It is only a different way of experiencing the cultural debate.

During these past months, more or less everywhere in Italy we have perceived the first signs. Perhaps it was a transitory phenomenon. If it lasts, we must examine, with the same coldness that has been used so far, what could happen when we attain the levels of institutionalized cultural showmanship that have been reached in the United States.

In that country, conferences are not organized for specialists alone; meetings, symposia, cultural marathons are frequently presented on every subject, from religion to literature to macrobiotics. The conferences are advertised in the papers, and (often considerable) admission is charged. The organization spends whatever is required to guarantee the presence of personalities who draw audiences, then the event proceeds like a theatrical event. The idea may horrify us. Sometimes it *must* horrify. I remember, in 1978, "The Event," organized by Jerry Rubin, former hero of '68 protest and hippie leader.

"The Event" lasted from nine in the morning until one the following morning, and it promised an "extravaganza of self-awareness," exhibitions, debates, lectures on Zen, macrobiotics, Transcendental Meditation, sex techniques, jogging, discovery of one's hidden genius, art, politics, religion of various types, popular philosophy. Among the stars were Dick Gregory, the sexologists Masters and Johnson, the prophet-architect Buckminster Fuller, preachers, entertainers. Tickets cost a fortune; advertising in all the leading papers promised happiness and radical discoveries for one's personal development, vegetarian buffets, books on Oriental doctrine, prostheses for sexual organs. The result was horrible because it had been conceived as a music hall, to make the public gape. There was no participation, and in any case the participants didn't know one another. The cultural show had been organized like a singles bar (for that matter it isn't rare in America to find advertising for a series of concerts, where it is suggested, in all seriousness, that the intermission is an ideal place to find your soulmate).

If cultural performance is going to follow this road, then we have little to be content about. Not because the show is "cultural," but because it is a "show" in the worst sense of the word: a false life depicted on the stage so that the witnesses, in silence, may have the illusion of living, through an intermediary.

But these are the degenerations of a society known, in fact, as "theatrical." Culture as show business, as we have been talking

156

of it, is not inevitably a product of a theatrical society; it can also be the alternative. A way of eluding organized entertainments, in order to create others for ourselves. And bearing this in mind, keep calm. We must wait and see.

1980

Sports
Chatter

There is one thing that—even if it were considered essential—no student movement or urban revolt or global protest or what have you would ever be able to do. And that is to occupy the football field on a Sunday.

The very idea sounds ironic and absurd; try saying it in public and people will laugh in your face. Propose it seriously and you will be shunned as a provocateur. Not for the obvious reason, which is that, while a horde of students can fling Molotov cocktails on the jeeps of any police force, and at most (because of the laws, the necessity of national unity, the prestige of the state), no more than forty students will be killed; an attack on a sports field would surely cause the massacre of the attackers, indiscriminate, total slaughter carried out by self-respecting citizens aghast at the outrage.

You can occupy a cathedral, and you'll have a bishop who protests, some upset Catholics, a fringe of approving dissidents, an indulgent left-wing, the traditional secular parties (secretly) happy. And you can occupy a party's headquarters, and the other parties, with or without a show of solidarity, will think it serves them right. But if a stadium is occupied, apart from the immediate reactions, the disclaiming of responsibility would be total: Church, Left, Right, State, Judiciary, Chinese, League for Divorce, anarchist unions, all would send the criminals to the pillory. So there is a deep area of the collective sensibility that no one, whether through conviction or demagogical calculation, will allow to be touched. And there is a profound structure of the Social whose Maximum Cement, if broken up, would cause a crisis in every possible associative principle, including the presence of man on earth, at least as he has been present in the last tens of thousands of years. Sport is Man, Sport is Society.

But if an overall revision of our human relationships is in process, let it also touch Sport. At this ultimate root it will discover the inconsistencies of Man as a social animal. Here what is not human in the relationship of sociality will emerge. Here the deceptive nature of Classical Humanism will become clear, founded on Greek anthropolalia, founded in turn not only on contemplation, the notion of the city or the primacy of Doing, but on sport as calculated waste, as masking of the problem, "chatter" raised to the rank of tumor. In short—and this will be explained below— sport is the maximum aberration of "phatic" speech and therefore, finally, the negation of all speech, and hence the beginning of the dehumanization of man or the "humanistic" invention of an idea of Man that is deceptive at the outset.

Sports activity is dominated by the idea of "waste." In principle, every sports act is a waste of energy: If I fling a stone for the sheer pleasure of flinging it—not for any utilitarian end—I have wasted calories accumulated through the swallowing of food, earned by work.

Now this waste—I must make myself clear—is profoundly healthy. It is the waste proper to play. And man, like every animal, has a physical and psychic need for play. So there is a recreational waste that we cannot renounce: It means being free, freeing ourselves from the tyranny of indispensable work. If, as I fling my stone, another man beside me aims to fling one still farther, the recreation takes on the form of "contest," also a waste, of physical energy and of intelligence, which provides the rules of the game. But this recreational waste proves a gain. Races improve the race, contests develop and control the competitive spirit, they reduce innate aggressiveness to a system, brute force to intelligence.

But in these definitions lurks the worm that undermines the action at the roots: Contest disciplines and neutralizes the aggressive charge, individual and collective. It reduces excess action, but it is really a mechanism to neutralize action.

From this nucleus of ambiguous healthiness (a healthiness that is "healthy" up to the point where a boundary is crossed—as you can die of an excess of that indispensable liberating exercise that is laughter, and Margutte explodes from exaggerated health) leads to the first degenerations of the contest: the raising of human beings dedicated to competition. The athlete is already a being who has hypertrophized one organ, who turns his body into the seat and exclusive source of a continuous play. The athlete is a monster, he is the Man Who Laughs, the geisha with the compressed and atrophied foot, dedicated to total instrumentalization.

But the athlete as monster comes into existence at the moment when sport is squared, when sport, that is, from a game played in the first person, becomes a kind of disquisition on play, or rather play as spectacle for others, and hence game as played by others and seen by me. Sport squared equals sports performance.

If sport (practiced) is health, like eating food, sport *seen* is a defrauding of health. When I see others play, I am doing nothing healthy, and I am only vaguely enjoying the health of others (which in itself would be a sordid exercise of voyeurism, like watching others make love), because in fact what I enjoy most are the accidents that will befall those who are healthily exercising, the illness that undermines this exercised health (like someone who watches not two human beings but two bees making love, while waiting to witness the death of the drone).

To be sure, someone who watches sport performed by others becomes excited as he watches; he yells and gesticulates, and so he is performing physical and psychic exercise, and reducing aggressiveness, and disciplining his competitivity. But this reduction is not compensated, as when one exercises sport, by an increase of energy or by an acquired control and self-mastery. On the contrary, for the athletes are competing in play, but the voyeurs compete seriously (and, in fact, they beat up one another or die of heart failure in the grandstands).

As for disciplining competitivity, which in exercised sport has the two aspects of increasing and losing one's own humanity, in athletic voyeurism it has only one aspect, the negative. Sport is presented then, as it has been over the centuries, as *instrumentum regni*. These things are obvious: The *circenses* restrain the uncontrollable energies of the crowd.

But this sport squared (which involves speculation and barter, selling and enforced consumption) generates a sport cubed, the discussion of sport as something seen. This discussion is in the first place that *of* the sports press, but it generates in turn discussion *on* the sports press, and therefore sport raised to the nth power. The discussion on the sports press is discourse on a discourse about watching others' sport as discourse.

Present-day sports, then, is essentially a discussion of the sports press. At several removes there remains the actual sport, which might as well not even exist. If through some diabolical machination of the Mexican government and chairman Avery Brundage, in agreement with all the TV networks in the world, the Olympics were not to take place, but were narrated daily and hourly through fictitious images, nothing in the international sports system would change, nor would the sports discutants feel cheated. So sport as practice, as activity, no longer exists, or exists for economic reasons (for it is easier to make an athlete run than to invent a film with actors who pretend to run); and there exists only chatter about chatter about sport. The chatter about chatter of the sports press constitutes a game with its full set of rules: You have only to listen to those Sunday morning radio broadcasts where they pretend (raising sport to the nth power) that some citizens gathered in the barber shop are discussing sport. Or else you can go and listen to such talk where it occurs.

It will be seen, as for that matter everyone knows already, that evaluations, judgments, arguments, polemical remarks, denigrations, and paeans follow a verbal ritual, very complex but with simple and precise rules. In this ritual, intellectual energies are exercised and neutralized; physical energies are no longer in play, so the competition shifts to a purely "political" level. In fact, the chatter about sports chatter has all the characteristics of a political debate. They say what the leaders should have done, what they did do, what we would have liked them to do, what happened, and what will happen. Only the object is not the city (or the corridors of the state house) but the stadium, with its locker rooms. Such chatter seems therefore the parody of political talk; but since in this parody the strength that the citizen had at his disposal for political debate is vitiated and disciplined, this chatter is the ersatz of political speech, but to such a heightened degree that it becomes itself political speech. Afterwards, there's no more room—because the person who chatters about sport, if he didn't do this, would at least realize he has possibilities of judgment, verbal aggressiveness, political competitiveness to employ somehow. But sports chatter convinces him that this energy is expended to conclude something. Having allayed his doubt, sport fulfills its role of fake conscience.

And since chatter about sport gives the illusion of interest in sport, the notion of *practicing sport* becomes confused with that of *talking sport*; the chatterer thinks himself an athlete and is no longer aware that he doesn't engage in sport. And similarly he isn't aware that he could no longer engage in it, because the work he does, when he isn't chattering, tires him and uses up both the physical energy and the time required for sports activities.

163

This chatter is the sort of thing whose function Heidegger examined in *Being and Time*, under the head of "idle talk":

Idle talk is the possibility of understanding everything without previously making the thing one's own. . . . If this were done, idle talk would founder; and it already guards against such a danger. Idle talk is something which anyone can make up; it not only releases one from the task of genuinely understanding but develops an undifferentiated kind of intelligibility for which nothing is closed off any longer. . . . [Idle talk does not] aim to deceive. Idle talk does not have the kind of Being which belongs to *consciously passing off* something as something else. . . . Thus, by its very nature, idle talk is a closing-off, since to go back to the ground of what is talked about is something which it *leaves undone*. *

Certainly Heidegger wasn't thinking of idle talk or chatter as totally negative: Chatter is the everyday manner in which we are spoken by preexistent language rather than our bending language to ends of comprehension and discovery. And it is a normal attitude. For it, however, "what matters is that there is talk." And here we come to that function of language that for Jakobson is the phatic function, that of contact. On the telephone (replying "Yes, no, of course, fine . . .") and in the street (asking "How are you?" of someone whose health doesn't interest us, and he knows it, and in fact he plays along, in answering "Fine, thanks"), we conduct phatic discourse indispensable to maintainng a constant connection among speakers; but phatic speech is indispensable precisely because it keeps the possibility of communication in working order, for the purpose of other and more substantial communications. If this function atrophies, we have constant contact without any message. Like a radio that is turned on but not tuned, so a

---

*Trans. John Macquarrie and Edward Robinson (New York: Harper and Row, 1962), p. 213.

background noise and some static inform us that we are, indeed, in a kind of communication with something, but the radio doesn't allow us to know anything.

Chatter then will be phatic discourse that has become an end in itself, but sports chatter is something more, a continuous phatic discourse that deceitfully passes itself off as talk of the City and its Ends.

Born as the raising to the nth power of that initial (and rational) waste that is sports recreation, sports chatter is the glorification of Waste, and therefore the maximum point of Consumption. On it and in it the consumer civilization man actually consumes himself (and every possibility of thematizing and judging the enforced consumption to which he is invited and subjected).

A place of total ignorance, it shapes the ideal citizen so profoundly that, in extreme cases (and they are many), he refuses to discuss this daily availability he has for empty discussion. And so no political summons could affect a practice that is total falsification of every political attitude. Thus no revolutionary would have the courage to revolutionize the availability for sports chatter; the citizen would take over the protest, transforming its slogans into sports chatter, or suddenly rejecting, and with desperate distrust, the intrusion of reason in his reasonable exercise of highly rational verbal rules.

Thus the Mexican students have died for nothing.* It seemed reasonable for an Italian athlete to say nobly: "If they kill any more, I refuse to jump." But it was not established how many they would have to kill for him not to jump. And if he then didn't jump, it would be enough, for the others, to talk about what would have happened if he had jumped.

1969

---

* While the 1968 Olympics were in progress in Mexico City, hundreds of Mexican students were killed when security forces opened fire on an antigovernment demonstration.

The World Cup
and Its Pomps

Many malignant readers, seeing how I discuss here the noble sport of soccer with detachment, irritation, and (oh, all right) malevolence, will harbor the vulgar suspicion that I don't love soccer because soccer has never loved me, for from my earliest childhood I belonged to that category of infants or adolescents who, the moment they kick the ball—assuming that they manage to kick it—promptly send it into their own goal or, at best, pass it to the opponent, unless with stubborn tenacity they send it off the field, beyond hedges and fences, to become lost in a basement or a stream or to plunge among the flavors of the ice-cream cart. And so his playmates reject him and banish him from the happiest of competitive events. And no suspicion will ever be more patently true.

I will say more. In an attempt to feel like the others (just as a terrified young homosexual may obstinately repeat to himself that he "has" to like girls), I often begged my father, a sober but loyal fan, to take me with him to the game. And one day, as I was observing with detachment the senseless movements down there on the field, I felt how the high noonday sun seemed to enfold men and things in a chilling light, and how before my eyes a cosmic, meaningless performance was proceeding. Later, on reading Otti-ero Ottieri, I would discover that this is the sense of the "everyday unreality," but at that time I was thirteen and I translated the experience in my own way; for the first time I doubted the existence of God and decided that the world was a pointless fiction.

Frightened, as soon as I had left the stadium, I went to confession to a wise Capuchin, who told me that I certainly had an odd idea, because reliable people like Dante, Newton, Manzoni, T. S. Eliot, and Pat Boone had believed in God without the slightest difficulty. Bewildered by this consensus, I postponed my religious crisis for about another decade—but I have been telling all this to indicate how, as far back as I can remember, soccer for me has been linked with the absence of purpose and the vanity of all things, and with the fact that the Supreme Being may be (or may not be) simply a hole. And perhaps for this reason I (alone, I think, among living creatures) have always associated the game of soccer with negative philosophies.

This having been said, the question could arise as to why I, of all people, should now discuss the World Cup. The answer is soon given: The editors of *L'Espresso*, in an excess of metaphysical vertigo, insist that the event be discussed from an absolutely alien point of view. And so they have turned to me. They couldn't have made a better or shrewder choice.

Now, however, I must say that I am not against the passion for soccer. On the contrary, I approve of it and consider it providential. Those crowds of fans, cut down by heart attacks in the grandstands, those referees who pay for a Sunday of fame by personal exposure to grievous bodily harm, those excursionists who climb, bloodstained, from the buses, wounded by shattered glass from windows smashed by stones, those celebrating young men who speed drunkenly through the streets in the evening, their banner poking from the overloaded Fiat Cinquecento, until they crash into a juggernaut truck, those athletes physically ruined by piercing sexual abstinences, those families financially destroyed after succumbing to insane scalpers, those enthusiasts whose cannon-crackers explode and blind them: They fill my heart with joy. I am in favor of soccer passion as I am in favor of drag racing, of competition between motorcycles on the edge of a cliff, and of wild parachute jumping, mystical mountain climbing, crossing oceans in rubber dinghies, Russian roulette, and the use of narcotics. Races improve the race, and all these games lead fortunately to the death of the best, allowing mankind to continue its existence serenely with normal protagonists, of average achievement. In a certain sense I could agree with the Futurists that war is the only hygiene of the world, except for one little correction: It would be, if only volunteers were allowed to wage it. Unfortunately war also involves the reluctant, and therefore it is morally inferior to spectator sports.

For I am speaking of spectator sports, mind you, not of sport. Sport, in the sense of a situation in which one person, with no financial incentive, and employing his own body directly, performs physical exercises in which he exerts his muscles, causes his blood to circulate and his lungs to work to their fullest capacity: Sport, as I was saying, is something very beautiful, at least as beautiful as sex, philosophical reflection, and pitching pennies.

But soccer has nothing to do with sport in this sense. Not for the players, who are professionals subjected to tensions not unlike those of an assembly-line worker (except for questionable differences in pay), not for the spectators—the majority, that is—who, in fact, behave like hordes of sex maniacs regularly going to see (not once in their lifetime in Amsterdam but every Sunday, and instead of) couples making love, or pretending to (something like the very poor children of my childhood, who were promised they would be taken to watch the rich eating ice cream).

Now that I have posited these premises, it is clear why these weeks I have been feeling very relaxed. Rendered neurotic, like everyone else, by recent tragic events during a three-month period* when we had to devour newspapers and stay glued to the TV, awaiting the latest message from the Red Brigades, or the promise of a new escalation of terror, I can now skip reading the papers, avoid TV, at most looking on page eight for news of the Turin trial, the Lockheed scandal, the referendum. For the rest, the papers and the TV talk about the thing I want to hear nothing about—and the terrorists, who have a keen sense of the mass media, know this very well and don't attempt anything interesting, because they'd end up in the local news or on the food page.

There's no need to ask ourselves why the World Cup has so morbidly polarized the attention of the public and the devotion of the mass media: From the famous story of how a comedy by Terence played to an empty house because there was a trained bear show elsewhere, and the acute observation of Roman emperors about the usefulness of *circenses*, to the shrewd use that dictatorships (including the Argentinian) have always made of great competitive events, it is so clear, so evident that the majority prefers soccer or bicycle racing to abortion, that it isn't even worth reflecting about. But since external pressure impels me to reflect, I might as well say that public opinion, especially in Italy, has never needed a nice international championship more than it does now.

In fact, as I have remarked in the preceding essay, sports debate (I mean the sports shows, the talk about it, the talk about the journalists who talk about it) is the easiest substitute for political debate. Instead of judging the job done by the minister of finance (for which you have to know about economics, among other things), you discuss the job done by the coach; instead of criticizing the record of Parliament you criticize the record of the athletes; instead of asking (difficult and obscure question) if such-and-such a minister signed some shady agreements with such-and-such a for-

---

*Written in 1978, the year of the kidnapping and eventual killing of former Italian Prime Minister Aldo Moro by Red Brigade terrorists.

eign power, you ask if the final or decisive game will be decided by chance, by athletic prowess, or by diplomatic alchemy. Talk about soccer requires, to be sure, a more than vague expertise, but, all in all, it is limited, well-focused; it allows you to take positions, express opinions, suggest solutions, without exposing yourself to arrest, to loyalty oaths, or, in any case, to suspicion. It doesn't oblige you to intervene personally, because you are talking about something played beyond the area of the speaker's power. In short, it allows you to play at the direction of the government without all the sufferings, the duties, the imponderables of political debate. For the male adult it's like little girls playing ladies: a pedagogical game, which teaches you how to occupy your proper place.

And at a moment like this, concerning oneself with the running of the government (the real one) is traumatic. So faced with such a choice, we are all Argentines, and that handful of Argentine nuisances who are still reminding us that, down there, people are "disappeared" from time to time, should be more careful not to mar our pleasure in this sacred mystery play. We listened to them before, and quite politely, so now what do they want? In other words, this World Cup has arrived like Santa Claus. Finally some news that has nothing to do with the Red Brigades.

But while we're on that subject: The reader who is not completely distracted knows that there are two theses in circulation (naturally I consider only the extreme hypotheses, but reality is always a bit more complicated). According to the first thesis, the Brigades are a group obscurely maneuvered by some Power, perhaps foreign. According to the second, they are "misled comrades," who behave execrably but, all things considered, for noble motives (a better world). Now if the first thesis is correct, Red Brigades and organizers of World Cups belong to the same articulation of power: The former destabilize at the right moment, the latter restabilize at the right moment. The public is asked to follow Italy-Argentina as if it were Curcio-Andreotti and, if possible, to place bets on the number of kneecaps involved in the next out-

171

burst of violence. If, on the contrary, the second thesis is correct, the Red Brigades are comrades who are really very misled indeed—because they insist so readily on assassinating political figures and blowing up assembly lines, but that, alas, is not where power is. It is in society's capacity for redistributing tension, immediately afterwards, on other poles, far closer to the soul of the crowds. Is the armed struggle possible on World Cup Sunday? Perhaps it would be best to engage in fewer political discussions and in more *circenses* sociology. Is it possible to have a revolution on a football Sunday?

1978

Falsification
and Consensus

The student I met last October in the Yale University Library
came from California. We were both reaching for the same copy
of an Italian paper, and so I discovered that he had lived in our
country. We went down to the café in the basement for a cigarette
and, in the course of our chat, he mentioned to me an Italian book
that had made a deep impression on him, though he couldn't remember the author or the title. "Wait a minute," he said, "I'll ask
my girlfriend in Rome. Have you got a dime?" He dropped the
dime into the nearby telephone, spoke for a moment with an operator, waited thirty seconds, and Rome was on the line. He chatted
with his girlfriend for a quarter of an hour, then came back and
handed me the dime, which the telephone had returned to him. I
thought he had called collect, but instead he told me that he used
the code number of a multinational.

In the American telephone system (about which the Americans, who know no other, are always complaining), you can call
Hong Kong, Sydney, or Manila by dialing the number of a special
personal credit card. Many executives of big firms use a collective

company card. The number is top secret, but countless students, especially in the technological departments, know it. I asked him if the multinational didn't eventually find out that everybody was using their number, when they checked their bills. Of course, they find out, but they have an annual fixed fee they pay the phone company, and running detailed checks would take too much time. They budget a few tens of thousands of dollars to cover illicit calls. But what if they did check? All you have to do is call from a public phone. But what if they checked the number being called? The other party is already in the know, and just has to say that one evening he or she did receive a long-distance call, but it must have been a joke (and this is also conceivable: Many people call random numbers, just for fun). It's not the immediate saving that counts, the student explained, it's the fact that you're screwing the multinationals, who support Pinochet and are all fascists.

The thousands of students who play tricks of this sort are not the only example of electronic dissent. Joseph La Palombara was telling me that a California protest group two years ago invited the public to pay their telephone bills regularly, but to add one cent to the sum on their checks. Nobody can sue you for paying your bill, especially if you overpay. But if large numbers do it the whole business management of the telephone company is thrown out of whack. Its computers, in fact, stop at every irregular payment, record the difference, send out a credit notice and a check for one cent to each customer. If the protest operation succeeds on a large scale, the system breaks down. In fact, for several months the phone company was in trouble and had to broadcast TV appeals to persuade the customers to stop the joke. The great systems are extremely vulnerable and a grain of sand suffices to send them into "paranoia." When you think about it, airline terrorism, hijacking, is based on this principle: You couldn't hijack a bus, but an airplane is like a baby. To bribe an accountant takes time, money, and perhaps beautiful women, whereas an electronic brain goes mad for much less: All you have to do is insert into its circuit, perhaps by telephone, a piece of "wild" information.

And so, in the era of electronic information, the call has gone out for a form of nonviolent (or at least nonbloody) guerrilla warfare: that of falsification.

Recently the papers told how easy it is for a color photocopier to counterfeit railroad tickets, and how you can drive the traffic lights of a whole city berserk. Someone produces by the dozen photocopies of a letter, whose signature is photocopied from another letter.

The theoretical idea behind these forms of falsification stems from the new criticisms of the idea of power. Never created by an arbitrary, top-level decision, Power lives thanks to thousands of forms of minute or "molecular" consensus. It takes thousands of fathers, wives, and children who recognize themselves in the family structure before a power can base itself on the family ethic as institution; it takes a myriad of people who find a role as physician, nurse, guard before a power can be based on the idea of the segregation of those who are different.

Only the Red Brigades, those last, incurable romantics of Catholic-papist origin, still think the state has a heart and that this heart can be wounded; and they fail because the kidnapping of one Moro, or ten or a hundred, doesn't weaken the system, but rather recreates the consensus around the symbolic ghost of its "heart," wounded and outraged.

The new forms of guerrilla protest are aimed instead at wounding the system, upsetting the fine network of consensus, based on certain rules of living together. If this network breaks down, collapse results. That is their strategic hypothesis.

About ten years ago, in Italy, there were two clamorous cases of falsification. First someone sent to *Avanti!* a fake poem of Pasolini. Later, someone else sent to the *Corriere della Sera* a fake article by Carlo Cassola. Both were published and caused a scandal. It did not spread far because the two episodes were exceptional. If they were to become the norm, then no paper could publish a piece that had not been hand-delivered by the author to the editor.

175

But this has already happened in the last two years: Political proclamations have been printed and posted by group A with the signature of group B; the fake correspondence of Berlinguer was published in a fake Einaudi edition; a fake text by Sartre was produced. We still notice them because the fakes are blatant and, for the most part, clumsy or too paradoxical—but what if it were all done better and at a faster pace? We could react to the falsifications only with other falsifications, spreading false news about everything, even about the falsifications; and—who knows?—perhaps the article you are now reading is only the first example of this new trend toward disinformation. But this very doubt shows the potential suicide inherent in the falsifying techniques.

Every top-level power is supported by a network of molecular consensus. But we have to distinguish between the kind of consensus that allows the spreading of macroscopic forms of control and that which satisfies what we might call a biological pace and doesn't come close to the establishment of power relationships in the true sense.

Let's take two examples. A modern state succeeds in making its citizens pay their taxes not by using force from above but through consensus. Consensus is born from the fact that the members of the group have accepted the idea that certain collective expenses (for example: Who's buying the sandwiches for the Sunday picnic?) must be redistributed collectively (answer: We all pay for the sandwiches at so much a head). We'll grant that this custom of microconsensus is mistaken: The sandwiches, let's say, should be paid for by the person who has derived the greatest benefit from the picnic, or who has the most money. If the base of microconsensus is destroyed, the ideology on which the taxation system is based also totters.

But let's look at the second example. A group of persons exists, united by normal relationships. Among these people, as in any group, the convention prevails that anyone who announces a piece of news is telling the truth. If a person lies once, he is reproached (he has deceived the others). If he lies habitually he is considered unreliable; the group no longer trusts him. At most the group takes its revenge and lies back to him. But let's suppose that the habit of ignoring the minimal condition of truth becomes widespread, and everybody lies to everybody else. The group breaks up, war begins—everyone against everyone else.

At this point power relationships have not been destroyed. The conditions of the group's survival have been destroyed. Each becomes in turn oppressor and victim, unless power is somehow reestablished in someone's favor—in favor of the group or person who works out some more effective technique, who lies better than the others, and more quickly, soon becoming master of the others. In a universe of falsifiers power is not destroyed; at most one holder of power is replaced by another.

To put it simply, a political group capable of broadcasting false news bulletins signed "Fiat" achieves an advantage over the Fiat company, causing a crisis of Fiat's power—but only until the company hires a more skillful falsifier who issues false news bulletins attributed to the group of falsifiers. Whoever wins this battle will be the new Boss.

The truth, actually, is less romantic. Certain forms of consensus are so essential to community life that they reestablish themselves despite every attempt to shake them. At most they are reestablished in a more dogmatic or, I would say, more fanatical way. In a group where the technique of disruptive falsification is spread, a very Puritan ethic of truth would be reestablished; the majority (to defend the ideological bases of consent) would become fanatical about "truth" and would cut off the tongue of anyone who lied, even in a figure of speech. The utopia of subversion would produce the reality of reaction.

Finally, is there any sense in proposing to break up the fine network of micropowers (mind you, not to create a crisis by criticism of its premises, but to break it up by making it suddenly untenable) once it has been assumed that a central Power doesn't exist and that power is distributed along the threads of a finespun, widespread cobweb? If this cobweb exists, it is capable of healing its local wounds, precisely because it has no heart, precisely because it is—let us say—a body without organs. For example:

The triumph of photocopying is creating a crisis in the publishing industry. Each of us if he can obtain, at less expense, a photocopy of a very expensive book avoids buying that book. The practice, however, has become institutionalized. Let's say a book of two hundred pages costs twenty dollars. If I copy it in a stationery store at twenty cents a page I spend forty dollars, and this is not economically feasible. If I use a machine that can reduce two pages onto a single sheet, I spend the price of the book. If I go in with some others and make a hundred copies, I cut the cost in half. Then the operation becomes feasible. If the book is scholarly, and is also two hundred pages long, it will cost forty dollars, then the cost of the photocopy is reduced to a fourth. Thousands of students in this way are paying a fourth of the list price of expensive books. An almost legal form of confiscation, or expropriation.

But the big German and Dutch publishing firms, who bring out scientific works in English, have already adapted to this situation. A two-hundred-page book now costs fifty dollars. They know full well that they will sell it only to libraries and research teams, and the rest will be xeroxes. They will sell only three thousand copies. But three thousand copies at fifty dollars comes out the same as fifty thousand copies at three dollars (except that production and distribution costs are lower). Further, to protect themselves, they don't pay the authors, claiming that these are scholarly publications destined for public-service organizations.

The example is only an example, and it applies exclusively to indispensable scientific works. But it serves to demonstrate that the capacity of the big systems for healing their wounds is considerable. And that, indeed, big systems and subversive groups are often twins, and one produces the other.

That is to say, if the attack on the presumed "heart" of the system (confident that a central Power exists) is bound to fail, likewise the peripheral attack on systems that have neither center nor periphery produces no revolution. At most it guarantees the mutual survival of the players of the game. The big publishing houses are ready to accept the spread of photocopying, as the multinationals can tolerate the phone calls made at their expense, and a good transportation system willingly accepts a fair number of counterfeit tickets—provided the counterfeiters are content with their immediate advantage. It is a more subtle form of "historic compromise," except that it's technological. It is the new form that the Social Contract is preparing to assume, to the extent that the utopia of the revolution is transformed into a scheme of short-range, but permanent, harassment.

1978

5

READING
THINGS

Two Families
of Objects

What would be a better way to initiate a column devoted to signs and myths—which we will try to carry forward without any obsession with regularity, responding instead to the suggestions that arrive from all sides—than by making a devout pilgrimage to one of the sanctuaries of mass communication, the Milan Trade Fair? And with the awareness that we are going there on a specific mission. Because it's one thing to enter as an economic operator: For him the Fair doesn't spout any false talk, it gives him a chance to find what he's looking for, touch it, buy it. This is a game with no double meanings, at least as honest as any commercial competition is honest in a market economy. But it's another thing to go there as spectator (as most visitors do): For him the Fair is a great kermesse of triumphant merchandise, and it takes on the characteristics, to a minor degree, of the big international expos, the world's fairs. If—as Marx said—"the wealth of those societies in which the capitalist mode of production prevails presents itself as an 'immense accumulation of commodities,'" then world's fairs are the temple in which this merchandise loses all real contact with its value in use and most of its contact with its barter value, to become a series of pure connotative signs, at an emotional fever pitch. The goods almost lose their concrete individuality to become so many notes in an anthem to progress, a hymn to the abundance and happiness of consumption and production.

But a trade fair is an international expo only halfway, because the merchandise is there to be sold. The products are signs of an undifferentiated desire, but they are also objective terms of an individuated and precise desire. The immense population of objects collected here refers us to that "sociology of objects" that is developing in France, of which we will speak on another occasion. But a sociology (or a semiology) of objects means that they must be seen within the concrete system of the society that creates them and receives them, so they must be seen as a language listened to as it is being spoken, and of which we try to discern the regulating system. Here, on the other hand, the objects appear lined up as if in a dictionary, or in a grammar, verbs with verbs, adverbs with adverbs, lamps with lamps, tractors with tractors. Wouldn't it be right to conclude that this collection of objects, which is a trade fair, actually leaves the visitor free, because it imposes on him no logic of the accumulation of objects and allows him to gaze coldly, to choose? On the contrary, however, the ideological message of a fair emerges only at second glance, when we have almost been taken in by the persuasive game it establishes.

The objects are of two types. The first are the "beautiful" objects, desirable, fairly accessible. They include easy chairs, lamps, sausages, liquors, motorboats, swimming pools. The visitor loves them and would like to own them. He cannot perhaps buy a motorboat but he can think of the remote possibility—one day, who knows?—of making such a purchase. But there is one thing he doesn't desire: to accumulate objects of a single type. He may want an ashtray, but not a hundred ashtrays; a rubber boat, but not a thousand rubber boats. So his desire is keen but not frantic; it can be postponed, but its difficulty never creates the drama of impossibility. When you think about it, these "beautiful" objects are all consumer goods.

Then there are the others. They are "ugly," because they are cranes, cement mixers, lathes, hods, excavators, hydraulic presses (actually, they are very beautiful, more beautiful than the first, but the visitor doesn't know this). Since they are ugly and cumbersome, they are undesirable, also because they seem strangely defunctionalized, with their wheels spinning pointlessly, their blades striking the air without slicing anything. . . . They are inaccessible, but the visitor doesn't care. He knows that even if he could buy a machine tool, it would be of no use to him. Because these objects, unlike the others, function only if they are accumulable. A thousand ashtrays are useless, but a thousand machine tools make big industry. At the end of his rounds, the ordinary visitor believes he has chosen. He desires beautiful objects, accessible, and not accumulable, and rejects those that are ugly and accumulable (but inaccessible). In reality, he has not chosen; he has only accepted his role as consumer of consumer goods since he cannot be a proprietor of means of production. But he is content. Tomorrow he will work harder in order to be able to buy, one day, an easy chair and a refrigerator. He will work at the lathe, which is not his because (the fair has told him) he doesn't want it.

1970

Lady
Barbara

More and more often I find myself hearing the refrain of some song, running through my mind—a thing everybody has experienced. But in the past few years the refrain has always come to me accompanied by a murmuring, the muttering of a crowd, an outburst of applause, with quite a distinct dynamic. It is not the refrain as it is, or as it should be—as you would hear it on a record, I mean, or translate it from printed music—it is a refrain that explodes violently, bursts as if from a telluric movement. In short, it erupts like a volcano. Before there was nothing, or a long dream of tectonic laziness without desires; then, all of a sudden, a roar, a spiral movement starts, a hornet that first flies from the distance then approaches with the sound of a missile, and then comes the refrain. It is more than a refrain, it is a coitus, a great satisfaction. Bzzz, bzzz, vrrr vrrr—and then suddenly the great aural effusion: "*Lady Barbara*, sei tu . . ." (I mention "Lady Barbara" because it's the first song that comes to mind, but the example is valid for almost all Italian pop festival songs, summer hits, and so on.)

This means that the style of festival songs has been influenced by a TV habit: The advent of the climax, in the comic gag as in the song, must be underlined by applause. But the applause mustn't come after the climax (as in the old days), but before. It must precede, announce, accompany it. The applause is a musical fact; it doesn't represent an opinion of the show or approval of it; it is one of the means the show uses to produce an overwhelming effect and achieve an enthusiastic reception.

In other words, applause no longer serves to demonstrate that the audience is pleased, but to command the public, "Be pleased, or rather, be enthusiastic. . . . Listen to what's just about to happen." This is a device that Poe deplored in the popular novels of Sue, when he said that Sue lacked the *ars celandi artem*, or rather that he excelled in alerting the audience, "Look out, in a moment something wonderful is going to happen that will fill you with amazement." How is anticipatory applause achieved? In two ways. One is the more squalid and mechanical: by flashing at the audience a luminous sign that orders "applause." This method is used in television, but only for shows with an invited public, politely called to collaborate in return for the free ticket. But the pre-applause, which proved quite productive, had to be transported, without reliance on cheap methods, also to big events with a paying public, like the San Remo Festival. The order to applaud thus had to be given, not by extrinsic means, but from within the song itself. They had to create a situation whereby the members of the public felt an inner urge to applaud and sustain the romantic outburst of the singer, under the impression that they were behaving freely, joyously.

Now, how do you achieve a feeling of liberation, surprise, or joy? By creating a situation of tension, boredom, repetition, monotony to the extreme degree, then finally giving a signal that signifies the end of boredom and dullness, promising new and more satisfying experiences. You only have to use the procedure a few times and to give the liberating signal certain recognizable characteristics; after that the public's behavior will not be unlike that of Pavlov's dog: bell, saliva. So the festival songs all begin with a first part (known as the "verse") that is very slow, hardly musical, unrhymed, with a vague tune that seems to bite its tail, in search of itself, or which is blatantly ugly and unpleasant. And thus when the moment of the refrain arrives, you have only to increase the intensity, or the pace, or give an indication of a recognizable tune, and the public explodes with an impassioned ovation that accompanies the opening of the aural calyx, expanding the orchestral fluid and the enraptured, listening hearts.

For example, there was Sergio Endrigo's song at San Remo. An unpleasant opening, with deliberately cultivated and mechanical images (kerosene, dead horses), and a tune that suggests ecclesiastical music, a marked absence of meter and rhyme. And then, all of a sudden, announced by a smile, by flung-out arms, and by the cooperation of the orchestra, we're off . . . "the ship, the ship will set sail," and you have tune, meter, rhyme, and everything tells the audience that the music, which previously wasn't present except negatively, has finally arrived.

But the destiny of the pop song, if styles have a logic and inventions have a manner, is traveling in a difficult direction, because to be so overwhelming and "informative" (in the cybernetic sense) the moment of the explosion should be (and will have increasingly to be) unique, punctual, isolated in the middle of the composition, which to be overwhelming will have to underline and prolong the waiting, the introductory frustration. The destiny of a beautiful song is thus to be all very ugly, except for one little, humble, marvelous central moment, which must die out at once, so that when it returns it will be hailed by the most intense ovation ever heard. Only when the song has become entirely unpleasant will the audience feel happy at last.

1972

Lumbar
Thought

A few weeks ago, Luca Goldoni wrote an amusing report from the Adriatic coast about the mishaps of those who wear blue jeans for reasons of fashion, and no longer know how to sit down or arrange the external reproductive apparatus. I believe the problem broached by Goldoni is rich in philosophical reflections, which I would like to pursue on my own and with the maximum seriousness, because no everyday experience is too base for the thinking man, and it is time to make philosophy proceed, not only on its own two feet, but also with its own loins.

I began wearing blue jeans in the days when very few people did, but always on vacation. I found — and still find — them very comfortable, especially when I travel, because there are no problems of creases, tearing, spots. Today they are worn also for looks, but primarily they are very utilitarian. It's only in the past few years that I've had to renounce this pleasure because I've put on weight. True, if you search thoroughly you can find an *extra large* (Macy's could fit even Oliver Hardy with blue jeans), but they are large not only around the waist, but also around the legs, and they are not a pretty sight.

Recently, cutting down on drink, I shed the number of pounds necessary for me to try again some *almost* normal jeans. I underwent the calvary described by Luca Goldoni, as the saleswoman said, "Pull it tight, it'll stretch a bit"; and I emerged, not having to suck in my belly (I refuse to accept such compromises). And so, after a long time, I was enjoying the sensation of wearing pants that, instead of clutching the waist, held the hips, because it is a characteristic of jeans to grip the lumbar-sacral region and stay up thanks not to suspension but to adherence.

After such a long time, the sensation was new. The jeans didn't pinch, but they made their presence felt. Elastic though they were, I sensed a kind of sheath around the lower half of my body. Even if I had wished, I couldn't turn or wiggle my belly *inside* my pants; if anything, I had to turn it or wiggle it *together with* my pants. Which subdivides so to speak one's body into two independent zones, one free of clothing, above the belt, and the other organically identified with the clothing, from immediately below the belt to the anklebones. I discovered that my movements, my way of walking, turning, sitting, hurrying, were *different*. Not more difficult, or less difficult, but certainly different.

As a result, I lived in the knowledge that I had jeans on, whereas normally we live forgetting that we're wearing undershorts or trousers. I lived for my jeans, and as a result I assumed the exterior behavior of one who wears jeans. In any case, I assumed a *demeanor*. It's strange that the traditionally most informal and anti-etiquette garment should be the one that so strongly imposes an etiquette. As a rule I am boisterous, I sprawl in a chair, I slump wherever I please, with no claim to elegance: my blue jeans checked these actions, made me more polite and mature. I discussed it at length, especially with consultants of the opposite sex, from whom I learned what, for that matter, I had already suspected: that for women experiences of this kind are familiar because all their garments are conceived to impose a demeanor—high heels, girdles, brassieres, pantyhose, tight sweaters.

I thought then about how much, in the history of civilization, dress as armor has influenced behavior and, in consequence, exterior morality. The Victorian bourgeois was stiff and formal because of stiff collars; the nineteenth-century gentleman was constrained by his tight redingotes, boots, and top hats that didn't allow brusque movements of the head. If Vienna had been on the equator and its bourgeoisie had gone around in Bermuda shorts, would Freud have described the same neurotic symptoms, the same Oedipal triangles? And would he have described them in the same way if he, the doctor, had been a Scot, in a kilt (under which, as everyone knows, the rule is to wear nothing)?

A garment that squeezes the testicles makes a man think differently. Women during menstruation; people suffering from orchitis, victims of hemorrhoids, urethritis, prostate and similar ailments know to what extent pressures or obstacles in the sacroiliac area influence one's mood and mental agility. But the same can be said (perhaps to a lesser degree) of the neck, the back, the head, the feet. A human race that has learned to move about in shoes has oriented its thought differently from the way it would have done if the race had gone barefoot. It is sad, especially for philosophers in the idealistic tradition, to think that the Spirit originates from these conditions; yet not only is this true, but the great thing is that Hegel knew it also, and therefore studied the cranial bumps indicated by phrenologists, and in a book actually entitled *Phenomenology of Mind*. But the problem of my jeans led me to other observations. Not only did the garment impose a demeanor on me; by focusing my attention on demeanor, it obliged me to *live towards the exterior world*. It reduced, in other words, the exercise of my interior-ness. For people in my profession it is normal to walk along with your mind on other things: the article you have to write, the lecture you must give, the relationship between the One and the Many, the Andreotti government, how to deal with the problem of the Redemption, whether there is life on Mars, the latest song of Celentano, the paradox of Epimenides. In our

193

line this is called "the interior life." Well, with my new jeans my life was entirely exterior: I thought about the relationship between me and my pants, and the relationship between my pants and me and the society we lived in. I had achieved heteroconsciousness, that is to say, an epidermic self-awareness.

I realized then that thinkers, over the centuries, have fought to free themselves of armor. Warriors lived an exterior life, all enclosed in cuirasses and tunics; but monks had invented a habit that, while fulfilling, *on its own*, the requirements of demeanor (majestic, flowing, all of a piece, so that it fell in statuesque folds), it left the body (inside, underneath) completely free and unaware of itself. Monks were rich in interior life and very dirty, because the body, protected by a habit that, ennobling it, released it, was free to think, and to forget about itself. The idea was not only ecclesiastic; you have to think only of the beautiful mantles Erasmus wore. And when even the intellectual must dress in lay armor (wigs, waistcoats, knee breeches) we see that when he retires to think, he swaggers in rich dressing-gowns, or in Balzac's loose, *drôlatique* blouses. Thought abhors tights.

But if armor obliges its wearer to live the exterior life, then the age-old female spell is due also to the fact that society has imposed armors on women, forcing them to neglect the exercise of thought. Woman has been enslaved by fashion not only because, in obliging her to be attractive, to maintain an ethereal demeanor, to be pretty and stimulating, it made her a sex object; she has been enslaved chiefly because the clothing counseled for her forced her psychologically to live for the exterior. And this makes us realize how intellectually gifted and heroic a girl had to be before she could become, in those clothes, Madame de Sévigné, Vittoria Colonna, Madame Curie, or Rosa Luxemburg. The reflection has some value because it leads us to discover that, apparent symbol of liberation and equality with men, the blue jeans that fashion today imposes on women are a trap of Domination; for they don't free the body, but subject it to another label and imprison it in other armors that don't seem to be armors because they apparently are not "feminine."

A final reflection — in imposing an exterior demeanor, clothes are semiotic devices, machines for communicating. This was known, but there had been no attempt to illustrate the parallel with the syntactic structures of language, which, in the opinion of many people, influence our view of the world. The syntactic structures of fashions also influence our view of the world, and in a far more physical way than the *consecutio temporum* or the existence of the subjunctive. You see how many mysterious paths the dialectic between oppression and liberation must follow, and the struggle to bring light.

Even via the groin.

1976

Casablanca:
Cult Movies and
Intertextual
Collage

Cult

"Was that artillery fire, or is it my heart pounding?" Whenever *Casablanca* is shown, at this point the audience reacts with an enthusiasm usually reserved for football. Sometimes a single word is enough: Fans cry every time Bogey says "kid." Frequently the spectators quote the best lines before the actors say them.

According to traditional standards in aesthetics, *Casablanca* is not a work of art, if such an expression still has a meaning. In any case, if the films of Dreyer, Eisenstein, or Antonioni are works of art, *Casablanca* represents a very modest aesthetic achievement. It is a hodgepodge of sensational scenes strung together implausibly, its characters are psychologically incredible, its actors act in a mannered way. Nevertheless, it is a great example of cinematic discourse, a palimpsest for future students of twentieth-century religiosity, a paramount laboratory for semiotic research into textual strategies. Moreover, it has become a cult movie.

What are the requirements for transforming a book or a movie into a cult object? The work must be loved, obviously, but this is not enough. It must provide a completely furnished world so that its fans can quote characters and episodes as if they were aspects of the fan's private sectarian world, a world about which one can make up quizzes and play trivia games so that the adepts of the sect recognize through each other a shared expertise. Naturally all these elements (characters and episodes) must have some archetypical appeal, as we shall see. One can ask and answer questions about the various subway stations of New York or Paris only if these spots have become or have been assumed as mythical areas and such names as Canarsie Line or Vincennes-Neuilly stand not only for physical places but become the catalyzers of collective memories.

Curiously enough, a book can also inspire a cult even though it is a great work of art: Both *The Three Musketeers* and *The Divine Comedy* rank among the cult books; and there are more trivia games among the fans of Dante than among the fans of Dumas. I suspect that a cult movie, on the contrary, must display some organic imperfections: It seems that the boastful *Rio Bravo* is a cult movie and the great *Stagecoach* is not.

I think that in order to transform a work into a cult object one must be able to break, dislocate, unhinge it so that one can remember only parts of it, irrespective of their original relationship with the whole. In the case of a book one can unhinge it, so to speak, physically, reducing it to a series of excerpts. A movie, on the contrary, must be already ramshackle, rickety, unhinged in itself. A perfect movie, since it cannot be reread every time we want, from the point we choose, as happens with a book, remains in our memory as a whole, in the form of a central idea or emotion; only an unhinged movie survives as a disconnected series of images, of peaks, of visual icebergs. It should display not one central idea but many. It should not reveal a coherent philosophy of composition. It must live on, and because of, its glorious ricketiness.

However, it must have some quality. Let me say that it can be ramshackle from the production point of view (in that nobody knew exactly what was going to be done next)—as happened evidently with the *Rocky Horror Picture Show*—but it must display certain textual features, in the sense that, outside the conscious control of its creators, it becomes a sort of textual syllabus, a living example of living textuality. Its addressee must suspect it is not true that works are created by their authors. Works are created by works, texts are created by texts, all together they speak to each other independently of the intention of their authors. A cult movie is the proof that, as literature comes from literature, cinema comes from cinema.

Which elements, in a movie, can be separated from the whole and adored for themselves? In order to go on with this analysis of *Casablanca* I should use some important semiotic categories, such as the ones (provided by the Russian Formalists) of theme and motif. I confess I find it very difficult to ascertain what the various Russian Formalists meant by motif. If—as Veselovsky says—a motif is the simplest narrative unit, then one wonders why "fire from heaven" should belong to the same category as "the persecuted maid" (since the former can be represented by an image, while the latter requires a certain narrative development). It would be interesting to follow Tomashevsky and to look in *Casablanca* for free or tied and for dynamic or static motifs. We should distinguish between more or less universal narrative functions à la Propp, visual stereotypes like the Cynic Adventurer, and more complex archetypical situations like the Unhappy Love. I hope someone will do this job, but here I will assume, more prudently (and borrowing the concept from research into Artificial Intelligence) the more flexible notion of "frame."

In *The Role of the Reader* I distinguished between common and intertextual frames. I meant by "common frame" data-structures for representing stereotyped situations such as dining at a restaurant or going to the railway station; in other words, a sequence of actions more or less coded by our normal experience. And by "intertextual frames" I meant stereotyped situations derived from preceding textual tradition and recorded by our encyclopedia, such as, for example, the standard duel between the sheriff and the bad guy or the narrative situation in which the hero fights the villain and wins, or more macroscopic textual situations, such as the story of the *vierge souillée* or the classic recognition scene (Bakhtin considered it a motif, in the sense of a chronotope). We could distinguish between stereotyped intertextual frames (for instance, the Drunkard Redeemed by Love) and stereotyped iconographical units (for instance, the Evil Nazi). But since even these iconographical units, when they appear in a movie, if they do not directly elicit an action, at least suggest its possible development, we can use the notion of intertextual frame to cover both.

Moreover, we are interested in finding those frames that not only are recognizable by the audience as belonging to a sort of ancestral intertextual tradition but that also display a particular fascination. "A suspect who eludes a passport control and is shot by the police" is undoubtedly an intertextual frame but it does not have a "magic" flavor. Let me address intuitively the idea of "magic" frame. Let me define as "magic" those frames that, when they appear in a movie and can be separated from the whole, transform this movie into a cult object. In *Casablanca* we find more intertextual frames than "magic" intertextual frames. I will call the latter "intertextual archetypes."

The term "archetype" does not claim to have any particular psychoanalytic or mythic connotation, but serves only to indicate a preestablished and frequently reappearing narrative situation, cited or in some way recycled by innumerable other texts and provoking in the addressee a sort of intense emotion accompanied by the vague feeling of a déjà vu that everybody yearns to see again. I would not say that an intertextual archetype is necessarily "universal." It can belong to a rather recent textual tradition, as with certain topoi of slapstick comedy. It is sufficient to consider it as a topos or standard situation that manages to be particularly appealing to a given cultural area or a historical period.

The Making of *Casablanca*

"Can I tell you a story?" Ilse asks. Then she adds: "I don't know the finish yet."

Rick says: "Well, go on, tell it. Maybe one will come to you as you go along."

Rick's line is a sort of epitome of *Casablanca* itself. According to Ingrid Bergman, the film was apparently being made up at the same time that it was being shot. Until the last moment not even Michael Curtiz knew whether Ilse would leave with Rick or with Victor, and Ingrid Bergman seems so fascinatingly mysterious because she did not know at which man she was to look with greater tenderness.

This explains why, in the story, she does not, in fact, choose her fate: She is chosen.

When you don't know how to deal with a story, you put stereotyped situations in it because you know that they, at least, have already worked elsewhere. Let us take a marginal but revealing example. Each time Laszlo orders something to drink (and it happens four times) he changes his choice: (1) Cointreau, (2) cocktail, (3) cognac, and (4) whisky (he once drinks champagne but he does not ask for it). Why such confusing and confused drinking habits for a man endowed with an ascetic temper? There is no psychological reason. My guess is that each time Curtiz was simply quoting, unconsciously, similar situations in other movies and trying to provide a reasonably complete repetition of them.

Thus one is tempted to read *Casablanca* as T. S. Eliot read *Hamlet*, attributing its fascination not to the fact that it was a successful work (actually he considered it one of Shakespeare's less fortunate efforts) but to the imperfection of its composition. He viewed *Hamlet* as the result of an unsuccessful fusion of several earlier versions of the story, and so the puzzling ambiguity of the main character was due to the author's difficulty in putting together different topoi. So both public and critics find *Hamlet* beautiful because it is interesting, but believe it is interesting because it is beautiful.

On a smaller scale the same thing happened to *Casablanca*. Forced to improvise a plot, the authors mixed a little of everything, and everything they chose came from a repertoire that had stood the test of time. When only a few of these formulas are used, the result is simply kitsch. But when the repertoire of stock formulas is used wholesale, then the result is an architecture like Gaudi's Sagrada Familia: the same vertigo, the same stroke of genius.

Stop by Stop

Every story involves one or more archetypes. To make a good story a single archetype is usually enough. But *Casablanca* is not satisfied with that. It uses them all.

It would be nice to identify our archetypes scene by scene and shot by shot, stopping the tape at every relevant step. Every time I have scanned *Casablanca* with very cooperative research groups, the review has taken many hours. Furthermore, when a team starts this kind of game, the instances of stopping the videotape increase proportionally with the size of the audience. Each member of the team sees something that the others have missed, and many of them start to find in the movie even memories of movies made after *Casablanca* — evidently the normal situation for a cult movie, suggesting that perhaps the best deconstructive readings should be made of unhinged texts (or that deconstruction is simply a way of breaking up texts).

However, I think that the first twenty minutes of the film represent a sort of review of the principal archetypes. Once they have been assembled, without any synthetic concern, then the story starts to suggest a sort of savage syntax of the archetypical elements and organizes them in multileveled oppositions. *Casablanca* looks like a musical piece with an extraordinarily long overture, where every theme is exhibited according to a monodic line. Only later does the symphonic work take place. In a way the first twenty minutes could be analyzed by a Russian Formalist and the rest by a Greimasian.

Let me then try only a sample analysis of the first part. I think that a real text-analytical study of *Casablanca* is still to be made, and I offer only some hints to future teams of researchers, who will carry out, someday, a complete reconstruction of its deep textual structure.

1. First, African music, then the *Marseillaise*. Two different genres are evoked: adventure movie and patriotic movie.

2. Third genre. The globe: Newsreel. The voice even suggests the news report. Fourth genre: the odyssey of refugees. Fifth genre: Casablanca and Lisbon are, traditionally, *hauts lieux* for international intrigues. Thus in two minutes five genres are evoked.

3. Casablanca–Lisbon. Passage to the Promised Land (Lisbon–America). Casablanca is the Magic Door. We still do not know what the Magic Key is or by which Magic Horse one can reach the Promised Land.

4. "Wait, wait, wait." To make the passage one must submit to a Test. The Long Expectation. Purgatory situation.

5. "Deutschland über Alles." The German anthem introduces the theme of Barbarians.

6. The Casbah. Pépé le Moko. Confusion, robberies, violence, and repression.

7. Pétain (Vichy) vs. the Cross of Lorraine. See at the end the same opposition closing the story: Eau de Vichy vs. Choice of the Resistance. War Propaganda movie.

8. The Magic Key: the visa. It is around the winning of the Magic Key that passions are unleashed. Captain Renault mentioned: He is the Guardian of the Door, or the boatman of the Acheron to be conquered by a Magic Gift (money or sex).

9. The Magic Horse: the airplane. The airplane flies over Rick's Café Américain, thus recalling the Promised Land of which the Café is the reduced model.

10. Major Strasser shows up. Theme of the Barbarians, and their emasculated slaves. "Je suis l'empire à la fin de la décadence/Qui regarde passer les grands barbares blancs/En composant des acrostiques indolents. . . ."

11. "Everybody comes to Rick's." By quoting the original play, Renault introduces the audience to the Café. The interior: Foreign Legion (each character has a different nationality and a different story to tell, and also his own skeleton in the closet), Grand Hotel (people come and people go, and nothing ever happens), Mississippi River Boat, New Orleans Brothel (black piano player), the Gambling Inferno in Macao or Singapore (with Chinese women), the Smugglers' Paradise, the Last Outpost on the Edge of the Desert. Rick's place is a magic circle where everything can happen—love, death, pursuit, espionage, games of chance, seductions, music, patriotism. Limited resources and the unity of place, due to the theatrical origin of the story, suggested an admirable condensation of events in a single setting. One can identify the usual paraphernalia of at least ten exotic genres.

12. Rick slowly shows up, first by synecdoche (his hand), then by metonymy (the check). The various aspects of the contradic-

tory (plurifilmic) personality of Rick are introduced: the Fatal Adventurer, the Self-Made Businessman (money is money), the Tough Guy from a gangster movie, Our Man in Casablanca (international intrigue), the Cynic. Only later he will be characterized also as the Hemingwayan Hero (he helped the Ethiopians and the Spaniards against fascism). He does not drink. This undoubtedly represents a nice problem, for later Rick must play the role of the Redeemed Drunkard and he has to be made a drunkard (as a Disillusioned Lover) so that he can be redeemed. But Bogey's face sustains rather well this unbearable number of contradictory psychological features.

13. The Magic Key, in person: the transit letters. Rick receives them from Peter Lorre and from this moment everybody wants them: how to avoid thinking of Sam Spade and of *The Maltese Falcon*?

14. Music Hall. Mr. Ferrari. Change of genre: comedy with brilliant dialogue. Rick is now the Disenchanted Lover, or the Cynical Seducer.

15. Rick vs. Renault. The Charming Scoundrels.

16. The theme of the Magic Horse and the Promised Land returns.

17. Roulette as the Game of Life and Death (Russian Roulette that devours fortunes and can destroy the happiness of the Bulgarian Couple, the Epiphany of Innocence). The Dirty Trick: cheating at cards. At this point the Trick is an Evil one but later it will be a Good one, providing a way to the Magic Key for the Bulgarian bride.

18. Arrest and tentative escape of Ugarte. Action movie.

19. Laszlo and Ilse. The Uncontaminated Hero and La Femme Fatale. Both in white — always; clever opposition with Germans, usually in black. In the meeting at Laszlo's table, Strasser is in white, in order to reduce the opposition. However, Strasser and Ilse are Beauty and the Beast. The Norwegian agent: spy movie.

20. The Desperate Lover and Drink to Forget.

21. The Faithful Servant and his Beloved Master. Don Quixote and Sancho.

22. Play it (again, Sam). Anticipated quotation of Woody Allen.

23. The long flashback begins. Flashback as a content and flashback as a form. Quotation of the flashback as a topical stylistic device. The Power of Memory. Last Day in Paris. Two Weeks in Another Town. Brief Encounter. French movie of the 1930's (the station as *quai des brumes*).

24. At this point the review of the archetypes is more or less complete. There is still the moment when Rick plays the Diamond in the Rough (who allows the Bulgarian bride to win), and two typical situations: the scene of the *Marseillaise* and the two lovers discovering that Love Is Forever. The gift to the Bulgarian bride (along with the enthusiasm of the waiters), the *Marseillaise*, and the Love Scene are three instances of the rhetorical figure of Climax, as the quintessence of Drama (each climax coming obviously with its own anticlimax).

Now the story can elaborate upon its elements.

The first symphonic elaboration comes with the second scene around the roulette table. We discover for the first time that the Magic Key (that everybody believed to be only purchasable with money) can in reality be given only as a Gift, a reward for Purity. The Donor will be Rick. He gives (free) the visa to Laszlo. In reality there is also a third Gift, the Gift Rick makes of his own desire, sacrificing himself. Note that there is no gift for Ilse, who, in some way, even though innocent, has betrayed two men. The Receiver of the Gift is the Uncontaminated Laszlo. By becoming the Donor, Rick meets Redemption. No one impure can reach the Promised Land. But Rick and Renault redeem themselves and can reach the other Promised Land, not America (which is Paradise) but the Resistance, the Holy War (which is a glorious Purgatory). Laszlo flies directly to Paradise because he has already suffered the ordeal of the underground. Rick, moreover, is not the only one who accepts sacrifice: The idea of sacrifice pervades the whole story, Ilse's sacrifice in Paris when she abandons the man she loves to return to the wounded hero, the Bulgarian bride's sacrifice when she is prepared to give herself to help her husband, Victor's sacrifice when he is prepared to see Ilse with Rick to guarantee her safety.

The second symphonic elaboration is upon the theme of the Unhappy Love. Unhappy for Rick, who loves Ilse and cannot have her. Unhappy for Ilse, who loves Rick and cannot leave with him. Unhappy for Victor, who understands that he has not really kept Ilse. The interplay of unhappy loves produces numerous twists and turns. In the beginning Rick is unhappy because he does not understand why Ilse leaves him. Then Victor is unhappy because he does not understand why Ilse is attracted to Rick. Finally Ilse is unhappy because she does not understand why Rick makes her leave with her husband.

These unhappy loves are arranged in a triangle. But in the normal adulterous triangle there is a Betrayed Husband and a Victorious Lover, while in this case both men are betrayed and suffer a loss.

In this defeat, however, an additional element plays a part, so subtly that it almost escapes the level of consciousness. Quite subliminally a hint of Platonic Love is established. Rick admires Victor, Victor is ambiguously attracted by the personality of Rick, and it seems that at a certain point each of the two is playing out the duel of sacrifice to please the other. In any case, as in Rousseau's *Confessions*, the woman is here an intermediary between the two men. She herself does not bear any positive value (except, obviously, Beauty): The whole story is a virile affair, a dance of seduction between Male Heroes.

From now on the film carries out the definitive construction of its intertwined triangles, to end with the solution of the Supreme Sacrifice and of the Redeemed Bad Guys. Note that, while the redemption of Rick has long been prepared, the redemption of Renault is absolutely unjustified and comes only because this was the final requirement the movie had to meet in order to be a perfect Epos of Frames.

The Archetypes Hold a Reunion

Casablanca is a cult movie precisely because all the archetypes are there, because each actor repeats a part played on other occasions, and because human beings live not "real" life but life as stereotypically portrayed in previous films. *Casablanca* carries the sense of déjà vu to such a degree that the addressee is ready to see in it what happened after it as well. It is not until *To Have and Have Not* that Bogey plays the role of the Hemingway hero, but here he appears "already" loaded with Hemingwayesque connotations simply because Rick fought in Spain. Peter Lorre trails reminiscences of Fritz Lang, Conrad Veidt's German officer emanates a faint whiff of *The Cabinet of Dr. Caligari*. He is not a ruthless, technological Nazi; he is a nocturnal and diabolical Caesar.

Casablanca became a cult movie because it is not *one* movie. It is "movies." And this is the reason it works, in defiance of any aesthetic theory.

For it stages the powers of Narrativity in its natural state, before art intervenes to tame it. This is why we accept the way that characters change mood, morality, and psychology from one moment to the next, that conspirators cough to interrupt the conversation when a spy is approaching, that bar girls cry at the sound of the *Marseillaise* . . .

When all the archetypes burst out shamelessly, we plumb Homeric profundity. Two clichés make us laugh but a hundred clichés move us because we sense dimly that the clichés are talking among themselves, celebrating a reunion.

Just as the extreme of pain meets sensual pleasure, and the extreme of perversion borders on mystical energy, so too the extreme of banality allows us to catch a glimpse of the Sublime.

Nobody would have been able to achieve such a cosmic result intentionally. Nature has spoken in place of men. This, alone, is a phenomenon worthy of veneration.

The Charged Cult

The structure of *Casablanca* helps us understand what happens in later movies *born in order to become cult objects*.

What *Casablanca* does unconsciously, other movies will do with extreme intertextual awareness, assuming also that the addressee is equally aware of their purposes. These are "postmodern" movies, where the quotation of the topos is recognized as the only way to cope with the burden of our filmic encyclopedic expertise.

Think for instance of *Bananas*, with its explicit quotation of the Odessa steps from Eisenstein's *Potemkin*. In *Casablanca* one enjoys quotation even though one does not recognize it, and those who recognize it feel as if they all belonged to the same little clique. In *Bananas* those who do not catch the topos cannot enjoy the scene and those who do simply feel smart.

Another (and different) case is the quotation of the topical duel between the black Arab giant with his scimitar and the unprotected hero, in *Raiders of the Lost Ark*. If you remember, the topos suddenly turns into another one, and the unprotected hero becomes in a second *The Fastest Gun in the West*. Here the ingenuous viewer can miss the quotation though his enjoyment will then be rather slight; and real enjoyment is reserved for the people accustomed to cult movies, who know the whole repertoire of "magic" archetypes. In a way, *Bananas* works for cultivated "cinephiles" while *Raiders* works for *Casablanca*-addicts.

The third case is that of *E.T.*, when the alien is brought outside in a Halloween disguise and meets the dwarf coming from *The Empire Strikes Back*. You remember that E.T. starts and runs to cheer him (or it). Here nobody can enjoy the scene if he does not share, at least, the following elements of intertextual competence:

(1) He must know where the second character comes from (Spielberg citing Lucas),

(2) He must know something about the links between the two directors, and

(3) He must know that both monsters have been designed by Rambaldi and that, consequently, they are linked by some form of brotherhood.

The required expertise is not only intercinematic, it is intermedia, in the sense that the addressee must know not only other movies but all the mass media gossip about movies. This third example presupposes a "*Casablanca* universe" in which cult has become the normal way of enjoying movies. Thus in this case we witness an instance of metacult, or of cult about cult—a Cult Culture.

It would be semiotically uninteresting to look for quotations of archetypes in *Raiders* or in *Indiana Jones*: They were conceived within a metasemiotic culture, and what the semiotician can find in them is exactly what the directors put there. Spielberg and Lucas are semiotically nourished authors working for a culture of instinctive semioticians.

With *Casablanca* the situation is different. So *Casablanca* explains *Raiders*, but *Raiders* does not explain *Casablanca*. At most it can explain the new ways in which *Casablanca* will be received in the next years.

It will be a sad day when a too smart audience will read *Casablanca* as conceived by Michael Curtiz after having read Calvino and Barthes. But that day will come. Perhaps we have been able to discover here, for the last time, the Truth.

Après nous, le déluge.

1984

A Photograph

The readers of *L'Espresso* will recall the tape of the last minutes of
Radio Alice,* recorded as the police were hammering at the door.
One thing that impressed many people was how the announcer,
as he reported in a tense voice what was happening, tried to convey the situation by referring to a scene in a movie. There was
undoubtedly something singular about an individual going through
a fairly traumatic experience as if he were in a film.

There can be only two interpretations. One is the traditional:
Life is lived as a work of art. The other obliges us to reflect a bit
further: It is the visual work (cinema, videotape, mural, comic strip,
photograph) that is now a part of our memory. Which is quite
different, and seems to confirm a hypothesis already ventured,
namely that the younger generations have absorbed as elements of
their behavior a series of elements filtered through the mass media

---

*An independent radical radio station closed down by the police after the Bologna student
riots of 1977, on the grounds that the station had incited the rioters and given them information about police movements.

(and coming, in some cases, from the most impenetrable areas of our century's artistic experimentation). To tell the truth, it isn't even necessary to talk about new generations: If you are barely middle-aged, you will have learned personally the extent to which experience (love, fear, or hope) is filtered through "already seen" images. I leave it to moralists to deplore this way of living by intermediate communication. We must only bear in mind that mankind has never done anything else, and before Nadar and the Lumières, it used other images, drawn from pagan carvings or the illuminated manuscripts of the Apocalypse.

We can foresee another objection, this time not from cherishers of the tradition: Isn't it perhaps an unpleasant example of the ideology of scientific neutrality, the way, when we are faced by active behavior and searing, dramatic events, we always try again and again to analyze them, define them, interpret them, dissect them? Can we define that which by definition eludes all defining? Well, we must have the courage to assert once more what we believe in: Today more than ever political news itself is marked, motivated, abundantly nourished by the symbolic. Understanding the mechanisms of the symbolic in which we move means being political. Not understanding them leads to mistaken politics. Of course, it is also a mistake to reduce political and economic events to mere symbolic mechanisms; but it is equally wrong to ignore this dimension.

There are unquestionably many reasons, and serious ones, for the outcome of Luciano Lama's intervention* at the University of Rome, but one particular reason must not be overlooked: the opposition between two theatrical or spatial structures. Lama presented himself on a podium (however makeshift), thus obeying the rules of a frontal communication characteristic of trade-union,

---

*Luciano Lama, leader of the Communist-oriented General Confederation of Labor, was violently rejected when he tried to speak to students occupying the University of Rome. The incident confirmed the rupture between the Communist Party and the student movement of 1977.

working-class spatiality, facing a crowd of students who have, however, developed other ways of aggregation and interaction, de-centralized, mobile, apparently disorganized. Theirs is a different way of organizing space and so that day at the University there was the clash also between two concepts of perspective, the one we might call Brunelleschian and the other cubist. True, anyone reducing the whole story to these factors would be mistaken, but anyone trying to dismiss this interpretation as an intellectual game would be mistaken, too. The Catholic Church, the French Revolution, Nazism, the Soviet Union, and the People's Republic of China, not to mention the Rolling Stones and soccer clubs, have always known very well that the deployment of space is religion, politics, ideology. So let's give back to the spatial and the visual the place they deserve in the history of political and social relations.

And now to another event. These past months, within that variegated and shifting experience that is called "the movement," the men carrying .38's have emerged. From various quarters the movement has been asked to denounce them as an alien body; and there were forces exerting pressure both from outside and from within. Apparently this demand for rejection encountered difficulties, and various elements came into play. Synthetically, we can say that many belonging to the movement didn't feel like labeling as outsiders forces that, even if they revealed themselves in unacceptable and tragically suicidal ways, seemed to express a reality of social protest that couldn't be denied. I am repeating discussions that all of us have heard. Basically what was said was this: They are wrong, but they are part of a mass movement. And the debate was harsh, painful.

Now, last week, there occurred a kind of precipitation of all the elements of the debate previously suspended in uncertainty. Suddenly, and I say suddenly because decisive statements were issued in the space of a day, the gunmen were cut off. Why at that moment? Why not before? It's not enough to say that recent events

215

in Milan* made a deep impression on many people, because similar events in Rome had also had a profound effect. What happened that was new and different? We may venture a hypothesis, once again recalling that an explanation never explains everything, but becomes part of a landscape of explanations in reciprocal relationship. A photograph appeared.

Many photographs have appeared, but this one made the rounds of all the papers after being published in the *Corriere d'Informazione*. As everyone will recall, it was the photograph of a young man wearing a knitted ski-mask, standing alone, in profile, in the middle of a street, legs apart, arms outstretched horizontally, with both hands grasping a pistol. Other forms can be seen in the background, but the photograph's structure is classical in its simplicity: The central figure, isolated, dominates it.

If it is licit (and it is necessary) to make aesthetic observations in such cases, this is one of those photographs that will go down in history and will appear in a thousand books. The vicissitudes of our century have been summed up in a few exemplary photographs that have proved epoch-making: the unruly crowd pouring into the square during the "ten days that shook the world"; Robert Capa's dying *miliciano*; the marines planting the flag on Iwo Jima; the Vietnamese prisoner being executed with a shot in the temple; Che Guevara's tortured body on a plank in a barracks. Each of these images has become a myth and has condensed numerous speeches. It has surpassed the individual circumstance that produced it; it no longer speaks of that single character or of those characters, but expresses concepts. It is unique, but at the same time it refers to other images that preceded it or that, in imitation, have followed it. Each of these photographs seems a film we have seen and refers to other films that had seen it. Sometimes it isn't a photograph but a painting, or a poster.

What did the photograph of the Milanese gunman "say"? I believe it abruptly revealed, without the need for a lot of digres-

---

*During a confrontation between rioters and police, a policeman was shot.

sive speeches, something that has been circulating in a lot of talk, but that words alone could not make people accept. That photograph didn't resemble any of the images which, for at least four generations, had been emblems of the idea of revolution. The collective element was missing; in a traumatic way the figure of the lone hero returned here. And this lone hero was not the one familiar in revolutionary iconography, which when it portrayed a man alone always saw him as victim, sacrificial lamb: the dying *miliciano* or the slain Che, in fact. This individual hero, on the contrary, had the pose, the terrifying isolation of the tough guy of gangster movies or the solitary gunman of the West—no longer dear to a generation who consider themselves metropolitan Indians.

This image suggested other worlds, other figurative, narrative traditions that had nothing to do with the proletarian tradition, with the idea of popular revolt, of mass struggle. Suddenly it inspired a syndrome of rejection. It came to express the following concept: Revolution is elsewhere and, even if it is possible, it doesn't proceed via this "individual" act.

The photograph, for a civilization now accustomed to thinking in images, was not the description of a single event (and, in fact, it makes no difference who the man was, nor does the photograph help in identifying him): It was an argument. And it worked.

It is of no interest to know if it was posed (and therefore faked), whether it was the testimony of an act of conscious bravado, if it was the work of a professional photographer who gauged the moment, the light, the frame, or whether it virtually took itself, was snapped accidentally by unskilled and lucky hands. At the moment it appeared, its communicative career began: Once again the political and the private have been marked by the plots of the symbolic, which, as always happens, has proved producer of reality.

1977

6

DE CONSOLATIONE
PHILOSOPHIAE

Cogito
Interruptus

Some books are easier to review, to explain, or comment on aloud, than they are simply to read; because it is only by applying yourself to a gloss that you can follow their argumentation without distraction, their implacable syllogistic necessities, or the precise knots of relation. This is why books like the *Metaphysics* of Aristotle or the *Critique of Pure Reason* have more commentators than readers, more specialists than admirers.

And there are, on the other hand, books that are extremely pleasant to read, but impossible to write about: because the minute you start expounding them or commenting on them, you realize that they refuse to be translated into the proposition "This book says that." The person who reads them for pleasure realizes he has spent his money well; but anyone who reads them in order to tell others about them becomes furious at every line, tears up the notes he took a moment before, seeks the conclusion that comes after his "therefore," and cannot find it.

Clearly it would be an unforgivable sin of ethnocentrism to consider "not thought out" a Zen tale that follows ideals of logic different from those to which we are accustomed; but it is also certain that if our ideal of reasoning is summed up in a certain Western model, consisting of "whereas" and "inasmuch as," then in these unreviewable books we find illustrious examples of *cogito interruptus* whose mechanism we must bear in mind. Since cogito interruptus is common both to the insane and to the authors of a reasoned "illogic," we must understand when it is a defect and when a virtue, and (against all Malthusian custom) a fertilizing virtue, what's more.

Cogito interruptus is typical of those who see the world inhabited by symbols or symptoms. Like someone who, for example, points to the little box of matches, stares hard into your eyes, and says, "You see, there are seven . . . ," then gives you a meaningful look, waiting for you to perceive the meaning concealed in that unmistakable sign; or like the inhabitant of a symbolic universe, where every object and every event translates into sign something hyper-Uranian that everyone already knows but wants only to see reconfirmed.

Cogito interruptus is also typical of those who see the world inhabited not by symbols but by symptoms: indubitable signs of something that is neither here below nor up above, but that sooner or later *will happen.*

The reviewer's torment lies in the fact that when a person stares at him and says, "You see, there are seven matches," the reviewer is already helpless to explain to others the scope of the sign or the symptom; but then when the same person adds, "And consider also, if you want to dispel any doubt, that four swallows flew past today," then the reviewer is really lost. None of this means that cogito interruptus is not a great prophetic, poetic, psychological technique. Only that it is ineffable. And it takes real faith in cogito interruptus—and a wish that readers understand me—for me to venture to speak of it, no matter what.

In discussions of the universe of mass communications and of the technological civilization, cogito interruptus is very fashionable among those whom, on other occasions, we have called the Apocalyptics, who see in the events of the past the symbols of a well-known harmony, and in those of the present the symbols of an inescapable fall (but always through clear references: Every girl in a miniskirt is entitled to exist only as a decipherable hieroglyph of the end of the world). This view was unknown until today to the so-called Adjusted, who, on the other hand, do not decipher the universe but live in it without problems. Still the attitude is observed by a category we could define as the Hyper-Adjusted, or pentecostal Adjusted, or still better as Parusiacs, affected by the Fourth Eclogue Syndrome, megaphones of the golden age. If the Apocalyptics were the sad relatives of Noah, the Parusiacs are jolly cousins of the Magi.

Recent Italian translations allow us to consider together two books that, in different ways and decades, have had a great success and are listed among the texts to be consulted for any discussion of contemporary civilization. *Art in Crisis: The Lost Center* by Hans Sedlmayr is a masterpiece of apocalyptic thought; *Understanding Media* by Marshall McLuhan is perhaps the most enjoyable and successful text offered us by the Parusiac school. The reader who deals with both of them is prepared for a dialectical kermesse, an orgy of comparisons and contradictions, in order to see how differently two men reason who see the world from such radically opposed standpoints; but instead he realizes that the two men reason in exactly the same way, and, what's more, they cite the same supporting arguments. Or rather, they cite the same events, one seeing them as symbols and the other as symptoms, one enduring them with grim, lamenting significance, the other with a light-hearted optimism, one writing on paper edged in black, the other on a lacy wedding invitation, one prefacing it all with a minus sign, the other with a plus sign—both, however, neglecting to articulate equations, for cogito interruptus demands that symbols and symptoms be flung by the handful, like confetti, and not lined up, bookkeeper style, like little balls on an abacus.

Art in Crisis dates from 1948. Fairly removed historically from the days of wrath when they burned works of degenerate art, it still retains (we are discussing the book, not the author's biography) some fiery echoes. And yet anyone ignorant of Sedlmayr's position in the context of the historiography of ideas, reading the first chapters now, would find himself following a discussion (conducted *sine ira et studio*) of the phenomena of contemporary architecture, from the English gardens and utopian architects of the Revolution, seen as supporting documents for a diagnosis of the period. The cult of reason that generates a monumental religion of eternity, a taste for the mausoleum, whether gardener's house or museum, that reveals a search for chthonic forces, occult and profound relationships with natural energies, the birth of an idea of the aesthetic temple from which the image of a determined God is absent; and then, with Biedermeier, a move away from the great themes of the sacred and a celebration of the cozy, the private, the individualistic; and finally, the birth of those secular cathedrals, the Universal Expositions.

From the worship of God to the worship of nature, from the worship of form to the cult of technology: This is the descriptive image of a "succession." But the moment this succession is described as "decreasing," the diagnostic conclusion becomes a part of the description: Man is plunging downwards, because he has lost the center. If you are clever enough at this point to skip several chapters of the book, many traumata of reading will be eliminated, because in the concluding chapters Sedlmayr supplies the key to understanding the symbols he handles in the middle chapters. The center is man's relationship with God. Once this affirmation is made (Sedlmayr, who is not a theologian, doesn't bother to tell us what God is, or what man's relationship with Him consists of), it becomes possible even for a child to conclude that the work of art in which God doesn't appear and in which there is no dialogue with God is a godless work of art. At this point there is a wealth of begged questions: If God is "spatially" up above, a work of art that you can look at even upside down (Kandinsky) is atheist. To be sure, Sedlmayr would have only to interpret in another key the same signs that he singles out in the course of Western art (Romantic demonism, Bosch-type obsession, Brueghel grotesques, and so on) to conclude that man, in his whole history, has apparently done nothing but lose the Center. But the author prefers to cling to philosophemes worthy of the rector of a seminary, on the order of "in any case we must bear firmly in mind the principle that, as man's essence is one and the same in all times, so also that of art is one, however different its external manifestations may seem." What can be said to that? Having defined man as "nature and supernature" and having defined supernature in the terms in which Western art depicted it for a certain period, the author obviously concludes that "this detachment is thus presented as contrary to the absence of man (and of God)" — inasmuch as the essence of both is deduced from a special iconographical interpretation that has been made of it once and for all.

But to arrive at these pages of laughable philosophy, the author has bid for the admiration of the literate masses and through some exemplary pages of tea-leaf reading.

How do you read tea-leaves? For example, you become terrified by the tendency of modern architecture to ignore the site, to confuse up with down, and your dejection reaches its nadir with the arrival of the cantilever, "a kind of materialistic canopy." The cantilever trauma pervades all of Sedlmayr's discussion: This horizontalization of architecture, which allows, between one floor and another, the emptiness of glass walls, this renunciation of vertical growth (except by the superimposition of horizontal levels) seems to him the "symptom of a negation of the tectonic element" and of "detachment from the earth." In terms of construction science, it never occurs to him that a skyscraper can stand up better than the apse of Beauvais, which kept collapsing until they had the idea of leaving it alone without adding the rest of the cathedral to it. After identifying architecture as a special kind of relationship with the surface, Sedlmayr observes the breakdown of architecture and puts his head under his wing. The fact that some men built in spheres rather than cubes or pyramids, from Ledoux to Fuller, leaves him gasping; like the madman's seven matches, the spheres of Ledoux or Fuller seem to him unmistakable signs of the end of architectonic time. When it comes to seeing in a sphere the epiphany of the loss of the center, Parmenides and Saint Augustine would not agree; but Sedlmayr is also prepared to switch archetypes in midstream if it will enable the events he chooses as symbols to mean what he has already known from the beginning.

As he moves on to the figurative arts, the caricatures of Daumier or of Goya seem to him the entrance of disfigured and demented man, as if Greek vase painters had not allowed themselves analogous pleasures and perhaps with less motive than the satirists of nineteenth-century progressivism. With Cézanne and Cubism, the clever reader will be able to anticipate the considerations Sedlmayr draws from this reduction of painting to a visual reconstruction of experienced reality; as for the rest of contemporary painting, the author is dazzled by apocalyptic signs such as the deformations "like those to be seen in a concave mirror" and photomontage, typical examples of "extra-human views." There is no point in replying that, since I am the one who sees in the concave mirror, which I have made, I consider this way of seeing just as human as the cyclopic deformation of the Renaissance perspective box: This is old stuff. But, for Sedlmayr, the image of chaos and death precedes the signs that he reports. Obviously nobody doubts that the phenomena listed by Sedlmayr really are the signs of something; but the task of the historiographer of art and of culture in general consists precisely in correlating these phenomena in order to see how they respond to one another. Sedlmayr's discussion, however, is paranoid because all the signs are made to refer back to an unmotivated obsession, philosophically alluded to; and therefore between the sphere that symbolizes detachment from the earth, the cantilever that exemplifies renunciation of ascent, and the unicorn that is the visible sign of Mary's virginity there is no difference.

Sedlmayr is a belated medieval man who imitates far keener and splendidly visionary decipherers. And the reason why his discussion is a distinguished example of cogito interruptus lies in the fact that having posited the sign, he nudges us, winks, and says "You see that?" And thus he identifies in three lines the trend toward the formless and the degenerate in modern science, and then (certifiable extrapolation) he deduces that the organ of degeneration is the intellect, whose weapons are symbolic logic and whose visual organs are microscopy and macroscopy; and, after mentioning macroscopy, Sedlmayr adds, in parentheses: "Here, too, note the loss of the center." Well, Professor Sedlmayr, I don't note; and you're cheating. If nobody else dares say it, I will: Either you must explain yourself or there is no difference between you and the man who tells me that the Ace of Spades means death.

Now let's open McLuhan. McLuhan says the same things as Sedlmayr: For him, too, man has lost the center. Only his comment is: High time.

McLuhan's thesis, as everyone knows by now, is that the various achievements of technology, from the wheel to electricity, should be considered media and therefore extensions of our corporality. In the course of history these extensions have caused traumata, blunting and restructuring our sensibility. Interfering or replacing, they have changed our way of seeing the world, and the change that a new medium involves makes irrelevant the content of experience that it can transmit. The medium is the message; what is given us through the new extension matters less than the form of the extension itself. Whatever you may write on the typewriter will always be less important than the radically different way in which the mechanics of typing will have caused you to consider writing. The fact that printing led to the widespread diffusion of the Bible depends on the fact that every technological achievement is added to what we already are; but printing could have developed in Arab countries, to bring the Koran within everyone's reach, and the kind of influence printing has had on modern sensibility would not have changed: the shattering of the intellectual experience into uniform and repeatable units, the establishment of a sense of homogeneity and continuity that generated, at a distance of centuries, the assembly line, and presided over the ideology of the mechanical age, as well as the cosmology of infinitesimal calculation. "Clock and alphabet, shattering the universe into visual segments, put an end to the music of interdependence" — they produced a man capable of dissociating his own emotions from what he sees aligned in space; they created the specialized man, accustomed to reasoning in a linear way, free with respect to the tribal envelopment of the "oral" epochs, where every member of the community belongs to a kind of undefined unit that reacts compactly and emotionally to cosmic events.

The press (to which McLuhan had dedicated perhaps his best work, *The Gutenberg Galaxy*) is a typically *hot* medium. Unlike what the adjective might suggest, the hot media develop a single sense (vision, in the case of the press) to a high power of definition, saturating the receiver with data, stuffing him with precise information, but leaving him free as far as his other faculties are concerned. In a way, the hot media hypnotize him, but fixing his sense on a single point. On the contrary, *cool* media supply information of low definition, oblige the receiver to fill in the gaps, and thus they engage all his senses and faculties, they make him a participant, but in the form of an overall hallucination that involves him completely. Press and movies are hot; television is cool.

With the advent of electricity certain revolutionary phenomena occurred: First of all, if it is true that the medium is the message, independently of content, then electric light was presented for the first time in history as a medium absolutely lacking in content; in the second place, electrical technology, replacing not an individual organ but the central nervous system, offered, as its primary product, *information*. The other products of mechanical civilization, in a period of automation, rapid communications, credit economy, financial operations, became secondary to the information product. The production and sale of information has overcome even ideological differences; at the same time the advent of television, the medium that is cool par excellence, destroyed the linear universe of mechanical civilization, inspired by the Gutenbergian model, reestablishing a sort of tribal unity, like a primitive village.

Just as television does not foster perspective in art, so, according to McLuhan, it does not foster linearity in living. "Since TV, the assembly line has disappeared from industry. Staff and line structures have dissolved in management. Gone are the stag line, the party line, the receiving line, and the pencil line from the backs of nylons." The visual sense, extended by phonetic literacy, stimulated the analytic habit of perceiving "the single facet in the life of forms" and enabled us to isolate the single incident in time and space, as happens with representational art. "Iconographic art," on the contrary, "uses the eye as we use our hand in seeking to create an inclusive image, made up of many moments, phases, and aspects of the person and thing." Such an "iconic mode" is not "visual," it is rather "tactual," total, synaesthetic, and involves all senses. "Pervaded by the mosaic TV image, the TV child encounters the world in a spirit antithetic to literacy." The young people born with TV "have naturally imbibed an urge towards involvement in depth that makes all the remote visualized goals of usual culture seem not only unreal but irrelevant, and not only irrelevant but anemic." It is abundantly clear that this kind of involvement has nothing to do with the *content* of TV messages; the quality of the program is irrelevant (chapter 31 of *Understanding Media*).

Speaking of automation (chapter 33), McLuhan insists on the fact that "our new electric technology now extends the instant process of knowledge by interrelation that has long occurred within our central nervous system." Such a phenomenon ends the mechanical age that started with Gutenberg. "With electricity as energizer and synchronizer, all aspects of production, consumption, and organization become incidental to communication."

This collage of quotations summarizes McLuhan's position and, at the same time, exemplifies his techniques of argumentation, which—paradoxically—are so illustrative of his thesis that they undermine its validity. We will try to make this clear.

Typical of our time, all-enveloping and shared, is the domination by cold media, one of whose properties, as we have said, is to present figures in low definition, not finished products but processes, and thus not linear successions of objects, moments, and arguments, but rather a kind of totality and simultaneity of the data involved. If this reality is transferred to methods of exposition, we will have discussion not through syllogisms, but through aphorisms. Aphorisms (as McLuhan reminds us) are incomplete and therefore require profound participation. Here his method of argumentation corresponds perfectly to the new universe in which we are invited to integrate ourselves—a universe that to men like Sedlmayr would seem the diabolical perfection of "loss of the center" (the notion of centrality and symmetry belong to the era of Renaissance perspective, supremely Gutenbergian), but for McLuhan it represents the future "broth" in which the bacilli of contemporaneity can develop to a degree unknown to the alphabet bacillus.

This technique, however, involves certain flaws. The first is that for every affirmation McLuhan aligns another, opposed to it, assuming both as congruent. In this way his book could offer valid arguments for Sedlmayr and for all the apocalyptic bunch as well as for the Adjusted & Co.; excerpts could be quoted by some Chinese Marxist who wants to excoriate our society; and there are demonstrative arguments for a theoretician of neocapitalistic optimism. McLuhan doesn't even worry about whether all his arguments are true; he is content that they *be*. What might, from our point of view, seem contradiction is, to him, simply co-presence. But, since he is writing a book, McLuhan can't elude the Gutenbergian habit of articulating consequent demonstrations. The consequentiality is fictive, however; he offers us the co-presence of arguments as if it were a logical succession. The speed with which he moves from the concept of linearity in business organization to the concept of linearity in the texture of a stocking is such that the juxtaposition cannot help but seem a causal nexus.

All McLuhan's book is there to prove to us that the "disappearance of the assembly line" and "disappearance of net stockings" must not be connected by a "therefore"—or at least not by the author of the message, but rather by the receiver, who will take care of filling in the gaps in this scantily defined chain. But the trouble is that, secretly, McLuhan *wants* us to put in that "therefore," also because he knows that, out of Gutenbergian habit, as we are reading the two data lined up on the printed page, we will be forced to think in "therefore" terms. So he is cheating just as Sedlmayr cheats when he tells us that microscopy means loss of the center, and as the madman cheats when he points to the seven matches. McLuhan requires an extrapolation, and imposes it on us in the most insidiously illegitimate way imaginable. We are in full cogito interruptus, which would not be interruptus if, in consequence, it were no longer presented as cogito. But McLuhan's whole book rests on the equivocation of a cogito that is denied, arguing in the modes of denied rationality.

If we are witnessing the advent of a new dimension of thought and of physical life, either this is total, radical—and has already conquered—and then books can no longer be written to demonstrate the advent of something that has made all books purposeless; or else the problem of our time is that of integrating the new dimensions of intellect and sensibility with those on which all our means of communication are still based (including television communication, which, at the outset, is still organized, studied, and programmed in Gutenbergian dimensions) and then the critic's job (as he writes books) is to act as mediator, and therefore to translate the situation of enveloping globality into terms of a Gutenbergian rationality, specialized and linear.

McLuhan has recently realized that perhaps books must no

longer be written; and with *The Medium Is the Massage*, his latest "nonbook," he suggests a discourse in which word is fused with image and the chains of logic are destroyed in favor of a synchronic, visual-verbal proposition, of unreasoned data set spinning before the reader's intelligence. The trouble is that *The Medium Is the Massage*, to be completely understood, needs *Understanding Media* as a code. McLuhan cannot elude the requirement of rational clarification of the process we are witnessing; but when he surrenders to that demand for cogito he is bound not to interrupt it.

The first victim of this ambiguous situation is McLuhan himself: He doesn't just line up disconnected data and make us swallow them as if they were connected. He also makes an effort to present us with data that seem disconnected and contradictory while he believes them to be connected by logical operations, but he is ashamed of showing these operations in action. Read, for example, this excerpt, which we have complemented with numbered parentheses, in order to separate the various propositions:

"It seems contradictory that the fragmenting and divisive power of our analytic Western world should derive from an accentuation of the visual faculty.

(1) This same visual sense is, also, responsible for the habit of seeing all things as continuous and connected.

(2) Fragmentation by means of visual stress occurs in that isolation of moment in time, or of aspect of space, that is beyond the power of touch, or hearing, or smell, or movement.

(3) By imposing unvisualizable relationships that are the result of instant speed, electric technology dethrones the visual sense and restores us to the dominion of synthesia and the close interinvolvement of the other senses."

Now, try rereading this incomprehensible excerpt, inserting at the indicated places these links: (1) *In fact*; (2) *Nevertheless*; (3) *On the other hand*. And you will see that the reasoning flows, at least formally.

But these observations still concern only the expositional

technique. More serious are the instances where the author sets actual traps of argumentation that can be summed up in a general category definable in terms dear to those schoolmen that Mc-Luhan, an old commentator of Thomas Aquinas, should know and imitate: the equivocation on the *suppositio* of the terms: or, equivocal definition, in short.

Gutenberg man and, before him, alphabet man had at least taught us to define precisely the terms of our speech. To avoid defining them in order to "involve" the reader further could be a technique (what else is the deliberate ambiguity of poetic discourse?), but in other cases it is a trick to throw sand in our eyes.

We won't go into the carefree change of a term's usual connotations: Thus *hot* means "capable of allowing critical detachment" and *cool* means "involving"; *visual*, "alphabetic"; *tactile*, "visual"; *detachment*, "critical involvement"; *participation*, "hallucinatory uninvolvement"; and so on. Here we are still at the level of a deliberate regeneration of terminology for provocatory purposes.

Let us look, instead, as examples, at some more criticizable games of definition. It is not true that—as McLuhan says—all the media are active metaphors because they have the power to translate experience into new forms. In fact, a medium—the spoken language, for example—translates experience into another form because it represents a code. A metaphor, on the contrary, is the replacement, within a code, of one term with another, a simile established and then covered. But the definition of medium as metaphor also covers a confusion in the definition of the medium. To say that it represents an extension of our bodies still means little. The wheel *extends* the capacity of the foot and the lever that of the arm, but the alphabet *reduces*, according to criteria of a particular economy, the possibilities of the sound-making organs in order to allow a certain codification of experience. The sense in which the press is a medium is not the same as that in which language is a medium. The press does not change the coding of experience, with respect to the written language, but fosters its diffusion and increments certain developments in the direction of precision, standardization, and so on. To say, as McLuhan says, that language does for intelligence what the wheel does for the feet (in so far as it allows us to move from one thing to another with ease and nonchalance) is little more than a *boutade*.

In effect, all of McLuhan's reasoning is dominated by a series of equivocations very troubling to a theoretician of communication, because the differences between the *channel* of communication, the *code*, and the *message* are not established. To say that roads and the written language are media is making a channel the same as a code. To say that Euclidean geometry and a suit of clothing are media means pairing a code (a way of formalizing experience) with a message (a way of signifying, through conventions of dress, something I want to say, a content). To say that light is a medium means not realizing that at least three definitions of "light" come into play here: (1) light as *signal* (I transmit impulses which, in Morse code, then mean certain messages); (2) light as *message* (the light burning in the girlfriend's window that means "come"); and (3) light as *channel of other communication* (if, in the street, there is a light burning, I can read the poster on the wall).

In these three cases light performs different functions, and it would be very interesting to study the constants of the phenomenon under such diverse aspects, or to examine the birth, thanks to the three different uses, of three phenomena-light. In conclusion, the happy and now famous formula, "The medium is the message," proves ambiguous and pregnant with a series of contradictory formulas. It can, in fact, mean:

(1) The *form* of the message is the real content of the message (which is the thesis of avant-garde literature and criticism);

(2) The *code*, that is to say, the structure of a language—or of another system of communication—is the message (which is the famous anthropological thesis of Benjamin Lee Whorf, for whom the view of the world is determined by the structure of the language);

(3) The *channel* is the message (that is, the physical means chosen to convey the information determines either the form of the message, or its contents, or the very structure of the codes—which is a familiar idea in aesthetics, where the choice of artistic material notoriously determines the cadences of the spirit and the argument itself).

All these formulas show that it is not true, as McLuhan states, that scholars of information have considered only the content of information without bothering about formal problems. Apart from the fact that here, too, McLuhan plays on terms and uses the word "content" in two different definitions (for him it means "what is said" while for the theory of information it means "the number of binary choices necessary to say something"), we discover that the theory of communication, formalizing the various phases of the passage of information, has offered instruments useful in differentiating phenomena that are different and must be considered as different.

Unifying these various phenomena in his formula, McLuhan no longer tells us anything useful. In fact, to discover that the advent of the typewriter, bringing women into business firms as secretaries, created a crisis for the manufacturers of spitoons, simply means repeating the obvious principle that every new technology imposes changes in the social body. But in the face of these changes it is highly useful to understand whether they occur because of a new channel, a new code, a new way of articulating the code, the things the message says in articulating the code, or the way a certain group is disposed to receive the message.

Here, then, is another proposition: The medium is *not* the message; the message becomes what the receiver makes of it, applying to it his own codes of reception, which are neither those of the sender nor those of the scholar of communications. The medium is not the message because, for the cannibal chief, the clock is not the determination to spatialize time, but a kinetic ornament to hang around the neck. If the medium is the message there is nothing to be done (the Apocalyptics know this): We are directed

235

by the instruments we have built. But the message depends on the reading given to it; in the universe of electricity there is still room for guerrilla warfare: The perspectives of reception are differentiated, the TV station is not attacked, the attack is against the first chair in front of every TV set. It may be that what McLuhan says (and the Apocalyptics with him) is true, but in this case it is a very harmful truth; and since culture has the possibility of shamelessly constructing other truths, it is worth proposing a more productive one.

In conclusion, three questions about the appropriateness of reading McLuhan.

Is it possible to understand *Understanding Media*? Yes, because even though the author seems to assail us with an enormous welter of data (Alberto Arbasino has splendidly suggested that this book was written by Bouvard and Pécuchet), the central information it gives us is still one and indivisible: The medium is the message. The book repeats this with exemplary stubbornness and with an absolute fidelity to the ideal of speech in the oral and tribal societies to which it invites us: As McLuhan says, the entire message is repeated frequently on the circles of a concentric spiral and with seeming redundance. Just one carp: The redundance is real, not apparent. As with the best products of mass entertainment, the confusion of collateral information serves only to make appetizing a central structure that is unrelentingly redundant, so that the reader will receive always and only what he has already known (or understood). The signs that McLuhan reads all refer to something that is given us from the start.

Having read authors like Sedlmayr, is it worth reading authors like McLuhan? Yes, actually. True, if you reverse the signs, both say the same thing (namely, the media do not transmit ideologies; they are themselves ideologies), but McLuhan's visionary rhetoric is not lachrymose, it is stimulating, high-spirited, and crazy. There is some good in McLuhan, as there is in banana smokers and hippies. We must wait and see what they'll be up to next.

Is it scientifically productive to read McLuhan? An embarrassing problem, because you have to take care not to liquidate in the name of academic common sense someone who writes the Canticle of Sister Electricity. How much fertility is concealed behind this perpetual intellectual erection?

McLuhan does not confine himself to saying to us "Ace of Spades equals death," but he makes further affirmations that, though still kabbalistic, are of the type of "legs: eleven": in which case we do not have a totally unmotivated relationship, as in the former statement, but a certain structural homology. And the search for homological structures frightens only narrow minds and alphabets incapable of seeing beyond their own primers. When Panofsky discovered a structural homology between the plan of Gothic cathedrals and the form of medieval theological treatises, he tried to compare two *modus operandi* that give life to relational systems that can be described by a single diagram, a single formal model. And when McLuhan sees a relationship between the disappearance of the Gutenbergian mentality and certain ways of conceiving organizational structures in a linear and hierarchical way, he is undoubtedly working on the same plane of heuristic happiness. But when he adds that the same process had led to the disappearance of the lines of porters waiting the arrival of guests in a hotel then he begins to enter the realm of the unverifiable, and when he comes to the disappearance of the vertical lines in nylon stockings he is in the realm of the imponderable. When he then cynically plays with current opinions, knowing they are false, he arouses our suspicions. McLuhan knows that a computer performs many operations at instantaneous speed, in a single second, but he also knows that this fact does not authorize him to declare that the instantaneous synchronization of numerous operations had put an end to the old syntax of linear sequences. In fact the *programming* of a computer consists precisely in the arranging of linear sequences of logical operations broken down into binary signals; if there is something not very tribal, enveloping, polycentric, hallucinatory, and non-Gutenbergian, it is precisely the programmer's job. It's wrong to take advantage of the ingenuousness of the average humanist, who has learned all he knows about electronic brains from science fiction. Precisely because his discussion offers some valid intuitions, we ask McLuhan not to play the shell game with us.

But—and this is a fairly melancholy conclusion—the popular success of his thought is due, on the contrary, to this very technique of nondefinition of terms and to that cogito-interruptus logic that has given such cheap celebrity also to the Apocalyptics, popularized in one-size-fits-all dimensions in well-intentioned newspapers. In this sense McLuhan is right: Gutenbergian man is dead, and the reader seeks in the book a message at low definition, in which to find hallucinatory immersion. At this point isn't it better to watch television?

That television is better than Sedlmayr is beyond any doubt. With McLuhan, things are different. Even when they are merchandised in a jumble, good and bad together, ideas summon other ideas, if only to be refuted. Read McLuhan; but then try to tell your friends what he says. Then you will be forced to choose a sequence, and you will emerge from the hallucination.

1967

Language,
Power,
Force

On January 17, 1977, Roland Barthes, before the kind of capacity audience attracted by great social and cultural occasions, delivered his inaugural lecture at the Collège de France, where he had just been invited to occupy the chair of literary semiology. This lecture, which the newspapers reported at the time .(*Le Monde* devoted an entire page to it), has now been published by the Editions du Seuil, under the humble and very proud title *Leçon.** Just over forty pages, it is divided into three parts. The first deals with language, the second with the function of literature with regard to the power of language, the third with semiology and, in particular, literary semiology.

I must immediately say that here I will not go into the third part (which, brief as it is, nevertheless would demand an extended discussion of method), and I will mention the second part only in passing. It is the first part that, I feel, raises a problem of far broader

---

*Available in *The Barthes Reader*, ed. Susan Sontag (New York: Hill and Wang, 1982) as "Inaugural Lecture," trans. Richard Howard.

scope, going beyond both literature and the techniques of enquiry into literature, to arrive at the question of Power—a question that informs also the other books referred to briefly in this article.

Barthes's inaugural lecture is constructed with splendid rhetoric and begins with praise of the position he is about to occupy. As many perhaps know, the professors of the Collège de France confine themselves to speaking: They give no examinations and have no power to promote or fail the students, who listen to them solely out of love for what they say. Hence Barthes's contentment (once both humble and very proud): I am entering a place beyond power. Hypocrisy, to be sure, because nothing confers more cultural power in France than teaching at the Collège de France, producing knowledge. But we are getting ahead of ourselves. In this lecture (which, as we shall see, focuses on play *with* language), Barthes, however innocently, is playing: He offers one definition of power and presupposes another.

In fact, Barthes is too subtle to ignore Foucault, whom he actually thanks for having been his patron at the Collège; therefore he knows that power is not "one" and that, as it infiltrates a place where it is not felt at first, it is "plural," legion, like demons. ". . . Power is present in the most delicate mechanisms of social exchange: not only in the State, in classes, groups, but even in fashion, public opinion, entertainment, sports, news, information, family and private relations, and even in the liberating impulses which attempt to counteract it." Whence: "I call the discourse of power any discourse which engenders blame, hence guilt, in its recipient." You carry out a revolution to destroy power, and it will be reborn, within the new state of affairs. ". . . Power is the parasite of a trans-social organism, linked to the whole of man's history and not only to his political, historical history. This object in which power is inscribed, for all its human eternity, is language, or, to be more precise, its necessary expression: the language we speak and write," the given language.

It is not the ability to speak that establishes power, it is the ability to speak to the extent that this ability becomes rigid in an order, a system of rules, the given language. The given language, Barthes says (in an argument that repeats broadly, I don't know how consciously, the positions of Benjamin Lee Whorf), obliges me to enunciate an action, placing myself as subject, so from that moment on what I do will be the consequence of what I am. The given language obliges me to choose between masculine and feminine, and forbids me to conceive a neuter category; it obliges me to engage the other by either "thou" or "you"; I have no right to leave my affective and social relationship unspecified. Naturally Barthes is speaking of French; English would restore to him at least the last two grammatical freedoms mentioned but (as he would rightly say) it would take others from him. Conclusion: "Thus by its very structure, my language implies an inevitable relation of alienation." To speak is to subject oneself; the given language is a generalized reaction. Moreover—"it is neither reactionary nor progressive, it is quite simply fascist; because fascism does not prevent speech, it compels speech."

From the polemical point of view, this is the affirmation that, since January of 1977, has provoked the most reaction. All the other affirmations which follow are its consequences; we must not be amazed then to hear people say that the given language is power because it compels me to use already formulated stereotypes, including words themselves, and that it is structured so fatally that, slaves inside it, we cannot free ourselves outside it, because outside the given language there is nothing.

How can we escape what Barthes calls, Sartre-like, this *huis clos*? By cheating. You can cheat with the given language. This dishonest and healthy and liberating trick is called literature.

Hence the outline of a theory of literature as writing, a game *of* and *with* words. A category involving not only so-called literary practices but also ones operative in the text of a scientist or historian. The model of this liberating activity, however, is for Barthes always that of the "creative" or "creating" activities. Literature puts language on stage, exploits its interstices, is not measured by the statements already made, but through the very game of the subject it states, it reveals the flavor of words. Literature says something and, at the same time, it denies what it has said; it doesn't destroy signs, it makes them play and it plays them. If and whether literature is liberation from the power of the given language depends on the nature of this power. And here Barthes seems to us very evasive. For that matter he mentioned Foucault not only as a friend, and directly, but also indirectly in a sort of paraphrase, when he spoke a few sentences on the "plurality" of power. And the notion that Foucault developed of power is perhaps the most convincing in circulation today, and certainly the most provocative. We find it, constructed step by step, in all his work.

Through the differentiation, from one work to the next, of the relations between power and learning, between practices of discourse and practices of nondiscourse, in Foucault a notion of power is clearly outlined that has at least two characteristics of interest to us here: First of all, power is not only repression and prohibition, it is also incitement to discourse and production of knowledge; in the second place, as Barthes also indicates, power is not single, but is massive; it is not a one-way process between an entity that commands and its subjects.

> In short this power is exercised rather than possessed; it is not the "privilege," acquired or preserved, of the dominant class, but the overall effect of its strategic positions—an effect that is manifested and sometimes extended by the position of those who are dominated. Furthermore, this power is not exercised simply as an obligation or a prohibition on those who "do not have it"; it invests them, is transmitted by them and through them; it exerts pressure upon them, just as they themselves, in their struggle against it, resist the grip it has on them.*

---

* Michel Foucault, *Discipline and Punish*, trans. Alan Sheridan (New York: Random House, 1979), pp. 16–17.

Further still:

> By power, I do not mean "Power" as a group of institu-
> tions and mechanisms that ensure the subservience of the cit-
> izens of a given state. . . . It seems to me that power must
> be understood in the first instance as the multiplicity of force
> relations immanent in the sphere in which they operate and
> which constitute their own organization; as the process which,
> through ceaseless struggles and confrontations, transforms,
> strengthens, or reverses them; as the support which these force
> relations find in one another, thus forming a chain or a sys-
> tem, or on the contrary, the disjunctions and contradictions
> which isolate them from one another; and lastly, as the strat-
> egies in which they take effect, whose general design or insti-
> tutional crystallization is embodied in the state apparatus, in
> the formulation of the law, in the various social hegemonies.

Power must be looked for not in one sovereign center but
in the

> moving substrate of force relations which, by virtue of their
> inequality, constantly engender states of power, but the latter
> are always local and unstable. . . . Power is everywhere; not
> because it embraces everything but because it comes from
> everywhere. . . . Power comes from below. . . . There is no
> binary and all-encompassing opposition between rulers and
> ruled at the root of power relations, and serving as a general
> matrix. . . . One must suppose rather that the manifold re-
> lations of force that take shape and come into play in the
> machinery of production, in families, in limited groups and
> institutions, are the basis for wide-ranging effects of cleavage
> that run through the social body as a whole.*

*Michel Foucault, *The History of Sexuality*, Vol. I: *An Introduction*, trans. Robert Hurley
(New York: Pantheon Books, 1978), pp. 92–94.

Now this image of power closely recalls the idea of the system that linguists call the given language. The given language is, true, coercive (it forbids me to say "I are him," under pain of being incomprehensible), but its coercion doesn't derive from an individual decision, or from some center that sends out rules in all directions: It is a social product, it originates as a constrictive apparatus precisely through general assent. Each individual is reluctant to have to observe the rules of grammar but consents and demands that others observe them because he finds his own advantage in such observance.

I'm not sure we can say that a given language is a device of power (even if, because of its systematic nature, it is a constituent of knowledge), but it is surely a model of power. We could also say that, being the semiotic apparatus par excellence or (as the Russian semioticians express it) the primary modelizing system, it is the model of those other semiotic systems that in the various cultures are established as devices of power, and of knowledge (secondary modelizing systems).

In this sense, therefore, Barthes is right in defining the given language as something connected with power, but he is wrong in then drawing two conclusions: that the given language is therefore fascist, and that it is the object in which power is inscribed, its threatening epiphany, in other words.

We can immediately liquidate the first, very clear error: If power is as Foucault defined it, and if the characteristics of power are found in the given language, to say that the given language is therefore fascist is more than a wisecrack, it is an invitation to confusion. Because fascism then, being everywhere, in every power situation, and in every given language, since the beginning of time, would no longer be anywhere. If the human condition is placed under the sign of fascism, all are fascists and no one is a fascist any longer. Whence we see how dangerous demagogical arguments are, which we find used abundantly in everyday journalism, and without Barthes's refinement, for he at least knows he is speaking in paradoxes and using them for rhetorical ends.

The second misunderstanding seems to me more subtle: The given language is not that in which power is inscribed. Frankly, I have never understood the French or frenchified affectation of inscribing everything and seeing everything as if inscribed: To put it simply, I'm not quite clear as to what inscribing means. It seems to me one of those expressions that resolve in an authoritative manner problems that nobody knows how to define otherwise. But even if we accept this expression as valid, I would say that the given language is the device through which power is inscribed where it establishes itself. I would like to make myself clearer, and for this reason I refer to the recent study of Georges Duby on the theory of the three orders.*

Duby starts out with the Estates General, at the dawn of the French Revolution: Clergy, Nobility, and Third Estate. And he asks where this theory (and ideology) of the three estates came from. And he finds it in very ancient Carolingian ecclesiastical texts, where the people of God is referred to as being divided into three orders, or parties, or levels: those who pray, those who fight, and those who work. Another metaphor in circulation during the Middle Ages was that of the flock: There are the shepherds, the sheepdogs, and the sheep. In other words, according to the traditional interpretation of this triple division, there is the clergy, which directs society spiritually, there are the soldiers who protect it, and there are the people, who support both. It is fairly simple, and you have only to think of the investiture conflict and the struggle between papacy and empire that we studied in school, to understand what is being discussed.

But Duby goes beyond the banal interpretation. In more than four hundred exceptionally closely argued pages, tracing the vicissitudes of this idea of the Carolingian period at the end of the twelfth century (and only in France), he discovers that this model of the ordering of society is never repeated exactly. It reappears

*The Three Orders: Feudal Society Imagined, trans. Arthur Goldhammer (Chicago: University of Chicago Press, 1980).

often, but with the terms arranged differently; sometimes, instead of a triangular form, it takes on a four-point shape; the words chosen to designate this party or that are changed, sometimes *milites* are spoken of, sometimes they are called *pugnatores*, sometimes cavaliers; sometimes, instead of clergy, the word is monks; sometimes they speak of farmers, sometimes simply of workers, sometimes of merchants.

The fact is that over a period of three centuries numerous evolutions of European society took place, and different alliances came into play: between the urban clergy and the feudal lords, to oppress the populace; between clergy and populace to escape the pressure of the knights; between monks and feudal lords against the urban clergy; between urban clergy and national monarchies; between national monarchies and great monastic orders. . . . The list could continue to infinity. To us Duby's book is like what a study of the relations between the Christian Democrats, the United States, the Italian Communist Party, and the Italian Manufacturers' Association in our century might seem to a reader in the year 3000. So you quickly realize that things are not always as clear as they look, that categorical expressions such as "opening to the left" or "economic development" take on different meanings not only as they pass from Andreotti to Craxi, but also within the confines of a Christian Democrat Party conference and in the space of two elections. Those medieval polemics which seemed so clear to us, with such well-defined party ploys, are actually very subtle. And the fact that Duby's book is so dense, so fascinating and boring at the same time, so difficult to unravel, lacking immediately comprehensible summarizations, is almost justified, because it puts before us a flux of sticky maneuvers. At a given moment, the Cluniac monk speaks of division among clerics, cavaliers, and peasants, but seems to stir up the specter of a four-part division, adding to the tripartite axis (which is concerned with earthly life) a binary axis that involves the supernatural life, and where the previous trio is set against the monks, who are mediators with the next world. The game is then ever so slightly altered and there is the hint of the domination that the monastic orders want to assume over the other three orders, in which the urban clergy would perform a purely vicarious function, and direct relations would be established between monasteries and feudal structure.

It happens that each of these formulas, so similar and yet so different, is structured on a network of relationships of strength: The knights sack the countryside, the populace seeks support and tries to defend the produce of the land, but among the populace are already emerging those who own their own property and tend to redirect the situation to their own advantage, and so on.

These relationships of strength, however, would remain purely aleatory if they were not disciplined by a power structure in which everyone is consentient and prepared to recognize himself as part of that structure. To this end, there intervenes rhetoric, the ordering and modelizing function of language, which with infinitesimal shifts of accent legitimizes certain relationships of strength and criminalizes others. Ideology takes shape: The power born from it becomes truly a network of consensus, beginning from below, because the relationships of strength have been transformed into symbolic relationships.

At this point in my reading of texts so different, an opposition between power and strength is outlined, an opposition that seems to me totally erased in the talk we hear every day now, in the school, the factory, the ghetto, about power. As we know, since '68 criticism of power and protest against it have greatly deteriorated, because they have become mass-produced. An inevitable process and we will not repeat (with a fine reactionary stance) that when a concept arrives within everyone's grasp it crumbles, and so it should have remained the property of a few. On the contrary, it is precisely because it had to be within everyone's grasp, though in the process it would risk crumbling, that the criticism of its degenerations becomes important.

So then, in mass political discussion of power there have been two ambiguous phases: the first, ingenuous, in which power had a center (the System, like an evil boss with a moustache who, at the keyboard of a maleficent computer, taps out the perdition of the working class). This idea has been sufficiently criticized, and Foucault's notion of power intervenes, in fact, to show its anthropomorphic naïveté. A trace of this revision of the concept can be found even in the internal contradictions of various terrorist groups: from those who want to strike at the "heart" of the state to those who, on the contrary, unravel the strands of power at its edge, in the points I would call "Foucaultian," where the prison guard, the petty merchant, the foreman are engaged.

But the second phase remains more equivocal; here strength and power are all too easily confused. I speak of "strength" instead of causality, which would come to me more spontaneously, for reasons that we will see; but we can begin at once with a fairly ingenuous notion of causality.

There are things that cause other things: The stroke of lightning burns the tree; the male member inseminates the female uterus. These relationships are not reversible: The tree does not burn the stroke of lightning, and woman does not inseminate man. There are, on the other hand, relationships where somebody makes somebody else do things because of a symbolic relationship: The man decides that in the home the woman washes the dishes; the Inquisition decides that heretics will be burned at the stake and assumes the right to define heresy. These relationships are based on a strategy of language that, once labile relationships of strength are recognized, institutionalizes them symbolically, achieving consensus from the dominated. Symbolic relationships are reversible. In principle the woman has only to say no to the man and he will have to wash the dishes, the heretics reject the authority of the Inquisition and they will not be burned. Naturally, things are not that simple, precisely because the discourse that symbolically represents power must deal not with simple causal relations but with complex interaction of forces. Still this seems to me the difference between power, as symbolic fact, and pure causality: The former is reversible, the latter is only capable of being contained or bridled, it allows reforms (I invent the lightning rod; the woman decides to go on the pill, to renounce sexual relations, to have only homosexual relations).

The inability to distinguish between power and causality leads to much childish political behavior. As we have seen, things are not all that simple. Let's replace the notion of causality (one-directional) with that of force. A force is applied to another force: They form a parallelogram of forces. They do not cancel one another; they are composed, according to a law. The play among forces is reformist: It produces compromises. But the game is never between two forces, it is among countless forces; the parallelogram gives rise to far more complex multidimensional figures. To decide which forces must be set against which other forces, decisions are made which are dependent not on the play of forces but on the play of power. A knowledge is produced, of the composition of forces.

To return to Duby: When knights exist, when the merchants appear on the scene with their wealth, when the peasants start migrating towards the city under the scourge of famine, you are dealing with forces: The symbolic strategy, the formulation of convincing theories of the three orders or the four, and thence the configuration of power relationships come into play in defining which forces must restrain which others, and in what direction the consequent parallelograms must march. But in Duby's book, at least for the idle reader, the play of forces risks disappearing in the face of the dominant argument, which is made up by the constant rearrangement of the symbolic figures.

We come to the last book in the pile, *War in European History*,* Michael Howard's study of weapons in the development of European history. We will speak of it only obliquely, inviting the

---

*New York: Oxford University Press, 1976.

reader to enjoy for himself this fascinating book that starts with the wars of the feudal period and arrives at those of the nuclear age, with a wealth of anecdote and unpredictable discoveries. In 1346, at Crécy, Edward III introduces, against the enemy cavalry, his longbow archers. These longbows, which shoot five or six arrows in the same time that a crossbow could fire only one of its large darts, engage a new force against the cavalry. They defeat it. From that moment on, cavalry is convinced that its armor must be heavier; the cavalry becomes less easily maneuvered and is totally useless when dismounted. The force of the armed cavalier is annulled.

These are relationships of force. The reaction to them is an attempt to check the new force. In other words, the entire structure of the army is reformed. Through adjustments of this sort, the history of Europe proceeds, and armies become something different. Remember the lament of Ariosto's paladins, complaining of the blindness of the harquebus? But now the new relationships of force, in reciprocally checking one another and in adjusting, create a new ideology of armed forces and produce new symbolic arrangements. Here Howard's book seems to proceed inversely from Duby's: from force, indirectly, to the new structures of power, whereas the other went from formulation of the images of power to the relations of new forces and old that underlay the images.

But if we don't reflect enough on this opposition, we fall into forms of political childishness. We do not say to a force: "No, I won't obey you"; we develop techniques of checking it. But we don't react to a relationship of power with a mere and immediate act of force. Power is far more subtle and exploits a far more widespread consensus, and heals the wound received at that point, always and necessarily marginal.

This is why we are usually fascinated by the great revolutions; to posterity they seem a sole act of force, which, applied at an apparently insignificant point, turns the whole axis of a power situation: the taking of the Bastille, the attack on the Winter Palace, the coup at the Moncada barracks. . . . And this is why the aspiring revolutionary is eager to repeat exemplary acts of this kind, and is amazed when they don't succeed. The fact is that the "historical" act of force was never an act of force, but a symbolic gesture, a theatrical finale that sanctioned, in a fashion also scenically pregnant, a crisis in power relationships that had been spreading, in a grass-roots way, for a long time. And without which the pseudo-act of force would again be a mere act of force, without symbolic power, destined to become adjusted in a little local parallelogram.

But how can a power, composed of a consensus network, disintegrate? This is the question Foucault asks, also in *The History of Sexuality*: "Should it be said that one is always 'inside' power, that there is no 'escaping' it, that there is no absolute outside where it is concerned, because one is subject to the law in any case?" If you think about it, this is Barthes's assertion when he says that we can never escape from language.

Foucault's answer is:

This would be to misunderstand the strictly relational character of power relationships. Their existence depends on a multiplicity of points of resistance: These play the role of adversary, target, support, or handle. . . . Hence there is no single locus of all rebellions, no pure law of the revolutionary. Instead there is a plurality of resistances, each of them a special case: resistances that are possible, necessary, improbable; others that are spontaneous, savage, solitary, concerted, rampant, or violent; still others that are quick to compromise, interested, or sacrificial. . . . The points, knots, or focuses of resistance are spread over time and space at varying densities, at times mobilizing groups or individuals in a definitive way, inflaming certain points of the body, certain moments in life, certain types of behavior. . . . But more often one is dealing with mobile and transitory points of resistance, producing

251

cleavages in a society that shift about, fracturing unities and effecting regroupings, furrowing across individuals themselves, cutting them up and remolding them. . . .*

In this sense power, in which we are, sees the crumbling of its fundamental consensus rise from its own inner being. What I want to point out most, within the limitations of this essay, is the homology between these continuous processes of breakdown described (in a fairly allusive form) by Foucault and the function Barthes assigns to literature inside the system of linguistic power. Which would lead us perhaps also to make some reflections on a certain aestheticism in Foucault's view, just as he (compare the 1977 interview in the appendix of the volume just mentioned) declares himself opposed to the end of the writer's activity and to the theorization of writing as eversive activity. Or to wonder if Barthes (when he says that it is a possibility open also to the scientist or to the historian) is not making literature an allegory of the relationships of resistance and criticism of power in the wider context of social life. What seems clear is that this technique of opposition to power, always from within and widespread, has nothing to do with the techniques of opposition to force, which are always external, and specific. Oppositions to force always obtain an immediate reply, like the clash of two billiard balls; those against power always obtain indirect replies.

We will venture an allegory, something like a good old American film of the '30's. In Chinatown a gang sets up a laundry racket. Acts of force. They come in, ask for money, and if the laundry doesn't fork over, they smash the place up. The proprietor of the laundry can oppose force with force: He punches a gangster in the face. The result is immediate. The gangster has to exercise greater force the next day. This game of forces can lead to some changes

---

*History of Sexuality, I, pp. 95–96.

in the restriction of the neighborhood life: iron bars on the laundry doors, alarm systems.

But gradually the inhabitants of Chinatown adjust to the atmosphere: The restaurants close earlier, the inhabitants stay home after dark, other storeowners agree that it's more reasonable to pay up than be harassed. . . . A relationship of legitimization of the gangsters' power has been established, and everyone collaborates, including those who would prefer a different system. Now the gangsters' power is beginning to be based on symbolic relationships of obedience, in which the obedient are as responsible as the obeyed. In a way, each finds something in it to his own advantage.

The first breakdown of the consensus could come from a group of young people who decide to organize a celebration every evening with firecrackers and paper dragons. As an act of force it could perhaps hinder the passage or the flight of the gangsters, but as far as that goes the action is minimal. As an aspect of resistance to power, the celebration introduces an element of self-confidence, which acts to disrupt the consensus dictated by fear. Its results cannot be immediate; and, furthermore, there can be no result unless other marginal attitudes correspond to the celebration, other ways of declaring, "Count me out." In our film it could be the courageous act of a local reporter. But the disrupting process could also abort. The tactics would have to be immediately denied, if the racket system were capable of absorbing them into the local folklore. . . . We will stop the allegory here before, being a movie, it obliges us to find a happy ending.

I don't know whether this festivity with the paper dragon is an allegory of literature according to Barthes or whether Barthes's literature and this festivity are allegories of the Foucaultian crises of the systems of power. Also because at this point a new suspicion arises: To what degree does Barthes's given language obey mechanisms homologous to the systems of power described by Foucault?

Let us posit then a given language as a system of rules: not only grammatical ones, but also those that today are called pragmatic. For example, the conversational rule that a question must be answered in a pertinent way, and whoever breaks this rule is judged, depending on the situation, rude, silly, provoking; or else it is assumed he is hinting at something else he doesn't want to say. Literature that cheats with the given language is presented as an activity that breaks down the rules and imposes others: temporary, valid in just one instance and for one current; and especially, valid in the context of the literary laboratory. This means that Ionesco cheats with the given language, making his characters speak the way they do in *The Bald Soprano*, for example. But if in a social relationship everyone spoke like the bald prima donna, society would break down. Mind you, there would not be a linguistic revolution, because revolution involves an upset of power relationships; a universe that talks like Ionesco wouldn't upset anything, it would establish a kind of nth degree (the opposite of zero, an indefinite number) of behavior. It would no longer be possible even to buy bread from the baker.

How does the given language defend itself against this risk? Barthes tells us, reconstructing a power situation faced by its own violation, absorbing it (the anacoluthon of the artist becomes common norm). As for society, it defends the given language by reciting the literature, which questions the given language's position, in certain set places. Thus it happens that there is never any revolution in a language: Either it is a pretense of revolution, on the stage, where all is licit, and then you go home speaking in a normal way; or else it is an infinitesimal movement of continuous reform. Aestheticism consists of believing that life is art and art, life, confusing the areas. Deceiving oneself.

The given language, therefore, is not a scenario of power, in Foucault's sense. Very well. But why do we seem to have found such strong homologies between linguistic devices and devices of power—and to have noted that the knowledge on which power is nourished is produced through linguistic means?

Here another suspicion arises. Perhaps it isn't that the given language is different from power because power is a place of revolution, something denied to language. It is that power is homologous to the given language because, as the former is described to us by Foucault, it can never be a place of revolution. That is, in power there is never any distance between reform and revolution, since revolution is the moment when a slow process of gradual adjustments suddenly undergoes what René Thom would call a catastrophe, a sudden turn; but in the sense in which a collecting of seismic movements suddenly produces an upheaval of the earth. A final breaking point of something already formed in advance, step by step. Revolutions then would be the catastrophes of the slow movements of reform, quite independent of the will of the subjects, casual effect of a final compounding of forces that obeys a strategy of symbolic adjustments ripening over a long time.

Which is tantamount to saying that it isn't clear if Foucault's view of power (which Barthes, with genius, exemplifies in the given language) is a neorevolutionary view or a neoreformist one. Except that Foucault's merit would lie in having abolished the difference between the two concepts, forcing us to rethink, along with the notion of power, also that of political initiative. I can already see the hunters of fashions charging me with having categorized Foucault as a typical reactionary thinker. Nonsense. The fact is that in this knot of problems new notions of power take shape, and of force, of violent upheaval and of progressive adjustment through slow, marginal shifts, in a centerless universe where all is margin and there is no longer any "heart" of anything. A fine plexus of ideas for a reflection that arises under the sign of a "leçon." We'll leave it suspended. These are problems, as Foucault would say, that the single subject does not resolve. Unless he confines himself to literary fiction.

1979

In Praise of
St. Thomas

The worst thing that happened to Thomas Aquinas in the course of his career was not his death, on March 7, 1274, in Fossanova, when he was barely forty-nine, and, fat as he was, the monks were unable to carry his body down the stairs. Nor was it what happened three years after his death, when the Archbishop of Paris, Etienne Tempier, published a list of heretical propositions (two hundred and nineteen of them) that included the majority of the theses of the followers of Averroes, some observations on terrestrial love advanced a hundred years earlier by André le Chapelain, and twenty propositions clearly attributable to him, Thomas, the angelic doctor himself, son of the lordly family of Aquino. For history soon dealt with this repressive act and in Thomas's favor; he received justice, even after his death, winning his battle while Etienne Tempier ended up, with Guillaume de Saint-Amour, Tommaso's other enemy, in the unfortunately eternal ranks of the great reactionaries. No, the disaster that ruined the life of Tommaso d'Aquino befell him in 1323, two years after the death of Dante and was perhaps also, to some degree, attributable to the poet: in other words, when John XXII decided to turn Tommaso into Saint Thomas Aquinas. These are nasty mishaps, like receiving the Nobel Prize, being admitted to the Académie de France, winning an Oscar. You become like the Mona Lisa: a cliché. It's the moment when the big arsonist is appointed Fire Chief.

This year marks the seventh centenary of the death of Thomas. Thomas is back in fashion, as saint and philosopher. We try to understand what Thomas would do today, with the faith, culture, and intellectual energy he had in his own day. But love sometimes clouds the spirit: To say that Thomas was great, that he was a revolutionary, it is necessary to understand in what sense he was one. For, though no one can say he was a reactionary, he is still a man who raised a construction so solid that no subsequent revolutionary has been able to shake it from within—and the most that could be done to it, from Descartes to Hegel to Marx and to Teilhard de Chardin, was to speak of it "from outside."

Especially since it is hard to understand how scandal could come from this person, so unromantic, fat, and slow, who at school took notes in silence, looked as if he weren't understanding anything, and was teased by his companions. And, in the monastery, as he sat at the table on his double stool (they had to saw off the central arm to make enough room for him) the playful monks shouted to him that outside there was an ass flying and he ran to see, while the others split their sides (mendicant friars, as is well known, have simple tastes); and then Thomas (who was no fool) said that to him a flying ass had seemed more likely than a monk who would tell a falsehood, and the other friars were insulted.

But then this student that his companions called the dumb ox became a professor, worshiped by his students, and one day he went out walking on the hills with his disciples and looked at Paris from above, and they asked him if he would like to be the master of such a beautiful city, and he said that he would much prefer to have the text of the Homilies of Saint John Chrysostom; but then when an ideological enemy stepped on his foot he became furious and in that Latin of his that seems laconic because you can under-stand it all and the verbs are exactly where an Italian expects them, he exploded in insults and sarcasm that sound like Marx when he is lashing out at Mr. Szeliga.

Was he good-natured, was he an angel? Was he sexless? When his brothers wanted to prevent him from becoming a Dominican (because in those days the cadet son of a good family became a Benedictine, which was something proper, and not a mendicant, which would be like entering a serve-the-people commune or going to work with Danilo Dolci), they captured him as he was on his way to Paris and shut him up in the family castle; then, to get the crazy notions out of his head and turn him into a respectable abbé, they sent a naked girl, ready and willing, into his room. And Thomas grabbed a firebrand and started running after her, clearly meaning to burn her buttocks. No sex, then? Who can say? Because the thing upset him so much that afterwards, as we are told by Ber-nard Gui, "Women, unless it were absolutely necessary, he avoided as if they were serpents."

In any case this man was a fighter. Sturdy, lucid, he conceived an ambitious plan, carried it out, and won. What then was the field of battle, what was at stake, what were the advantages he achieved? When Thomas was born, the Italian communes had won the battle of Legnano against the empire fifty years earlier. Ten years before his birth England received the Magna Charta. In France the reign of Philippe Auguste had just ended. The empire was dying. Within five years the seafaring and trading cities of the north would join to form the Hanseatic League. The Florentine economy was expanding, about to issue the gold florin; Fibonacci had already invented double-entry bookkeeping; the flourishing medical school of Salerno and the law school of Bologna were a century old. The Crusades were in an advanced state; in other words, contacts with the East were in full development. Further, the Arabs in Spain were fascinating the Western world with their scientific and philosophical discoveries. Technology was making great strides: There were new ways of shoeing horses, driving mills, steering ships, yoking oxen for bearing burdens and plowing. National monarchies in the north, and free communes in the south. In short, this was not the Middle Ages, at least not in the popular sense of the term. Polemically, we might say that if it weren't for what Thomas was about to do, it would already be the Renaissance. But Thomas actually had to do what he was going to do if things were then to proceed as they did.

Europe was trying to create for itself a culture that would reflect a political and economic plurality, dominated, true, by the paternal control of the church, which nobody called into question, but also open to a new sense of nature, of concrete reality, of human individuality. Organizational and productive processes were being rationalized: It was necessary to find the techniques of reason.

When Thomas was born, the techniques of reason had been operative for a century. In Paris, at the Faculty of Arts, they still taught music, arithmetic, geometry, and astronomy, but also dialectic, logic, and rhetoric, and in a new way. Abelard, a century before, had been there; for private reasons he was deprived of reproductive organs, but his head lost none of its vigor. The new method was to compare the opinions of the various traditional authorities, and decide, according to logical procedures based on a secular grammar of ideas. Linguistics, semantics were being employed; scholars asked themselves what a given word meant and in what sense it was used. Aristotle's writings on logic were the study manuals, but not all of them had been translated and interpreted; few knew Greek, except for the Arabs, who were far ahead of the Europeans both in philosophy and in science. But already a century before, the school of Chartres, rediscovering the mathematical texts of Plato, had constructed an image of the natural world based on geometrical laws, on measurable processes. This was not yet the experimental method of Roger Bacon, but it was theoretic construction, an attempt to explain the universe through natural bases, even if Nature was seen as a divine agent. Robert Grosse-teste developed a metaphysics of luminous energy that suggests partly Bergson and partly Einstein: The study of optics was born. In short, the problem of the perception of physical objects was broached, a line was drawn between hallucination and sight.

This is no small matter. The universe of the early Middle Ages was a universe of hallucination, the world was a symbolic forest peopled with mysterious presences; things were seen as if in the continuous story of a divinity who spent his time reading and devising the *Weekly Puzzle Magazine*. This universe of hallucination, by Thomas's time, had not disappeared under the blows of the universe of reason: On the contrary, the latter was still the product of intellectual élites and was frowned upon. Because, to tell the truth, the universe of terrestrial things was frowned upon. Saint Francis talked to the birds, but the philosophical foundation of theology was neo-Platonic. Which means: Far, far away there is God, in whose unattainable totality the principles of things, ideas, stir; the universe is the effect of a benevolent distraction of this very distant One, who seems to trickle slowly downward, abandoning traces of his perfection in the sticky clumps of matter that he defecates, like traces of sugar in the urine. In this muck that represents the more negligible margin of the One, we can find, almost always through a brilliant puzzle-solution, the imprint of germs of comprehensibility, but comprehensibility lies elsewhere, and if all goes well, along comes the mystic, with his nervous, stripped-down intuition, who penetrates with an almost drugged eye into the *garçonnière* of the One, where the sole and true party is going on.

Plato and Aristotle had said all that was needed to understand the problems of the soul, but the nature of a flower or of the maze of guts the Salerno doctors were exploring in the belly of a sick man, and the reason why the fresh air of a spring evening was good for you: Here things became obscure. So it was better to know the flowers in the illuminated texts of the visionaries, ignore the fact that guts exist, and consider spring evenings a dangerous temptation. Thus European culture was divided: If they understood the heavens, they didn't understand the earth. If somebody then wanted to understand the earth and not take an interest in heaven, he was in big trouble. The Red Brigades of the period were roaming around: heretical sects that, on the one hand, wanted to renew the world, set up impossible republics, and on the other hand, practiced sodomy, pillage, and other horrors. Reports might or might not be true, but in any case it was best to kill the lot of them.

At this point the men of reason learned from the Arabs that there was an ancient master (a Greek) who could supply a key to join these scattered limbs of culture: Aristotle. Aristotle knew how to talk about God, but he also classified animals and stones, and concerned himself with the movement of the stars. Aristotle knew logic, studied psychology, talked about physics, classified political systems. But above all Aristotle offered the keys (and in this sense Thomas was to make the fullest use of him) to overturning the relationship between the essence of things (that is, to the extent that things can be understood and said, even when those things are not here, before our eyes) and the matter of which things are made. We can leave God out of it: He is living happily on his own and has provided the world with excellent physical laws so that it can go ahead by itself. And we needn't waste time trying to recover the trace of essences in that sort of mystic cascade of theirs whereby, losing the best along the way, they come and get all muddled up in matter. The mechanism of things is here, before our eyes; things are the principle of their movement. A man, a flower, a stone are organisms that have grown up obeying an internal law that moved them: The essence is the principle of their growth and their organization. It is a something already there, ready to explode, that moves matter from inside, and makes it grow and reveal itself: This is why we can understand it. A stone is a portion of matter that has assumed form: Together, from this marriage, an individual substance has been born. The secret of being, as Thomas was to gloss with a bold intellectual leap, is the concrete act of existing. Existing, happening are not accidents that occur to ideas, which for themselves would be better off in the warm uterus of the distant divinity. First, thank heaven, things exist concretely, and then we understand them.

Naturally two points have to be clarified. First of all, according to the Aristotelian tradition, understanding things does not mean studying them experimentally: You had only to understand that things count, theory took care of the rest. Not much, if you like, but still a huge step forward from the hallucinated world of the previous centuries. In the second place, if Aristotle had to be Christianized, more space had to be given to God, who was a bit too much off to one side. Things grow thanks to the inner force of the life principle that moves them, but it must also be admitted that if God takes all this great movement to heart, he is capable of thinking the stone as it becomes stone by itself, and if he were to decide to cut off the electricity (which Thomas calls "participation") there would be a cosmic blackout. So the essence of the stone is in the stone, and it is grasped by our mind, which is capable of thinking it; but it existed already in the mind of God, which is full of love and spends its days not doing its fingernails but supplying energy to the universe. This was the game to be played; otherwise Aristotle wouldn't enter Christian culture, and if Aristotle remained outside, nature and reason remained outside, too.

It was a difficult game because the Aristotelians that Thomas found had preceded him, when he began to work, had taken another path, which might even be more pleasing to us, and which an interpreter fond of historical short-circuits might even define as materialistic: But it was a very slightly dialectical materialism; indeed, it was an astrological materialism, and it rather upset everybody, from the keepers of the Koran to those of the Gospel. The man responsible, a century earlier, had been Averroes, Mos-

263

lem by culture, Berber by race, Spanish by nationality, and Arab by language. Averroes knew Aristotle better than anybody and had understood what Aristotelian science led to: God is not a manipulator who sticks his nose into everything at random; he established nature in its mechanical order and in its mathematical laws, regulated by the iron determination of the stars. And since God is eternal, the world in its order is eternal also. Philosophy studies this order: nature, in other words. Men are able to understand it because in all men one principle of intelligence acts; otherwise each would see things in his own way and there would be no reciprocal understanding. At this point the materialistic conclusion was inevitable: The world is eternal, regulated by a predictable determinism, and if a sole intellect lives in all men, the individual immortal soul does not exist. If the Koran says something different, the philosopher must philosophically believe what his science shows him and then, without creating too many problems for himself, believe the opposite, which is the command of faith. There are two truths and the one must not disturb the other.

Averroes carried to lucid conclusions what was implicit in rigorous Aristotelianism, and this was the reason for his success in Paris among the masters at the Faculty of Arts, in particular with Sigier of Brabant, whom Dante puts in Paradise with Saint Thomas, even if it is Thomas's fault that Sigier's scholarly career collapsed and he was relegated to the footnotes in popular handbooks of philosophy.

The game of cultural politics that Thomas tried to play was a double game: on the one hand, to make Aristotle accepted by the theological learning of the time; and on the other, to detach him from the use the followers of Averroes were putting him to. But in doing this, Thomas encountered a handicap: He belonged to the mendicant orders, who had the misfortune of having put Joachim of Fiore in circulation along with another band of apocalyptic heretics who represented a grave danger for the established order, for the Church and for the State. So the reactionary masters of the Faculty of Theology, with the fearsome Guillaume de Saint-Amour at their head, could easily say that mendicant friars were all Joachimite heretics, and wanted to teach Aristotle, the master of the Averroes-inspired atheistic materialists.

But Thomas, on the contrary, was neither a heretic nor a revolutionary. He has been called a "concordian." For him it was a matter of reconciling the new science with the science of revelation, changing everything so that nothing would change.

In this plan he showed an extraordinary amount of good sense and (master of theological refinements) a great adherence to natural reality and earthly equilibrium. Mind you, Thomas did not aristotelianize Christianity; he christianized Aristotle. He never thought that with reason everything could be understood, but that everything is understood through faith; he wanted to say only that faith was not in conflict with reason, and that therefore it was possible to enjoy the luxury of reason, emerging from the universe of hallucination. And so it is clear why in the architecture of his works the main chapters speak only of God, angels, the soul, virtues, eternal life; but, within these chapters, everything finds a place that is, more than rational, "reasonable." Within the theological architecture you understand why man knows things, why his body is made in a certain way, why he has to examine facts and opinions to make a decision, and resolve contradictions without concealing them, trying to reconcile them openly. With this Thomas gave the church once more a doctrine that, without taking away a fraction of its power, left the communities free to decide whether to be monarchist or republican, and it distinguishes for example among the various types and rights in property, going so far as to say that the right to property does exist, but for possession, not use. Or, in other words, I have the right to possess a building, but if there are people living in hovels, reason demands that I grant the use to those who do not possess the equivalent (I remain owner of the building, but the others must live there even if this offends my egoism). And so on. These are all solutions based on equilibrium and on that virtue that he called "prudence," whose job was to "retain the memory of gained experience, to have an exact sense of ends, prompt attention to situations, rational and progressive investigation, circumspection of opportunities, precaution in complexities, and discernment of exceptional conditions."

It works, because this mystic who was so eager to lose himself in the beatific contemplation of God to whom the human soul aspires "by nature" was also alert, in a human way, to natural values and respected rational discourse.

It must be remembered that, before him, when the text of an ancient author was studied, the commentator or the copyist, when he came upon something that clashed with revealed religion, either scratched out the "erroneous" sentences or marked them with a question mark, to alert the reader, or else they shifted the words to the margin. But what did Thomas do, instead? He aligned the divergent opinions, clarified the meaning of each, questioned everything, even the revealed datum, enumerated the possible objections, and essayed the final mediation. Everything had to be done in public, just as, in his day, the *disputatio* was public: The tribunal of reason was in operation.

Then, if you read closely, in every case the datum of faith came to prevail over everything else and led to the untangling of the question; in other words, God and revealed truth preceded and guided the movement of secular reason. This has been made clear by the most acute and affectionate Thomas scholars, like Etienne Gilson. Nobody has ever said that Thomas was Galileo. Thomas simply gave the church a doctrinal system that put her in agreement with the natural world. And he won, at lightning speed. The dates are explicit. Before him it was asserted that "the spirit of Christ does not reign where the spirit of Aristotle lives"; in 1210 the Greek philosopher's books of natural history were still forbidden, and the ban continued through the following decades, as Thomas had these texts translated by his collaborators and commented on them. But in 1255 all of Aristotle was allowed.

After the death of Thomas, as we mentioned, there was an attempt at reaction, but finally Catholic doctrine was aligned along Aristotelian positions. The dominion and spiritual authority of Benedetto Croce over fifty years of Italian culture was as nothing compared to the authority Thomas displayed by changing in forty years the whole cultural policy of the Christian world. Hence Thomism. That is to say, Thomas gave Catholic thought such a complete frame that, since then, Catholic thought can no longer shift anything. At most, with the scholastic Counter-Reformation, it developed Thomas, gave us a Jesuit Thomism, a Dominican Thomism, even a Franciscan Thomism, where the shades of Bonaventure, Duns Scotus, and Ockham stir. But Thomas cannot be touched. Thomas's constructive eagerness for a new system becomes, in the Thomistic tradition, the conservative vigilance of an untouchable system. Where Thomas swept away everything in order to build anew, scholastic Thomism tries to touch nothing and performs wonders of pseudo-Thomistic tightrope walking to make the new fit into the frame of Thomas's system. The tension and eagerness for knowledge that the fat Thomas possessed to the maximum degree shift then into heretical movements and into the Protestant Reformation. Thomas's frame is left, but not the intellectual effort it cost to make a frame that, then, was truly "different."

Naturally it was his fault: He is the one who offered the church a method of conciliation of the tensions and a nonconflictual absorption of everything that could not be avoided. He is the one who taught how to distinguish contradictions in order to mediate them harmoniously. Once the trick was clear, they thought that Thomas's lesson was this: Where yes and no are opposed, create a "nes." But Thomas did this at a time when saying "nes" signified not stopping, but taking a step forward, and exposing the cards on the table.

So it is surely licit to ask what Thomas Aquinas would do if he were alive today; but we have to answer that, in any case, he would not write another *Summa Theologica*. He would come to

267

terms with Marxism, with the physics of relativity, with formal logic, with existentialism and phenomenology. He would comment not on Aristotle, but on Marx and Freud. Then he would change his method of argumentation, which would become a bit less harmonious and conciliatory. And finally he would realize that one cannot and must not work out a definitive, concluded system, like a piece of architecture, but a sort of mobile system, a loose-leaf *Summa*, because in his encyclopedia of the sciences the notion of historical temporariness would have entered. I can't say whether he would still be a Christian. But let's say he would be. I know for sure that he would take part in the celebrations of his anniversary only to remind us that it is not a question of deciding how still to use what he thought, but to think new things. Or at least to learn from him how you can think cleanly, like a man of your own time. After which I wouldn't want to be in his shoes.

1974

The Comic
and the Rule

Of the many questions that make up the panorama of problems connected with the comic, I will confine myself to just one, for reasons of space, and will take the others for granted. The question may be badly formulated; it may even be contested as a question. Nevertheless, it is, in itself, an *endoxon* that has to be borne in mind. Crude as it may be, it contains some germ of problematic truth.

The tragic (and the dramatic)—it is said—are *universal*. At a distance of centuries we still grieve at the tribulations of Oedipus and Orestes, and even without sharing the ideology of Homais we are distressed by the tragedy of Emma Bovary. The comic, on the other hand, seems bound to its time, society, cultural anthropology. We understand the drama of the protagonist of *Rashomon*, but we don't understand when and why the Japanese laugh. It is an effort to find Aristophanes comic, and it takes more culture to laugh at Rabelais than it does to weep at the death of the paladin Orlando.

It is true, one may object, that a "universal" comic does exist:

custard-pie-in-the-face, for example, or the braggart soldier falling into the mud, the white nights of the husbands frustrated by Lysistrata. But at this point it could be said that the tragic that survives is not only the equally universally tragic (the mother who loses her child, the death of the beloved), but also the more individual tragic. Even without knowing the accusation against him, we suffer as Socrates dies slowly from the feet toward the heart, whereas without a degree in classics we don't know exactly why the Socrates of Aristophanes should make us laugh.

The difference exists even when contemporary works are considered: Anyone is distressed in seeing *Apocalypse Now*, whatever his nationality; whereas for Woody Allen you have to be fairly cultivated. Danny Kaye did not always make people laugh; and Cantinflas, the idol of Mexican audiences in the '50's, left us non-Mexicans cold; the comedians of American TV are not for export (no one in Italy has ever heard the name of Sid Caesar; Lenny Bruce is equally unknown), just as our Italians Alberto Sordi and Totò cannot be exported to a number of countries.

So, in reconstructing a part of the lost Aristotle, it is not enough to say that in tragedy we have the downfall of a person of noble condition, neither too wicked nor too good, for whom we can in any case feel sympathy, and at his violation of the moral or religious code we feel pity for his fate and terror at the suffering that will strike him but could also strike us, and so finally his punishment is the purification of his sin and of our temptations; and, conversely, in the comic we have the violation of a rule committed by a person of lower degree, of bestial character, toward whom we feel a sense of superiority, so that we do not identify ourselves with his downfall, which in any case does not move us because the outcome will not be bloody.

Nor can we be satisfied with the reflection that in the violation of the rule on the part of a character so different from us we not only feel the security of our own impunity but also enjoy the savor of transgression by an intermediary. Since he is paying for us, we can allow ourselves the vicarious pleasure of a transgression that offends a rule we have secretly wanted to violate, but without risk. All these aspects are unquestionably at work in the comic, but if these were all then we would be unable to explain why this difference in universality exists between the two rival genres.

So the point does not (not only) lie in the transgression of the rule and in the inferior character of the comic hero. The point that interests me is, on the contrary, this: What is our awareness of the violated rule?

We can eliminate the first misunderstanding: that in the tragic the rule is universal, hence its violation involves us, while in the comic the rule is particular, local (limited to a given period, a specific culture). To be sure this would explain the loss of universality: An act of cannibalism would be tragic, a comic act would be a Chinese cannibal's eating one of his fellows with chopsticks instead of knife and fork (and naturally it would be comic for us, but not for the Chinese, who would still find the act fairly tragic).

Actually, the violated rules of the tragic are not necessarily universal. Universal, they say, is the horror of incest; but Orestes' obligation to kill his own mother would not be universal. And we may ask ourselves why today, in a period of great moral permissiveness, we should find the situation of a Madame Bovary tragic. It would not be so in a polyandrous society, or even in New York; let the good lady indulge her extramarital whims without making such a fuss about it. This excessively repentant provincial woman should make us laugh today as much as the main character in Chekhov's "The Death of a Civil Servant," who, having sneezed on an important person sitting in front of him at the theater, then goes on repeating his apologies beyond all reasonable limits.

What is typical of the tragic, before, during, and after the enactment of the violation of the rule, is a long examination of the nature of the rule. In tragedy it is the chorus itself that offers us the depiction of the social "frames" in whose violation the tragic consists. The function of the chorus is precisely that of explaining to us at every step what the Law is: This is the only way we can understand its violation and its fatal consequences. And *Madame*

271

Bovary is a work that, first of all, explains how adultery is to be condemned, or at least how severely the contemporaries of the protagonist condemned it. And *The Blue Angel* tells us, first and foremost, how a middle-aged professor *should not* run amok with a chorus girl; and *Death in Venice* tells us chiefly how a middle-aged professor *should not* fall in love with an adolescent boy.

The second step (not chronological, but logical) is then to tell how they couldn't avoid doing wrong, and couldn't help but be swept away. And precisely because the rule is reiterated (either as assertion in terms of ethical value, or as recognition of a social constriction).

The tragic justifies the violation (in terms of fate, passion, or whatever) but doesn't eliminate the rule. This is why it is universal: It explains *always* why the tragic act must inspire pity and fear. Which amounts to saying that every tragic work is also a lesson in cultural anthropology, and allows us to identify with a rule that perhaps is not ours.

The tragic can describe the situation of a member of an anthropophagous community who rejects the cannibalistic ritual, but it will be tragic to the degree that the story convinces us of the majesty and weight of the duty of anthropophagy. A story that narrates the sufferings of a dyspeptic and vegetarian anthropophagist who doesn't like human flesh, but fails to explain to us at length and convincingly how noble and proper anthropophagy is, will be only a comic story.

The confirmation of these theoretical proposals would lie in showing that comic works take the rule for granted, and don't bother to restate it. And this, in fact, is what I believe and what I suggest investigating. Translated into terms of textual semiotics, the hypothesis could be formulated in this way: There exists a rhetorical device, which concerns the figures of thought, in which, given a social or intertextual "frame" or scenario already known to the audience, you display the variation without, however, making it explicit in discourse.

The fact that suppressing the violated norm is typical of figures of thought seems evident in irony. Which, as it consists of asserting the opposite (of what? of what is or what is believed socially), dies when the opposite of the opposite is made explicit. At most, the fact that the opposite is being asserted may be suggested by the inflection, but irony must not be commented on, there must be no assertion of "not-A," bearing in mind that "instead-of-A" is the case. For the fact that instead-of-A is the case is something everyone must know, but no one must say.

What are the scenarios that the comic violates without having to repeat them? First of all, the common scenarios, the pragmatic rules of symbolic interaction that society takes for granted. The pie in the face makes us laugh because we normally assume that, at a party, pies are eaten and not thrown at other people. Because we know that kissing a lady's hand means lightly grazing it with the lips, a comic situation arises when someone seizes the hand and covers it greedily with wet, smacking kisses. (Or he may proceed from the hand to the wrist and then to the arm—a situation no longer comic and perhaps even tragic in an erotic relationship, an act of carnal violence.)

Look at the conversational maxims of H. P. Grice. It is pointless to say that in everyday interaction we violate them constantly. Not so. We observe them, or else we accept them to give flavor, against the background of their unheeded existence, to conversational implicature, rhetorical figure, artistic license. Precisely because rules, even unconsciously, are accepted, their unmotivated violation becomes comic.

(1) *Maxim of quantity*: Make your contribution as informative as is required. Comic situation: "Excuse me, do you know what time it is?" "Yes."

(2) *Maxim of quality*: (a) Do not say what you believe to be false. Comic situation: "My God, I beseech thee, give me some

proof of thy nonexistence!" (b) Do not say that for which you lack adequate evidence. Comic situation: "I find Maritain's thought unacceptable and irritating. Thank God I've never read any of his books!" (declaration by a university professor of mine, personal communication, February 1953).

(3) *Maxim of relation*: Be relevant. Comic situation:
"Can you drive a motorboat?" "Why, you bet your life! I did my military service in Death Valley!"

(4) *Maxim of manner*: Avoid obscurity of expression and ambiguity. Be brief and avoid unnecessary prolixity. Be orderly. I don't believe it necessary to suggest comic results of this violation. Often they are involuntary.

Naturally, I insist, this requisite is not sufficient. Conversational maxims can be violated with normal results (implicature), with tragic results (depiction of social maladjustment), with poetic results. Other requisites are necessary, and I refer the reader to other typologies of the comic effect. What I want to insist on here is that in the above-mentioned instances comic effect is achieved (*ceteris paribus*) if the rule is not cited but assumed as implicit.

The same thing happens with the violation of intertextual scenarios. Years ago *Mad* magazine specialized in little cartoon scenes from "the movies we would like to see." For example, outlaw bands in the West tying a girl to the train tracks in the prairie. Successive frames, in a Griffith-like sequence, the train approaching, girl weeping, the good guys riding to the rescue, progressive acceleration of the cross-cutting, and, at the end, the train crushing the girl. Variations: the sheriff who prepares for the final duel obeying all the rules of the Western, and in the end is shot by the villain; the swordsman who gains admittance to the castle where the bad guy is keeping the beauty prisoner, he swings across the splendid great hall on the chandelier and the drapery, engages in a fantastic duel with the villain, and at the end is run through. In all these cases, to enjoy the violation, the rule of the genre must be presupposed, and considered inviolable.

If this is true, and I believe it would be difficult to declare the hypothesis false, then the metaphysics of the comic should also change, including the Bakhtinian metaphysic or meta-anthropology of carnivalization. The comic seems to belong to the people, liberating, subversive, because it gives license to violate the rule. But it gives such license precisely to those who have so absorbed the rule that they also presume it is inviolable. The rule violated by the comic is so acknowledged that there is no need to reaffirm it. That is why carnival can take place only once a year. It takes a year of ritual observance for the violation of the ritual precepts to be enjoyed (*semel* — in fact — *in anno*).

In a world of absolute permissiveness and complete anomie no carnival is possible, because nobody would remember what is being called (parenthetically) into question. Carnival comic, the moment of transgression, can exist only if a background of unquestioned observance exists. Otherwise the comic would not be liberating at all. Because, in order to display itself as liberation, it would require (before and after its appearance) the triumph of observance. And this would explain why the mass-media universe is, in fact, at once a universe of control and regulation of the consensus and a universe based on the commerce and consumption of comic patterns. Laughing is allowed precisely because before and after the laughing, weeping is inevitable. The comedian doesn't need to reiterate the rule because he is sure it is known, accepted without discussion, and it will remain all the more so after the comic license has allowed — within a given space and through an intermediary mask — violating it in jest.

"Comic" is, in any case, an umbrella term, like "play." We must still ask ourselves if, in the various subspecies of this highly ambiguous genre, there isn't room for a kind of activity that plays differently with the rules, to allow exercises also in the interstices of the tragic and, eluding by surprise, this murky commerce with the code, which would condemn the comic in general to act as the best safeguard and celebration of the code.

I believe we can identify this category with the one Pirandello opposed to the comic, or articulated with respect to it, calling it humor.

The comic is the perception of the opposite; humor is the feeling of it. We need not discuss this still-Crocian terminology. An example of the comic might be a decrepit old woman who makes herself up like a young girl; humor would insist on asking also why the old woman acts like that.

In this development I no longer feel superior and detached toward the bestial character who acts against the proper rules; I begin to identify with him, I suffer his drama, and my laugh is transformed into a smile. Another example that Pirandello offers is that of Don Quixote as opposed to the Astolfo of Ariosto. Astolfo arriving on the moon riding a fabled hippogriff and, at nightfall, seeking a hotel as if he were a commercial traveler, is comic. But not Don Quixote, because we realize that his battle with the windmills reproduces the illusion of Cervantes, who fought and lost a limb and suffered imprisonment for his illusions of glory.

I would say, furthermore, that the illusion of Don Quixote is humorous, when he knows or should know, as the reader knows, that the dreams he is pursuing are by now confined in the possible worlds of an outmoded chivalrous literature. But then, at this point, Pirandello's hypothesis meets ours. It is not by chance that *Don Quixote* begins with a library. Cervantes' work does not assume knowledge of the intertextual scenarios on which the adventures of the madman of La Mancha are modeled, reversing their outcomes. It explains them, repeats them, discusses them again, just as a tragic work recalls the rules that will be violated.

Humor thus acts like the tragic, with perhaps this difference: In the tragic the reiterated rule is part of the narrative universe

(Bovary), or, when it is reiterated at the level of the structure of discourse (the tragic chorus) it still is uttered by the characters; in humor, on the other hand, the description of the rule should appear as an intrusion, though concealed, of the author, who reflects on the social scenarios in which the enunciated character should believe. Humor then would be excessive in metalinguistic detachment.

Even when a single character speaks of himself and upon himself, he is split into judge and judged. I am thinking of the humor of Woody Allen, where the threshold between the "voices" is hard to distinguish, but, so to speak, makes itself heard. This threshold is more evident in the humor of Manzoni, marking the detachment between the author, who judges the moral and cultural world of Don Abbondio, and the actions (interior and exterior) of Don Abbondio himself.

In this way humor would not be, like the comic, victim of the rule it presupposes, but would represent the criticism of it, conscious and explicit. Humor would always be metasemiotic and metatextual. The comic of language would belong to the same breed, from Aristotelian witticisms to the puns of Joyce. To say, "Green ideas without color sleep furiously" could be (if it didn't resemble poetry) a case of verbal comic, because the grammatical norm is presupposed, and it is only by presupposing it that its violation appears evident (hence this sentence makes grammarians laugh, but not literary critics, who are thinking of other rules, already of a rhetorical nature, and hence of second degree, that would make the sentence normal).

But to say that *Finnegans Wake* is a "Scherzarade" reconfirms, as it conceals, the presence of Scheherazade, of the charade and the scherzo in the very body of the transgressive expression. And it shows the kinship, the basic ambiguity of the three repeated and denied lexemes, and the paranomastic possibility that made them fragile. For this reason anacoluthon can be comic and the lapsus for which we are not asked the reasons (buried in the very structure of what others call the signifying chain, but which is actually the ambiguous and contradictory structure of the encyclopedia). Wit, on the other hand, and the pun are already kin to humor: They do not arouse pity for human beings, but distrust (which involves them) of language, in its fragility.

But perhaps I am confusing categories that must be further distinguished. In reflecting on this fact, and on the relationship between reflection and its times (chronological times, that is), I am perhaps opening the door, just a crack, onto a new genre, the humorous reflection on the mechanism of symposia, where one is asked to reveal in thirty minutes what is *le propre de l'homme*.

1980

7

DE INTERPRETATIONE

De Interpretatione

The Difficulty of Being Marco Polo
(On the Occasion of Antonioni's China Film)

What happened in Venice last Saturday fell somewhere between science fiction and comedy *all'italiana*, with a dash of Western thrown in. In the wagon train circle, desperately resisting, were the Venice Biennale officials. Around them galloped Chinese diplomats, the Italian foreign minister, the Italian ambassador to Peking, the Italian-Chinese Association, the police, firemen, and other Sinophiles. The story is noteworthy: China was protesting the imminent showing of Antonioni's documentary *Chung Kuo* at La Fenice. The Italian government had done everything possible to prevent the showing, while the Biennale had resisted the government in the name of the right to know and of freedom of artistic expression; at the last moment the prefect, coming to the aid of Peking, discovered that La Fenice was unusable as a movie hall (after nothing but films had been seen there all week). The president of the Biennale let drop at a press conference a few well-chosen words of "pity" for the prefect, "forced into such a vile business," and got on the phone to his colleagues. Within half an hour he got hold of the Olimpia movie house, where Barbra Streisand was fleeing, pursued by stampeding cattle. Here the screening took place while police held an enormous, tense crowd at bay so that no incident could give the prefect (their direct superior) an excuse to cancel even this last expedient. Antonioni, nervous and troubled, was once again suffering his personal and paradoxical drama—the antifascist artist who went to China inspired by affection and respect and who found himself accused of being a fascist, a reactionary in the pay of Soviet revisionism and American imperialism, hated by 800 million persons.

Now the Biennale did with firmness and dignity what should have been done long ago: It gave us the chance to see and see again the three and a half hours of incriminated documentary, so that now we can finally open a political and aesthetic debate about it.

What is Antonioni's China? Those who saw it on TV remember it as a work that displayed, from the start, an attitude of warm and cordial participation in the great saga of the Chinese people; an act of justice on TV's part which finally revealed to millions of viewers a real China, human and peaceful beyond any Western propagandistic schema. All the same, the Chinese have denounced this film as an inconceivable act of hostility, an insult to the Chinese people.

It has been said that Antonioni's film is only a pretext, a casus belli chosen by a Peking power group to advance the anti-Confucian campaign. But even if that were true, the fact remains that a casus belli, to work, must be credible: A world war can be started by the murder of an archduke, but not by the murder of a footman. Where is the archduke in Antonioni's documentary?

So we must look at the entire work from a different viewpoint: not from an Italian point of view, but from a Chinese point of view. This is not easy, since it amounts to activating all one's anthropological antennae, alert to the fact that words and images acquire different meanings according to the cultures which interpret them. Saturday night I got lucky, because I had the opportunity to see the film while a young Chinese movie critic from Hong Kong—who regarded and still regards this work sternly and polemically, identifying himself with the values and culture of the People's Republic—provided a shot-by-shot commentary on it.

Now serious ideological objections can unquestionably be made to Antonioni's work. A Western artist, inclined to plumb the depths of existential problems and to emphasize the representation of personal relationships rather than abstract dialectical problems and the class struggle, tells us about the daily life of the Chinese within the revolution instead of showing the revolution as the moment of a primary contradiction, within which poles of secondary contradiction develop. Furthermore, a director capable of speaking with masterly skill by stressing the inessential, the secondary episode charged with multiple meanings and subtle ambiguities, tries to open a dialogue with an audience better accustomed to great frontal oppositions, symbolic characterizations in clear ideological cipher. Here is enough to start a serious debate about the ends and means of revolutionary art, and it is no use for Antonioni to defend the rights (for us, incontestable) of his poetic vision, of his artistic eye's special interpretation; another aesthetic opposes him, an aesthetic which seems to negate the rights of art, an aesthetic which in reality reaffirms them but in a way that is foreign to Western tradition. If this were all, a splendid chance for confrontation would have presented itself, and *China* would have become an occasion for mass showings followed by political debate. Instead *China* unleashed an almost physical reaction, a violent and offended rejection.

The *China* question reminds us that when political debate and artistic representation involve different cultures on a worldwide scale, art and politics are also mediated by anthropology and thus by semiotics. We cannot initiate a dialogue between different cul-

283

tures on identical class problems if we do not first resolve the problem of the symbolic superstructures through which different civilizations represent to themselves the same political and social problems.

What discourse did Antonioni address to the Western public with his film? In a few words, I would say the following: "Here is a vast and unknown country that I can only look at, not explain in depth. I know that this country used to live under immensely unjust feudal conditions, and now I see the beginnings, through daily struggle, of a new justice. To Western eyes this justice might have the look of widespread, austere poverty. But this poverty creates the possibility of dignified survival, it produces people who are calm and much more human than we are, at times it comes close to our ideal of serenity, harmony with nature, affection in personal relationships, tenacious inventiveness that resolves with simplicity the problem of redistribution of wealth in an often greedy territory. I am not so much interested in seeing those cases where the Chinese were able to construct industries like Western ones (we know that they even have the atomic bomb); it seems to me more interesting to show you how they were able to construct a factory, or hospital, or child-care center from a few scraps, under working conditions based on reciprocal respect. I want to tell you how much sorrow and how much work that task cost, and suggest to you the measure of happiness—different from ours—that it all could encompass, perhaps also for us."

All this entailed the search for China as a potential utopia by the frenetic, neurotic West. When our art critics speak of *arte povera* they mean a kind of art rescued from the commercial gallery circuit, and when they say *medicina povera* they mean a medicine that substitutes the rediscovery of the relationship between human beings and medicinal herbs, and the possibility of a new, popular knowledge, for the poisoning of our pharmaceutical industries. But what sense can the same words have for a country where "poverty" meant, only a few decades ago, death by starvation for entire generations of children, class genocide, sickness, ignorance? And while the Chinese see a suddenly acquired collective "fortune," the film commentary speaks about a serene and just "poverty." Where the film means "simplicity" for "poverty," the Chinese viewer reads "failure." When his Chinese escorts told Antonioni, with pride, that a refinery had been built from nothing, using scavenged material, the film emphasizes the miracle of "this humble factory, made with discarded materials"—and Western taste for the ingeniousness of bricolage, to which we currently attribute aesthetic value, is at play in this linguistic formula. But the Chinese see in it an insistence on an "inferior" industry, just at the historical moment when they are successfully closing their industrial gap. When the film celebrates fealty to the past and proposes a model of integration between development and tradition, the Chinese (engaged in a struggle to destroy an unjust past) see praise of feudalism and an insinuation that nothing has changed.

The root of the misunderstanding becomes evident in a theatrical presentation with which Antonioni ends his documentary: Smiling Chinese athletes, dressed in vivid colors, guns slung on their shoulders, make their way up tall poles with acrobatic energy. This is Revolutionary China, which presents a strong picture of itself. But Antonioni's film offers a tender, docile picture. For us, gentleness is opposed to neurotic competition, but for the Chinese that docility decodes as resignation. Antonioni explores with realistic gusto the faces of the old and of children; but Chinese revolutionary art is not realistic, it is symbolic, and presents, in posters as in film, an "ideal type" that goes beyond ethnic characteristics (as if Sicilians decided, and with justification, to represent themselves through the faces of Sicilians of Norman ancestry, blond and blue-eyed). Doesn't it occur to us Italians to feel betrayed when a foreign film depicts us with the faces of Southern immigrants or Sardinian shepherds in costume, while we tend to identify our country with freeways and factories? The narration states (and it is a positive thing in our eyes) that the Chinese sur-round suffering and sentiment with shame and reserve. And a culture that rewards dynamism, enthusiasm, and extroverted competitiveness reads "reserve" as "hypocrisy." Antonioni thinks about the individual dimension and speaks of sufferings as an uneliminable constant in the life of every person, bound up with passion and death; the Chinese read "suffering" as a social ill and see in it the insinuation that injustice has not been eliminated, but rather covered up.

Thus we see how the now famous criticism in *Renmin Ribao* could regard the shot of the Nanking bridge as an attempt to make it appear distorted and unstable, because a culture that prizes frontal representation and symmetrical distance shots cannot accept the language of Western cinema, which, to suggest impressiveness, foreshortens and frames from below, prizing asymmetry and tension over balance. And the shot of Peking's T'ien An Men Square is seen as a denunciation of swarming mass disorder, whereas for Antonioni such a shot is the picture of life, and an ordered shot would be the picture of death or would evoke the Nuremberg stadium.

Antonioni depicts the vestiges of feudal superstition, and then immediately afterward he shows students returning to work in the fields, spades slung over their shoulders, and the post-'68 viewer thinks that is justice: The Chinese critic sees another logic (today students work as hard in the fields as they did in the past) and becomes indignant. Cutting, too, is a language, and this language is historical, linked to different material conditions of life; the same shots can portray different things and different people. The same thing happens with colors, denounced by the Chinese as unbearably pale and cold, and rightly so, if you compare *China* with a film like *The Red Detachment of Women*, where extremely bright colors acquire a precise linguistic value and directly symbolize ideological positions.

I could go on at length and point out that the dialogue between people (and between people of the same class who live in different cultures) must be sustained by a historical and social awareness of cultural differences. We must not blame Antonioni, for he made a film for the Western public; but he might have realized that his film could not remain a work of art and would immediately acquire the weight of a diplomatic note—in which every word is fraught with ambivalence. The consultants of the People's Republic should have realized it too, since they showed Antonioni the places and things to film, insisting on the peaceful aspects of their society; and it was a year before those consultants were denounced by other critics who in their turn are now displaying remarkable ethnocentrism and proving incapable of seeing the different effects that the film can have inside and outside China.

But perhaps the greatest responsibility rests with the Italy-China Association, whose task is precisely that of resolving these misunderstandings, supporting on more than one level of "translation from culture to culture" the cause of understanding between peoples. In introducing the Chinese protest into Italy, the Association acted objectively as a factor of misunderstanding; it widened the gap and fomented a reactionary game (which enlisted willing ministers, prefects, police superintendents, and old-school diplomats for whom it is important for the Chinese to remain yellow, treacherous, inscrutable, and pig-tailed).

Finally, if useful mediation had been undertaken, we would then have been able to clarify the grossest misunderstandings. For example, the notorious scene of the pigs over which—for pure reasons of sound mix—a musical fragment is inserted. Unfortunately this fragment happened to resemble somewhat a well-known Chinese patriotic song, evoking in the Chinese viewer the same reaction that a bishop might experience seeing a clinch accompanied by the hymn *Tantum Ergo*. It seems there was a consultant from the People's Republic on hand who realized nothing and told no one about the blunder. And then there is the fact that the narration, intending to be dry and objective, leaves too much room to isolated words, which thus acquire a disproportionate value:

When it is said that a certain restaurant (rather modest from the outside) is the best in the city, probably the meaning is that it serves the best food, but the viewer could infer that it is the most imposing. And when a historical truth is related, such as the fact that modern Shanghai was laid out by colonial powers, a handbill distributed in Italy by the Italy–China Association maintains (in fact, without justification) that industrial Shanghai was built by the People's Republic "with the help of the imperialists." All these are slights that Antonioni could easily have avoided if only someone had brought them to his attention. But by now the situation has deteriorated beyond repair.

Now Chinese and Sinophiles have become rigid in their rejection. Antonioni has closed himself up again in his personal sorrow of the artist-in-good-faith and accepts only with difficulty the idea that from now on the debate will go far beyond his film and will involve on both sides — apart from political questions which elude us — unexorcised phantoms of ethnocentristic dogmatism and aesthetic exoticism, and symbolic superstructures that obscure material relations and delay the course of history. The Venice Biennale pointed a way; it reopened critical discussion. We hope that this will not be in vain.

Already last Saturday evening, after the showing, a more open debate was in the air, beyond scandalmongering. And to illustrate that fact, journalists' eyes were fixed on Antonioni and the young Chinese critic, who, at two in the morning, at a restaurant table, were polemically exchanging ideas and impressions. And in the corner, ignored by everyone, a young woman with soft, sensual eyes was following the discussion, accepting the fact that more important considerations were at stake and that the protagonist of the evening was the Chinese. This was the film actress Maria Schneider, but few would have recognized her.

1977

8

A THEORY OF
EXPOSITIONS

A Theory of
Expositions

What does Expo '67 — that unsurpassed, quintessential, classic World's Fair — mean in today's world? There are many possible answers, depending on the point of view from which we look at the phenomenon. We could give an interpretation in terms of cultural history, in sociological terms, in architectural terms, or from the point of view of visual, oral, or written communication. Since an exposition presents itself as a phenomenon of many faces, full of contradictions, open to various uses, we are probably entitled to interpret it from all these points of view. Perhaps in the end we shall discover that though the interpretations are different, they are complementary and not contradictory.

Expositions as Inventories

Spires, geodesic domes, molecular structures enlarged millions of times, cathedrals, shacks, monorails, space frames, astronauts' suits and helmets, moon rocks, rare minerals, the King of Bohemia's crown, Etruscan vases, Pompeiian corpses, a Magdeburg sphere, incense burners from Thailand, Persian rugs, Giuseppe Verdi's cravat, cars, TV sets, tractors, jewelry, transistors, wooden statues from the Renaissance, panoramic views of fairytale landscapes, electronic computers, boomerangs, an Ethiopian lion, an Australian kangaroo, Donatello's *David*, a photo of Marilyn Monroe, a mirror-labyrinth, a few hundred prefabricated dwellings, a plastic human brain, three parachutes, ten carousels . . .

At first contact and first reaction, exhibitions assume the form of an inventory, an enormous gathering of evidence from Stone to Space Age, an accumulation of objects useless and precious, an immense catalogue of things produced by man in all countries over the past ten thousand years, displayed so that humanity will not forget them. They seem to be a final recapitulation in the face of a hypothetical end of the world. Considering this aspect, we realize that the exhibition technique antedated the nineteenth century, when expositions were actually born, by several centuries. We can cite famous collections of objects gathered in past eras, when uncertainty about the future and fear of the apocalypse were dominant, when church and state attempted to summarize all the memorabilia of the past in a collection, in a fantastic accumulation of strange and marvelous objects, to save them from oblivion and the avalanche of history.

"We felt the need to transmit the description of the ornaments of the church with which God's hand, during our administration, has embellished his house, his beloved wife, fearing that Oblivion, jealous rival of Truth, will steal in and erase for the future this worthy example. . . ." In this way Suger, abbot of St. Denis in the twelfth century, began his description of liturgical objects, of ampulae, holy crosses, gems of a goblet "made of 140 ounces of gold, decorated with precious stones, amethysts, and topazes," and also of "a porphyry vase that was fashioned into a wondrous thing by the hand of a sculptor; after it had been in storage unused for many years, he transformed it from an amphora into the shape of an eagle." That was the period when cathedrals and princely courts assembled great collections of treasures, like that of the Archduke of Bavaria who owned 3,407 objects, including "an egg that an abbot had found inside another egg, some manna divinely supplied during a famine, a stuffed elephant, a hydra, and a basilisk," or the treasure of the Duc de Berry, which included a unicorn's horn; or the *Wunderkammern* of the sixteenth century, collections of diverse and wondrous objects, unconsciously anticipating the taste for the assemblage, for the "bricolage" of the pop artist who juxtaposes things out of context. (These collections also had a prestige function, to celebrate a dynasty or a town as a commercial, cultural, or religious center.) Only one thing made these classic collections different from modern expositions: the fact that they concerned the past and contained nothing which pointed to the future. It was only with the expositions of the nineteenth century that the marvels of the year 2000 began to be announced. And it is only with Disneyland and Disney World that concern with the Space Age is combined with nostalgia for a fairytale past.

But is an exposition today anything more than an adult Disneyland? Having been reminded that the zest for collection and assemblage is ancient and that it also represented apocalyptic insecurity and hope for the future, we realize that cultural history is no longer a guide for us. We can move on to a discussion of expositions in sociological terms.

A Collection of Goods

Entering any pavilion of Expo '67, entering a pavilion of any international trade fair, mentally reconstructing almost any of the pavilions from expositions of the last century, one inevitably recalls the opening phrase of Karl Marx's *Das Kapital*, "The wealth of those societies in which the capitalist mode of production prevails presents itself as 'an immense accumulation of commodities.' " But these goods, which generally are represented as visible signs of exchange value overcoming use value, take on in expositions another aspect, which was emphasized by Walter Benjamin in the essays he wrote some decades ago on nineteenth-century expositions and their influence on the culture of that period.

The world exhibitions glorify the exchange value of commodities. They create a framework in which commodities' intrinsic value is eclipsed. They open up a phantasmagoria that people enter to be amused. The entertainment industry facilitates this by elevating people to the level of commodities.*

The merchandise is "enthroned," as Benjamin says, "with an aura of amusement surrounding it." A boat, a car, a TV set are not for sailing, riding, watching, but are meant to be looked at for their own sake. They are not even meant to be bought, but just to be absorbed by the nerves, by the taut, excited senses, as one absorbs the vortex of projected colors in a discothèque. The fact that the goods exist does not make one want to own them; it is enough to look and listen, but to goods instead of to colors and music. Or else we "experience" goods with music and colors, but here the goods take on the value of a chromatic area, of a note or a scent. At such a display even those who possess few worldly goods do not feel humiliated. The merchandise becomes play, color, light, show. The objects are not desired in themselves, although the show is enjoyed as a whole; every wish is gone and what remains is pure amusement and excitement.

In this sense of an enormous collection of goods, an exposition could be seen as representing the Missa Solemnis of traditional capitalist society; thus it is ironic that in Montreal it was the Soviet Union's pavilion that conveyed the most feeling. There are many possible explanations. The first and most obvious is that

---

* *Reflections*, trans. Edmund Jephcott (New York: Harcourt Brace Jovanovich, 1978), p. 152.

a large part of the exhibition was designed by Western Europeans, from Italian companies, in fact, who generally work on trade fairs. In designing the Soviet pavilion, they used the same exhibition techniques employed for commercial fairs. The second explanation is that in its struggle for prosperity and for more consumer goods, Soviet society has returned to the formal idiom of the industrialized society of the last century, just as realism in Soviet painting represented a return to the realism of the salons, the Beaux Arts of the nineteenth century. In this sense the Soviet pavilion, even if it looked dated (especially after the Lausanne exposition), represented progress in comparison with the style of official state art. This progress could be seen if one compared the pavilion itself with the big stone hammer and sickle in front of it, which was pure Stalin style.

But the third explanation is the simplest and the least flattering: The bug of grandeur kills invention. When a government wants to emphasize its productive hyperefficiency, it ends up suffocating the inventiveness of the designers. The Soviet pavilion, in its exhibitionism, became the pathetic brother of the French pavilion, which seemed more modern but was equally bombastic and false. The French interior showed the same self-satisfaction in displaying an immense collection of merchandise, even if the display was more sophisticated. The references to the future and to outer space in the French pavilion deceived no one. Externally its steel edifice, which appeared to be both powerful and delicate, was a construction of slender, nervous plates, and the interior displayed tensed steel cables, as in a sculpture by Lippold or Gabo, but these elements had no structural function: They did not support anything; they were added as pure ornamentation, pretending to have a function. In such cases architecture is killed. Styling remains. The collection of goods inside confirmed this: A pompous display of a multitude of objects does not necessarily create anything. The Russian and French pavilions seemed old because they were inspired by the concept of the last century's expositions (although these broke the ground for the architecture of the future with the Eiffel Tower and the Crystal Palace). They seemed old because they still displayed objects, whereas in our century industrial society has invented another kind of exposition. The exposition today does not display goods, or if it does, it uses the goods as a means, as a pretext to present something else. And this something else is the exposition itself. As in Lausanne in 1964, the Montreal exposition exposed itself.

How an Exposition Exposes Itself

In contemporary expositions a country no longer says, "Look what I produce" but "Look how smart I am in presenting what I produce." The "planetary society" has already standardized industrial production to such a degree that the fact of showing a tractor or a space capsule no longer differentiates one image of civilization from another. The only solution left is symbolic. Each country shows itself by the way in which it is able to present the same thing other countries could also present. The prestige game is won by the country that best tells what it does, independently of what it actually does. The architectural solutions confirm this view of expositions.

In order to understand the problem better, let us assume that architecture (and design, in its overall sense) is an act of communication, a message, of which the parts or the whole can perform the double action of every communication, connotation and denotation. A word or a phrase can denote something. The word "moonlight," for example, means, unequivocally, the light that the earth's satellite gives off. At the same time it has a broader connotation depending on the historical period and education of the person who communicates or receives a message using the word. Thus it could connote "a romantic situation," "love," "feeling," and so on. In architecture, it seems at first that the inherent function of every item prevents us from regarding it as a message, as a medium of communication (a staircase is used for going up, a chair for sitting); if architecture communicates something, it is in the form of a symbol. The colonnade by Bernini in St. Peter's Square in Rome can be interpreted as an immense pair of arms, open to embrace all the faithful. Aside from this, a product of architecture or design is simply like a mechanism that suggests a function and acts on the user only as a stimulus that requires a behavioral response: A staircase, because it is one step after another, does not allow one to walk on a plane, but stimulates the walker to ascend. A stimulus is not a symbol; a stimulus acts directly at the physiological level and has nothing to do with culture.

But as Roland Barthes wrote in his *Elements of Semiology*, as soon as society can be said to exist, every use also becomes the sign of that same use. The staircase becomes for everybody the conventional sign to denote ascending, whether or not anyone ascends a given staircase in fact. The known connection between form and function mainly means this: The form of the object must fundamentally and unequivocally communicate the function for which the object was designed, and only if it denotes this function unambiguously is one stimulated to use it the way it was intended. The architectural product acts as a stimulus only if it first acts as a sign. So the object, according to the linguistic theory of de Saussure, is the signifier, denoting exactly and conventionally that signified which is its function. Nevertheless, even if a chair communicates immediately the fact of sitting, the chair does not fulfill only this function and does not have only this meaning. If the chair is a throne, its use is not only to have somebody sitting on it; it has to make somebody sit with dignity, and should stress the act of sitting with dignity, through various details appropriate to royalty. For example, it might have eagles on the arms of the chair and a crown surmounting the back. These connotations of royalty are functions of a throne and are so important that as long as they are there, one can minimize or even forget the primary function of sitting comfortably. Frequently, for that matter, a throne, in order to indicate royalty, demands that the occupant sit stiffly (that is, uncomfortably) because providing a seat is only one of the meanings of a throne and not the most important one. More important are the symbolic connotations that the throne must communicate and whose communication reinforces its social function.

This continuous oscillation between primary function (the conventional use of the object, or its most direct or elementary meaning) and secondary functions (its related meanings, based on cultural conventions, and mental and semantic associations) forms the object as a system of signs, a message. The history of architecture and design is the history of the dialectic between these two functions. The history of civilization influences the history of architecture in such a way that objects in which the two functions were harmoniously integrated are in time deprived of one of these functions, so that the other becomes dominant; or else the original functions change, creating quite a different object. The ruins of the Greek and Roman temples and amphitheaters provide an example of the first case, where the primary function, which was to gather people for prayer or entertainment, is largely absent from the mind of the contemporary viewer, who sees them in terms of their secondary functions, in the light of notions like "paganism" and "classicism" and the expression of a particular sense of harmony, rhythm, and monumentality. The Egyptian pyramids offer an example of the second case. Not only is their primary function that of a tomb, lost to us today; even their original connotation, based on astrological and mathematical symbolism, in which the pyramidal shape had exact communicative functions, has lost its meaning. What is left is a series of connotations established by history and "carried" by the monument. We recognize these connotations in the monument because we are educated to the same symbolism.

With its voracious vitality, history robs architecture of its meaning and endows it with new meaning. Some massive forms that have lost all original capacity to communicate, such as the statues on Easter Island or the stones of Stonehenge, now appear to be enormous messages, overcomplex in relation to the actual information they can communicate to us. But they may spur us to find new meanings instead, just as Chateaubriand, who could not understand the original social function of the Gothic cathedrals, interpreted them in new ways.

The architecture of the contemporary exposition is used to connote symbolic meanings, minimizing its primary functions. Naturally, an exposition building must allow people to come in and circulate and see something. But its utilitarian function is too small in comparison with its semantic apparatus, which aims at other types of communication. In an exposition, architecture and design explode their dual communicative nature, sacrificing denotation to very widespread connotation. If we look at the buildings in an exposition as structures to live in or pass through, they are out of scale, but they make sense if we look at them as media of communication and suggestion. The paradox in an exposition is that the buildings, which are supposed to last just a few months, look as if they have survived, or will survive, for centuries. In an exposition, architecture proves to be message first, then utility; meaning first, then stimulus. To conclude: In an exposition we show not the objects but the exposition itself. The basic ideology of an exposition is that the packaging is more important than the product, meaning that the building and the objects in it should communicate the value of a culture, the image of a civilization.

What Kind of Communication?

We know that the image of a culture can be communicated in various ways. Even the process of connotation has its own rules. It is based on a conventional code, which is less rigid than the code for denotation. "Moonlight" connotes "romantic moment" on the basis of a fairly widespread cultural code and connotes "Beethoven" on the basis of more complex cultural assumptions, which are less conventional in that they are accessible only to a few. An exposition can also communicate rather ambiguously, through "open symbols," giving a broad possible field of interpretation to the perceiver (because of this broad field such symbols are, of course, open to misinterpretation), or through less equivocal means. Let us give four different examples. First, in the British pavilion in Montreal, in the center of a massive and irregular building, there was a tall, tapered tower, seemingly cut off before reaching its pointed apex. On the flat roof was a three-dimensional abstract composition inspired by the Union Jack. Some might interpret this as "tension in progress," like a still moment in the process of growth, but others might recall a Celtic menhir. The interior, presenting a view of the progress of British civilization from Stonehenge to great contemporary scientists and writers, could suggest either interpretation; but the system of connotations worked inevitably at other levels, and it was difficult to make a connection between the building's suggestions and the image of contemporary Britain that we all have. For the building, full of ingrown architectural recollections, appeared oddly opposed to the idea of the dynamic and open-minded country that produced Mary Quant, Bertrand Russell, and the Beatles, and seemed more to communicate an imperial pompousness, a Babylonian style, a taste for the monument *aere perennius*, for the Tower of Babel erected as a challenge to heaven and the centuries. So the fame of symbolic connotations generated continuous meanings, all quite contrary to the image that the country wanted to give of itself and tried to present in the interior. When a symbol is too open, it becomes ambiguous, overstepping the limits of communication.

Secondly, symbols can be conventionalized visually when their various graphic components are based on a unified, commonly understood code. For instance, a medieval allegory originates from the development of a metaphor, and the metaphor originates from a condensed similitude. When we compare the proud and farsighted eye of a king to the eye of an eagle, the eagle becomes in itself a symbol of triumphant royalty. This analogy could be used in allegorically depicting the story of a king. A similar procedure was used in the pavilion of the Province of Quebec. The external architecture of the building, clear and simple, was related to the interior, which had the same quality of rational simplicity. Here, a series of geometric volumes—cubes, cylinders, and so on—was chosen to represent elements of the natural landscape, such as trees and water. Through a consistent use of these forms, the story of the inhabitants of Quebec was told—for example, how they harnessed the natural elements: water, forest, mines. The consistency of the symbolic, allegorical key reduced confusion, making the visit easy. Naturally the visitor should have had the key; but if he did not, he could simply enjoy the pleasant composition of volumes, of forms in space, and the contrast of colors. In this second case, moreover, the visitor could have a certain aesthetic experience, as if he were reading an ancient heroic poem without understanding its allegorical meaning, but nevertheless enjoying the flow of images and the rhythm of the story.

There is a third solution. It also involves using a series of symbols and a kind of allegorical representation, but symbols that are coded and recorded in the collective mind by long reiteration, as in a tale with familiar characters like a wolf, a shepherd, and a flock of sheep. In this case, well-rooted traditions make the allegory easily understood by a large group of people, as was true in medieval sculpture, especially in the portals and windows of cathedrals, which depicted religious representations using characters so standardized that they could be used as if they were linguistic signs. This was true of the United States pavilion, perhaps the best one at the exposition. The large geodesic dome by Buckminster Fuller reflected its surroundings and at the same time revealed something of what was happening inside. Inside, it was visually open, but the objects and interior structures were still enclosed in a dome of light. Mystical and technical, past and future, open and closed, this dome communicated the possibility of privacy without eliminating the rest of the world, and suggested, even achieved an image of power and expansion. The exhibited objects told, by their sequence, the history of the country and its myths. But to recognize these American myths, we did not need private keys because what were shown were typical symbols of the frontier, the Civil War, the '20's, the Western movie, the Broadway musical, pop art, the Space Age. Every display was universally recognized as a connotation of "Americanism." The United States told its history clearly, in a way immediately comprehensible to everyone. But, as in every act of communication, directness had its drawbacks. Clear communication was achieved at the cost of exaggerating the obvious and reducing the "information," the surprise, the unexpected. The more straightforward the communication, the greater the danger of telling the recipient something he already knows. To a certain extent this happened in the U.S. pavilion. The symbols were recognizable, but in the end they told us what we already knew, and thus they underscored a typical image of the United States, an image suggested to us by literature and film where, as in this pavilion, ironic observation and self-criticism are found along with the pride and optimism appropriate to any mythic vision. The only element that did not communicate what we already knew, but added something new, even if intangible and ambiguous, was the Fuller dome. In other words, the dome was aesthetically the strongest element of the pavilion, and it was so full of nuance, so open to different interpretations, that it affected the symbols inside and added depth to their easily identifiable, more superficial qualities.

Finally there is the case of a more traditional and direct denotative communication, based on codified symbols and the redundant integration of words and images, as in the very fine Israeli pavilion, where the story of the Jewish people was told clearly through a series of maps, pictures, captions, quotations, and so on. Only once in this pavilion was the picture-caption system abandoned, and symbolic suggestion used instead. This occurred in a large, otherwise empty room whose walls were struck by dramatic shadows. Here there was a memorial to the Jews exterminated by Hitler, and it was composed of only two prominent elements: a photograph of a concentration camp and, in a glass case, a pair of children's shoes, clearly found in a crematorium. But here, as in the American pavilion, the images were so charged with strong connotations, given them by long familiarity and repetition, that the mechanics of communication allowed no ambiguous connotations. We should say, though, that the way in which these well-known symbols were displayed revived them, and we saw them in a new light, through a sort of *Verfremdung*.

Three Possibilities for an Exposition of the Future

Through these various methods of communication we can envisage three possibilities for an exposition of the future, beyond the conception of an exposition as a collection of goods. The first is an exposition as a collection of symbolic objects, in the sense of open symbols, as we have discussed them. This sort of exposition will be similar to much of contemporary art: Communication will be ambiguous, and there will be many possible interpretations. We know that when this form of communication takes place it can have good results and increase the freedom and creativity of the recipient of the message, but the question is whether an exposition should simply repeat, on a larger scale, the same thing that a painting or sculpture does.

The second possibility is the exposition as an educational instrument, a teaching device. This was the purpose behind the Canadian theme pavilions, in which difficult scientific and social problems were explained. But there are some "aesthetic fallacies" here. Some of the pavilions demonstrated how architects and designers employ teaching téchniques but used them as composing elements for their own personal works of art. When a graphic artist designing a book jacket insists on omitting the author's name or making the title barely visible in order to have a "beautiful" jacket, legibility is sacrificed to "aesthetics" and the primary function of the book cover is completely betrayed. The case is obviously different when the artist abandons educational purposes and uses didactic elements to compose his own collage, whose meaning is no longer explanatory but, again, symbolic. This category includes collages or assemblages made out of pieces of posters, street signs, book jackets, and the like, the purpose of which is to suggest a critique of that material but certainly not to teach anything that could be clearly put into words or sentences. However, when the aim is to teach and the method is that of the suggestive collage, the aim is betrayed. This is what characterized the theme pavilion "Man in the Community," where, in order to suggest modern man alienated by today's city, there were plaster figures à la George Segal enclosed in cages lined up along the walls of an enormous room. It is clear that in this case the symbolic communication was weaker than that of the original work of art, and it did not teach anything.

Other attempts of this kind, even if more successful, were still debatable. An example of this was the pavilion called "Man and Life," where the functions of the brain and nervous system were represented. Here, without any doubt, the enormous model of the human brain, the diagrams of the nervous system, and the explanatory captions wanted to teach something. But graphic and architectural (and again, aesthetic) concerns made the visual experience stronger and more important than the didactic process; even the explanatory diagrams were used as elements in an architectural collage that existed for its own sake. Consequently, the explanation was sometimes too difficult, sometimes too detailed, and sometimes just sketchy, and it was understandable only to those who already knew the material. This pavilion, though one of the most pleasant to visit, did not say enough to people who already knew how the brain functions and spoke too elliptically to the person who did not know. The same criticism could be made of other theme pavilions, such as "Man, His Planets and Space" and "Man and the Ocean."

In these cases avant-garde art used pedagogic methods, but did not become educational. At best it reached the level of experiment, proposing new exhibition techniques not yet fully investigated. The solution to this contradiction lies not in these avant-garde forms, valid in their own sphere, but in avant-garde didactics, in a developing pedagogy, a revolutionary way of teaching. Thus expositions should utilize systems of popularized communication, valid for any visitor, which other means of communication, from TV to newspapers, cannot employ with equal intensity. I think we found a hint of these possibilities in some of the pavilions, such as Labyrinth, and in the section Man and His Environment in the pavilion "Man, His Planets and Space." Film was used in both pavilions, but not in the usual way. The Canadians, masters of experimental and documentary moviemaking, used different systems of projection on many screens or on panoramic screens of unusual sizes and format. Something similar had been attempted at the fair in Lausanne, but I think that here the simultaneous projection of many movies, the sense of rhythm, the contradictory or complementary play of competing images, the suggestion of new spatial effects, were superior to any known Cinerama techniques. Here the visitors, to whom humanity's history on earth was told with beautiful images, received a clear, informative message. They felt aesthetic emotion from communication that gave them ideas and data to think about, decisions to make, conclusions to draw. In this case, we can talk about a pedagogy of the avant-garde, because the communication was directed to educated and naive visitors alike, in such a way that both could get what they understood and were struck by.

We still must ask ourselves if the enormous size of Expo '67 justified this sort of result. But in a sense, this question is unfair. Even the least successful experiments contained some lessons, some suggestions for the art, architecture, and education of the future. It is in this sense that we can point to the true justification for an exposition: It is like an enormous experimental laboratory, not to be criticized for its immediate results, but for its bequest of suggestions and ideas for architecture and design. The best example of this experimental legacy was Habitat '67, designed by Moshe Safdie and David, Barott, Boulva. Habitat was an aggregation of 158 prefabricated cubic or rectangular units of different dimensions, assembled in an apparently free and spontaneous way to form a continuous rhythm, where the module led not to uniformity but to continuous variety. In reality the criteria of combination were rigorous; each unit formed the terrace of the unit above, thus giving it more space and possibility for green areas. Habitat seemed to have reconciled the limitations of prefabrication and industrial mass production with those of a free and inventive way of living, full of fantasy, variety, and asymmetric vitality. Without doubt, Habitat was an example of intervention on the landscape. Its form was integrated with the surroundings, and, deriving its own irregular profile from Mediterranean terraces, it presented a fascinating silhouette against a Northern background.

Naturally we must still ask whether Habitat was so impressive because, with its diverting forms, it was so different from everything else surrounding it. Perhaps an area composed only of such Habitats would result in a monotonous and regimented landscape. But who knows? An exposition does not give final answers; it suggests experimental directions. Habitat performed this task, justifying (since it was charged with stimuli) the many useless forms which surrounded it.

A Perplexing Conclusion

Even if an exposition could be a perfect teaching device, as we have suggested, is it worth the expense and effort? To organize an exposition means to organize a teaching machine dedicated to all the peoples of the world. But, as we know very well, the visitors to Expo (with the possible exception of the Canadians) were well-to-do people, and these people generally can obtain ideas from innumerable cultural sources. They are the ones who least need these universal teaching devices. The world is able to produce splendid expositions but cannot allow all its children to move freely (politically and economically) to attend the Expo school. An exposition anywhere inevitably becomes a sort of mass communication for élites. In a pessimistic moment we might thus become convinced of the uselessness of expositions (though still recognizing their experimental and stimulating value). But we can draw other conclusions and make other hypotheses. For example: Isn't it absurd that in our century we still build stationary expositions? Shouldn't the designers of future expositions confront again the problem of Mohammed and the Mountain?

1967

BY UMBERTO ECO
ALSO AVAILABLE IN VINTAGE

☐ Five Moral Pieces	0099276968	£6.99
☐ Foucault's Pendulum	0099287153	£7.99
☐ How to Travel With a Salmon	0099428636	£7.99
☐ The Island of the Day Before	0749396660	£7.99
☐ Kant and the Platypus	009927695X	£8.99
☐ The Name of the Rose	0749397055	£7.99
☐ Baudolino	0099422395	£7.99